Durkheim

Also available:

Marx:
The Alternative to Capitalism
Kieran Allen

Weber:
Sociologist of Empire
Kieran Allen

Durkheim

A Critical Introduction

Kieran Allen and Brian O'Boyle

First published 2017 by Pluto Press
345 Archway Road, London N6 5AA

www.plutobooks.com

British Library Cataloguing in Publication Data
A catalogue record for this book is available from the British Library

ISBN   978 0 7453 3741 8   Hardback
ISBN   978 0 7453 3740 1   Paperback
ISBN   978 1 7868 0195 1   PDF eBook
ISBN   978 1 7868 0197 5   Kindle eBook
ISBN   978 1 7868 0196 8   EPUB eBook

Typeset by Stanford DTP Services, Northampton, England
Printed and bound by CPI Group (UK) Ltd, Croydon, CR0 4YY

Contents

Preface

This idea for this book arose out of complementary frustrations. Kieran Allen has worked as a sociologist for well over two decades. In that time, he became increasingly exasperated at the treatment of the disciplines 'founding fathers' in the secondary literature. In the case of Emile Durkheim, this treatment revolves around his supposed abilities as a working scientist. According to the standard narrative, Durkheim was the quintessential empirical observer, laying down canonical rules for serious-minded, value-free research. Over many years, Kieran concluded that this narrative is neither accurate nor defensible given the nature of Durkheim's output. Brian O'Boyle is an economist who has specialised in the areas of political economy and the philosophy of science. His PhD thesis looked at the links between politics and scientific perspectives, arguing that conventional social science ends in major problems due to its defence of the status quo. Two theorists in particular were used to exemplify this perspective – Anthony Giddens and Emile Durkheim.

The idea for this book therefore flowed from a joint concern about the ways that Durkheim's work gets (mis)represented in the secondary literature. Each year, hundreds of thousands of students hear about the partisan ideas of Karl Marx, while Durkheim is presented as a value-free observer. Scholars such as Steven Lukes and Lewis Coser have highlighted the fact that Durkheim defended the interests of the French Third Republic, but there is not yet a book that takes up this defence in any great detail. *Durkheim: A Critical Introduction* is designed to fill that gap in the existing literature. The opening chapters look at the various ways in which Durkheim's work was moulded by his own society. Thereafter, the book engages in a close reading of Durkheim's primary texts, focusing on the links between his Republican politics and his central categories.

Durkheim's desire to shore up the institutions of the Third Republic dictated the selection of his sociological questions, the construction of his key concepts and the way that he marshalled the available evidence. In each of these areas, moreover, Durkheim's politics resulted in major sociological weaknesses that we seek to explain in these pages.

Writing a book of this nature requires considerable help from various quarters. To this end, Brian would like to acknowledge the support of Professor Terrence McDonough with whom he discussed the central ideas in this work over many years. He would also like to thank Deirdre O'Boyle, John O'Boyle, Brendan O'Boyle, Anne Martin and Colin Brennan who, each in their own way, helped to support him in the writing of this work. Finally, he would like to thank Emma Hendrick for her patience, love and understanding.

Kieran would like to thank those colleagues who share his concerns about the nature of modern-day sociology and, particularly, the staff at University College Dublin Library, without whom the writing of this book would have been considerably more difficult. He would also like to thank Sean Moraghan (earthsoulrocknroll@gmail.com) for indexing the book and proofreading.

Brian O'Boyle and Kieran Allen
April 2017

1

Durkheim Declassified

Emile Durkheim is regarded as one of the founding fathers of sociology. His writings form part of the canon of classical sociology and each year tens of thousands of undergraduate students are provided with short, textbook-style summaries of his four major books on *The Division of Labour in Society*, *The Rules of Sociological Method*, *Suicide* and *The Elementary Forms of Religious Life*. Throughout his career, Durkheim strove to improve the standard of sociological output. Assessing the work of his most important predecessors, he complained that much of their analysis remained at the level of empty speculation. In place of the empirical research that Durkheim advocated, thinkers like Auguste Comte and Herbert Spencer merely imposed abstract philosophical categories onto reality.[1] This impoverished their analysis and invalidated their prescriptions.

The idea of detailed empirical investigation became a central theme in Durkheim's work. Whether he was investigating the division of labour or suicide rates, Durkheim sought to apply the scientific method in a way that moved his understanding beyond that of the common individual. Where others had built abstract conceptual systems, moreover, Durkheim would 'allow the facts to speak for themselves'.[2] This helped to build the reputation of his sociology for a generation of French intellectuals, who, like Durkheim, aspired to make sociology more scientific.

In 1887, Durkheim was given the title of Professor of Social Science at the University of Bordeaux. This was the first such chair in the whole of France, signalling Durkheim's growing standing amongst his contemporaries. Fifteen years later, Durkheim took the Chair of Education at the Sorbonne, the pre-eminent university in France at the time. He became a full professor there in 1906, taking the Chair of Education and Sociology in 1913. Durkheim's academic career propelled him to the head of a distinct school of sociology, replete with its own journal – the *L'Année Sociologique*. The *L'Année*, first published in 1898, further cemented Durkheim's influence by drawing together the most important sociological literature emerging at the time.[3] Inspired by Durkheim's sociological practice, the journal married detailed empirical work with the development of a corpus of sociological categories that were used to investigate social reality. Over time, the *L'Année* also became the home of a gifted group of young researchers, united in their devotion to empirically grounded and methodical research. Together with Durkheim, thinkers like Marcel Mauss worked tirelessly to establish sociology as an academic discipline with the standing of physics and chemistry.

In order to cultivate this academic legitimacy, Durkheim stood deliberately above the fray of contemporary controversies. Indeed, with the exception of the Dreyfus affair of 1894, he painstakingly cultivated the image of a serious scholar, detached from the cut and thrust of daily politics. This conscious projection of neutrality was to prove extremely successful. Both in his own day and in our own, it has led to a conception of Durkheim as the detached scientific observer *par excellence*. Craig Calhoun recently spoke for many within the profession when he argued that Durkheim is, above everyone, the founder of sociology as a serious academic discipline.[4] This mantle has traditionally been shared with Karl Marx and Max Weber, but unlike the former's defence of workers' rights or the latter's overt German nationalism, Durkheim is generally seen as the defender of 'empirical research' over 'political polemics'.

His work has thereby become synonymous with objectivity and serious scholarship in a way that, we believe, completely misrepresents it. In stark contrast to many orthodox interpretations, this book aims to root Durkheim's sociological practice firmly within the political institutions of the French Third Republic. Durkheim's meteoric rise is one indication of his alignment with the values of French Republicanism, but his link to the French ruling classes went much deeper than mere academic patronage. Durkheim's republicanism was, rather, heartfelt and enduring. Throughout his life, he believed passionately in the republican precepts of reason, liberty and individual rights. Against the clericalism of the monarchist right and the utopianism of the revolutionary left, Durkheim posited these ideals as the rightful inheritors of the French Revolution. Modern defenders of the *ancien régime* were, therefore, completely anachronistic. A return to the clericalism of the eighteenth century would stifle the individual liberty and undermine the collective solidarity of the French Republic. From the other side of the political spectrum, revolutionary socialists sought to replace scientific reason with, what Durkheim considered to be, a dangerous utopia. Rather than uniting citizens in social partnership, socialism preached class hatred, endless struggle and social disorder. The solution to these twin evils was to revive the benign form of civic patriotism that Durkheim associated with the Third Republic. Every society has a morality that is shaped by and appropriate to those who produce it, but this needs to be properly brought out through scientific investigation. Instead of looking into the ancient past or striving for a utopian future, Durkheim promised to root his sociology in the nature of reality itself.[5]

This meant investigating the nature of the contemporary moral order and then diffusing it through a republican education programme. If morality was the means by which people came into proper alignment with each other, then Durkheim's role was to make this clearer to the general population. This quest for a scientifically informed moral regeneration was evident in the questions that Durkheim posed, the concepts he created and the political positions that he – implicitly – advocated.

In order to defend this assertion, Chapter 2 highlights the extent to which Durkheim's sociology was, in fact, influenced by French Republicanism. This chapter works as the fulcrum for the entire book, as it sets the stage for the detailed textual investigations that run from Chapters 3 to 8. In Chapter 3, we take up Durkheim's assessment of the forms of solidarity underpinning French society, highlighting the extent to which his categories rely on a republican marshalling of the empirical evidence. In Chapter 4, we look at Durkheim's methodological pronouncements, critically appraising his attempt to differentiate between healthy (republican) and pathological (non-republican) social facts. In Chapter 5, we investigate Durkheim's work on suicide rates as proxies for the ways that individuals become detached from their own society. Durkheim famously claimed to investigate the social causes of individual self-destruction, but his republican politics once again biased his central categories in discernible ways.

In Chapter 6, we take up Durkheim's writings on the solidarity underpinning aboriginal communities. This study was meant to shed light on contemporary society, as the moral regeneration of the French Third Republic once again became the key driver of his work on religion. Having looked at Durkheim's canonical texts, we turn to his writings on the French education system (Chapter 7) and his critique of socialism (Chapter 8). In each case the focus remains firmly on the political influences that shaped the output of this supposedly neutral sociologist. In the final chapter, we once again take up the question of Durkheim's republicanism, this time highlighting the limitations of a sociology rooted in a class defence of French society. Our fundamental conclusion is that Durkheim's greatest theoretical achievement lay in his ability to translate the class interests of the French elites into a scientific framework that claimed universal application.

HOW DURKHEIM ENTERED THE CANON OF SOCIOLOGY

Indeed, in many ways, it was his ability to present republican values as neutral and objective that made his sociology so successful. It also made it appealing to later sociologists, who, like Durkheim, aspired to use sociology in the interests of the status quo.

This success hasn't always been the case, however. After his death in 1917, Durkheim's sociology had fallen into relative disrepute, even in his own country. Durkheim had been a vigorous supporter of the war and his reputation suffered as the disillusionment grew. Over time, the younger generations tended to reject the 'pompous rhetoric of the Durkheimians' as a relic of the pre-First World War era.[6] Moreover, many of the sociological team that surrounded Durkheim never survived the war. Durkheim was, however, to re-enter the canon of sociology that is taught in many university courses today.

Parsons was the leading sociologist in America from the mid-1930s to the mid-1960s. After his undergraduate studies, he spent a short time at the London School of Economics where he studied under the anthropologist Bronislaw Malinowski and encountered the ideas of Emile Durkheim. Parsons soon discovered a number of themes in Durkheim that related to his own concerns. On his return to America, Parsons was hired by the first sociology department to be founded at Harvard University. All around him, however, his country was being ravaged by unemployment and mass dissent. The American dream seemed to be in tatters and many had started to look to the left and the unions for answers. A new organisation, the Commission for Industrial Organization, was recruiting lots of unskilled factory workers into its particular brand of militant unionism. In 1935, there were mass sit-down strikes where workers took over their plants and sometimes engaged in pitched battles with the police. Marxism appeared to be making considerable headway among intellectuals with 52 prominent writers endorsing the candidacy of the Communist Party leader for US president in 1932. Parsons became increasingly concerned about the stability of his own country and the growing attraction of the left. He claimed reason and scientific knowledge were being attacked by an anti-intellectualism that was coming from 'socialistic, collectivistic and organic theories of all sorts'.[7] What was needed was a grand theory that both challenged Marxism and pointed to sources of stability and order in society.

The Structure of Social Action which was published in 1937 was Parsons' response. The book was based on an intellectual survey of European social thinkers who had addressed the 'Hobbesian problem of order'. Thomas Hobbes was a seventeenth-century British thinker who challenged the idea that society has been designed by God with inherent stability guaranteed. He had asked: How was social order possible in a world of self-interest? In Parsons' era, this seemed a deeply relevant question – particularly for those who wished to maintain social stability. Hobbes and the subsequent utilitarian school had argued that order was founded on social contracts. In what became known as the 'contract theory of social order', they assumed that individuals entered into contracts with each other and agreed to forego some of their freedoms in order to achieve their most important goals.

Parsons drew on Emile Durkheim to challenge this view. He used Durkheim's work on social solidarity as the template for his own functionalist approach to US capitalism. This made for a deeply conservative sociology that mirrored Durkheim's own concern with defending the interests of the native elites. Parsons argued two points in particular. First, that shared values had to be at the centre of social cohesion. These common values were necessary before people could even begin to establish contracts with each other. Without a 'non-contractual' element based on trust and commitment to carry out one's promises, there could be no contract. There had to be a social element that stood behind individual interactions consisting of: 'a common system of rules, of moral obligation, of institutions, governing the actions of men in the community'.[8] Second, that the non-rational and non-economic elements of these values played a crucial role in maintaining order. Whereas the Enlightenment figures before the French Revolution had mocked traditional rituals as unnecessary anachronisms, Durkheim, according to Parsons, saw 'the function of ritual as a stimulant to solidarity and energy of action.'[9] Parsons was particularly impressed with Durkheim's study of religion as the prime example of a non-rational value system that made society more coherent by pointing beyond the self.

The aim of *The Structure of Social Action* was to show that there was a convergence of European thinkers on the importance of common values as a source of social stability. Parsons argued that their analysis did not go far enough and thus framed their writing as a contribution to his own 'voluntarist theory of social action', which focused more on how individuals internalised values which made their own goals and the goals of society complementary.

Nevertheless, the central point was that Durkheim had been resurrected and declared to be very much alive within the new canon that Parsons was creating. This was an extremely conscious process of framing 'required readings' that would later form the core of sociological textbooks. Not only was Parson's the major intellectual influence for generations of American sociologists, he also actively participated in the translation and selection of books for publication by the Free Press – a publishing house that had huge influence over the direction of American sociology.[10] Parsons aim was to create a professional, scientific sociology which was apparently value free and yet could function as an intellectual counterweight to Marxism.

But by sociology he meant something quite different to the general category of social thought which could trace its origins back to ancient Greece. He defined sociology as: 'a science which attempts to develop analytical theory of social action systems in so far as these systems can be understood in terms of the property of common value integration.'[11] In other words, his was a science whose focus was on the manner in which values and culture could be used to integrate people into society. This definition marked out sociology as a distinct space from economics and politics. But it also created its own bias because it bracketed out economic relations and political institutions and, by implication, assumed an uncritical stance towards them. What mattered was social stability not the conflicts that undermined cohesion.

The canon that Durkheim entered was thus a distinctly American one, shaped by the anti-Marxist ethos of McCarthyism and the Cold War. Durkheim was hailed as a founding father because his primary concern was with order and stability. The writings of Robert Nisbet, a professor of sociology and member of the right-wing American Enterprise Institute, gives a flavour of the discourse about Durkheim in the post-Second

World War period. According to Nisbet, Durkheim was hailed the 'complete sociologist' and the 'first among equals' due to his insistence on rooting sociology in scientific objectivity. Yet Nisbet wanted to have it both ways, simultaneously praising Durkheim for a sociology that drew on a conservative tradition that stretched back to Edmund Burke in its 'profound stress upon the functional interdependence of all parts of society' and the 'collective representations' that held society together.[12] Thus, Durkheim was a 'value-free scientist' who viewed science as a tool for maintaining a conservative social cohesion.[13] This image of functionalist sociology could not survive the social revolt of the 1960s. As a result, Durkheim's influence within the discipline has waxed and waned with the wider levels of social struggle against capitalist oppression and exploitation. This, yet again, speaks to the political nature of his sociology as we seek to show in the rest of this introduction.

THE FALL AND RISE OF DURKHEIMIAN SOCIOLOGY

The war in Vietnam and the rise of the black civil rights movements tore apart the image of America as a society integrated around common values. The consensus that America was the 'land of the free' confronting a communist tyranny came under particular question in the colleges. As the profession of sociology grew throughout the 1960s, it also became more radicalised. One sign of this radicalisation was the emergence of a Sociology Liberation Movement which challenged the upper caste of the profession. It denounced the way in which figures like Talcott Parsons were tied into the US state-machine. Inspired by writers like C.W. Mills, it also challenged the combination of 'grand theory', which gave ideological support for the system and 'abstract' empiricism, which provided the ruling class with factual knowledge to help control their population.[14] In the words of Martin Nicolaus, 'the eyes of sociologists ... have been turned downward ... to study the activities of the lower classes', while 'the professional palm of the sociologists is stretched [upwards] toward' the dominant classes who provide research funds.[15]

The attacks on Parsons soon led to a more critical approach to Durkheim himself. He came to be seen as the founder of a functionalist approach to sociology which had dominated American sociology since the 1930s. This, its critics argued, studied society as if it were an organic unit like a plant or living organism. Pointing to his many biological metaphors, Durkheim was seen as an ideologue who saw each element of a social system working together to provide a function for the whole. He failed to recognise the reality of social conflict and tended to regard it as a pathological problem in need of cure. A new generation of conflict theorists drew on the work of Max Weber and Karl Marx to challenge Durkheim's notion that society invariably moved to a position of equilibrium around shared values. They raised the question of whose values dominated society and saw political struggle over these values as a normal part of society.[16]

Others took a more radical stance, challenging the objectivity of Durkheim's scientific pretensions. In particular, he came to be seen as a follower of the positivist, Auguste Comte, who wished to put scientific methods at the service of the ruling elite. Comte modelled his studies of society on the natural sciences and Durkheim built on this, claiming that sociologists could study social facts in the same manner that a geologist could study rocks. By seeing social facts as things which were external to both individuals and masses of people, Durkheim was effectively proclaiming that the lower orders had to accept their fate. He was accused of 'supplying scientific sanction for a patriotic posture towards the facts of social compulsion'.[17] Against the very idea of value-free sociology, these radicals called for an engagement that took the side of the oppressed and critiqued the powerful.[18]

However, while Durkheim's reputation declined somewhat, his position inside the canon of sociology was never seriously assailed. For one thing, the radical sociology movement had its own limitations. Developing at the high point of the boom in Western capitalism, it assumed that the working class were well and truly incorporated into the system and saw itself primarily as giving voice to more marginal and oppressed groups. Because its own critique lacked any revolutionary agent that could overthrow the system, it slid into promoting forms of identity politics that sought a space for such groupings within the system. The writings of C.W. Mills, moreover, tended to project the sociologist as one of the main agents for 'conscientising' the masses. This, in turn, meant that the radicals tried to recuperate the wider sociological tradition for the purpose of a softer critique of the system.

As the revolutionary tide began to ebb from the mid-1970s, the impetus from radical sociology itself declined. Symbolically, the journal of the radicals, *The Insurgent*, changed its name to *Critical Sociology* and many of its supporters took up positions within the higher echelons of American academia. Far from overthrowing the canon created by Parsons, the 1968 generation – as in so many other areas of society – recovered traditions they once opposed and gave them a more modern tinge.

One indication of the shift was the manner in which there was an attempt to rescue Durkheim from the discredited theories of Parsons. A number of publications suddenly appeared to stress the radical side of his sociology. Thus, Susan Stedman Jones claimed that: 'although he has a clear critique of Marxism, the interests and sympathy of the early and late Durkheim are supportive of socialism.'[19] Mike Gane also saw Durkheim as a genuine radical who merely criticised the concept of revolution as a form of 'witchcraft' for bringing social change.[20] Frank Pearce meanwhile produced a book with the straightforward title, Radical Durkheim, and claimed it was written from a post-structuralist-Marxist viewpoint.[21] The strength of this new Durkheim was, apparently, that he had a subtle understanding of the non-economic forms of representation and was thus able to create a 'more humanistic alternative to instrumental Marxism'.[22]

The shifting fortunes of Durkheim thus reflect the broader changes within the discipline of sociology itself. The original canon as developed by Parsons was explicit in defining Durkheim as an upholder of order and stability. During the post-war era in America, sociologists were more or less shamelessly plugged into the branches of state power. They assisted the Pentagon; drew up surveys of mass communication; examined the morale of soldiers; and attempted to provide practical solutions for social problems. In the new post-1968 Durkheim, the plus and minus signs have been reversed. Conservatism is now a negative and progressive has become a positive. Durkheim appears now as a mild anaemic social democrat who has a concern for greater regulation and social justice. This shift, however, merely reflects the current perception of those working within the discipline.

ROOTING DURKHEIM IN FRENCH REPUBLICANISM

Many of those who enrol for sociology in universities around the world do so from a motivation to improve their society. They often have a sense of the injustice and inequality that pervades modern society and want to learn how to do something about it. Implicitly, at least, they may also have rejected the neoliberal message once trumpeted so shrilly by Margaret Thatcher – that there is no such thing as society. Yet having spent some time in modern academia, many emerge with a cynicism about the very possibilities for radical social change. Sociology helps to create this sense of helplessness. Indeed, the new establishment within sociology encourages students to focus on the 'complexity' of social structures; to be suspicious of the 'simplistic' reductionism' of Marx; and to examine how many items within society are due to a 'social construction' as opposed to exploitation and oppression. Change, it is suggested, can only come piecemeal from gradual shifts in culture or, if the lecturers use some leftist rhetoric, a shift in 'hegemony'. Moreover, despite the older rhetoric of 'engagement' and the more recent one about 'emancipatory research', there appears to be very little connection between these broader cultural changes and day-to-day struggles. Hegemony is only changed, it appears, through the media or the lecterns in universities.

This message is, of course, not automatically received as it is pronounced. As in every area of life, the contradictions between proclaimed aims and present-day hypocrisies are always evident. The more discerning student often takes some of the more critical points raised by current sociologists and turns them against the very system that so comfortably envelopes their mentors. But in so doing, they will come up against the limits set up by the ideological boundaries of sociology itself. Foremost among those limits is a notion that theorising is developed in the abstract without any relation to the social relations of a particular society. To challenge this view we must consistently look at the structures of our own society in order to assess whether they can be adequately explained through the central concepts in Durkheim's sociology. This inevitably means subjecting Durkheim's entire corpus – including his views on capitalism, education, religion and social cohesion – to a critical examination. It also means challenging the manner in which Durkheim fashioned his own image as a neutral scientist standing above social conflicts to offer cures for social ills. The mere fact someone claims that they have no political stance does not mean they are neutral in the conflicts that pervade their society. Once we examine Durkheim in the context of these struggles, we will find that the labels 'conservative' or 'radical' are abstract, timeless categories that do not capture his viewpoint. A far more precise description of where he stood in relation to his own society is needed and this means situating Durkheim's sociology within the context of his republican politics.

Indeed, as we shall see, Durkheim's great talent was to take problems of the moment and generalise them into a framework that corresponded to the outlook of a section of the ruling classes in his own time and for decades afterwards. More specifically, he was writing at a time when the claims of classical economics had run aground. These had assumed that a harmony of interests would emerge between the different classes as a result of the hidden hand of the market. It had also assumed that the state could operate as a 'nightwatchman' – or in modern parlance – a security guard who patrolled the perimeter of the economy but was not involved. As France approached the twentieth century, these assumptions made little sense. The era when an individual capitalist who lived by the market alone and believed that he had a common interest with his workers was over. Conventional bourgeois thought therefore fragmented between those who wanted to uphold the 'science' of a self-regulating economy (bracketing out all social relations) and those who wanted to open new avenues to discuss the residual questions that economics could not deal with. Durkheim fell squarely into the second category. His explicit project was to forge a professional, academic discipline known as sociology. His implicit agenda was to forge a theory of social relations which promoted social partnership as a means of integrating workers into the capitalist economy and into its state. It is from these two vantage points that we shall examine the key components of his various theories.

2

Durkheim's French Republicanism

When Durkheim was aged twelve, his country suffered a calamitous defeat in the Franco-Prussian War. The Emperor Napoleon II and 80,000 of his troops were captured at Sedan in 1870. As news of the shameful defeat reached Paris, a popular uprising occurred which tore down the whole edifice of the Bonapartist Second Empire. A government of national defence took power and a new republic was proclaimed. But from its very inception, it was covered in blood and class conflict. Elections based on very limited franchise were quickly held in January 1871 and they returned a conservative assembly dominated by royalists. When the new government, headed by the elder statesman, Adolphe Thiers, attempted to impose the humiliating surrender terms they had agreed with the Prussians on Paris, they were met by an uprising of the National Guard, effectively a citizens' militia. In what subsequently became known as the Paris Commune, workers took control of the city and ruled there for two months. Their activities shocked both the old aristocratic notables and the new republican middle class, who ordered the remnants of the French national army to invade the city. The suppression of the Commune became one of the bloodiest massacres of the nineteenth century. Yet it ranks as a 'minor' event in mainstream history when compared to the much repeated story of the Robespierre terror during the French Revolution, one hundred years previously. More than 20,000 people were slaughtered during the battle to retake Paris; others were executed summarily in the jails and prison camps of the new regime; more were exiled for life to New Caledonia.[1]

Durkheim's sympathies with French republicanism were instinctive and deep. According to Lukes' classic biography, he was 'entirely persuaded by the rhetoric of republicanism and convinced of the need to establish a national creed based on "liberty, equality and fraternity".'[2] Born into a Jewish family in Alsace Lorraine, Durkheim was aware of how the French Revolution had emancipated Jews from feudal ostracisation. Moreover, he saw how the enduring campaigns of anti-Semitism, which culminated in the notorious Dreyfus case, were led by monarchists and reactionary Catholics. Durkheim approved of republican policies which promised the middle classes and the peasantry new avenues of social ascent. The aim of republican leaders such as Léon Gambetta and Jules Ferry was to displace the monopoly that the big landowners and the wealthy bourgeoisie held on state power and patronage.[3] In Gambetta's words, ultimately, 'the rich financier who lives today withdrawn behind his formidable signature will see his son acknowledge the grocer around the corner who has become a millionaire'.[4] This was particularly appealing to the broad layers of the petty bourgeoisie, who numbered about 8 or 9 million people, and who belonged neither to the 1 million strong 'authentic bourgeoisie' nor to the workers or peasants.[5] The republican vision was for a property owning democracy, underpinned by meritocratic ascent.

REPUBLICANISM AND SCIENTIFIC EDUCATION

Durkheim was a direct beneficiary of the latter path. A bright student in school, he entered the École Normale Supérieure in Paris, which was an elite university that trained students to become teachers. Under the republican regime, there were increased opportunities as a huge investment in higher education took place. The number of primary teachers doubled from 64,000 in 1876–77 to 125,000 in 1912–13 – and their status grew as well.[6] These strata of society became strong supporters of the republican cause and used their new-found status to disseminate its ideals throughout the countryside.

Upon graduating, Durkheim held a meeting with the key architect of higher education reform, Louis Liard, who urged him to go to Germany to report on how social science had contributed to its national regeneration. His encounter with the more 'scientific' form of German education convinced him that it was time to end the practice whereby French education was dominated by a vague appreciation of the classics and a spiritualist philosophy which distinguished between the body and the soul. This system was devised by Victor Cousins in the 1830s as a method of undermining the negative critiques made by Enlightenment writers before the French Revolution. By the late nineteenth century, it had become a major obstacle to the development of a scientific ethos. Without a thorough grounding in the newer forms of science, France would continue to lose out to Germany in industrial and military competition as evidenced in the Franco-Prussian War.

Durkheim's first academic position was in the University of Bordeaux and once again he owed this post to his close association with the republican elite. A ministerial decree in 1887 appointed him a junior lecturer in the University of Bordeaux where he succeeded a fellow republican sociologist, Alfred Espinas.[7] Liard saw Bordeaux as a place where new innovations could be tried out before they were introduced into Paris. His aim was to introduce social science into the wider system of training for future teachers. Durkheim was, therefore, appointed to lecture in both social science and education.

Here we come to the first major thread that shows Durkheim's adherence to French republicanism. The republican tradition was based on a concept of citizens who were equal before the law. However, the abstract nature of the citizenry hid the fact that they were deeply divided according to social class and political orientation. This meant that on occasion the citizens might endorse political positions that were either to the right or the left of the republicans. During the 1850s, for example, the dictator Louis Napoleon held power through regular plebiscites where he won mass support from the peasantry. In the 1890s, the socialists, who were led by Jules Guesde, were making major gains at the ballot box in the north of France. The republican answer to this conundrum was to put resources into educating the population so that they became 'proper' citizens able to take a responsible part in democracy. Thanks to a huge budgetary effort, they made public schooling free of charge and this allowed it to become compulsory.[8] Their aim was to inculcate the citizens with republican values. Léon Bourgeois, in his address to a congress of the Ligue Française de L'enseignement, stated that: 'minds need hygienists and doctors as much as bodies do'.[9] The aim of republican education was to help unify the nation and create harmony and consensus. Durkheim was an enthusiastic supporter of this project from the very outset. Thus he wrote that,

> all good citizens had the same idea; we must re-build the country. In order to re-build it we first had to educate it. A country that aspires to governing itself needs 'enlightenment' above all else. A democracy would be untrue to itself if it did not have faith in science.[10]

The link between republicanism and science had previously been made in the positivist tradition of Auguste Comte. Science was to become the means to replace both religious indoctrination which supported a monarchy and 'metaphysical' slogans such as liberty, equality and justice, which were the cries of the Enlightenment. But whereas Comte had conceived of science as mainly assisting the elite to govern society in a harmonious fashion, Durkheim and the latter-day republicans wanted to spread scientific education to the masses. A number of reasons were advanced for this project. One was a need for education to strengthen the solidarity of the French nation. Durkheim noted that social reality was not always clear to everyone. In terms of immediate appearances, it did not exist as only individuals could be seen as sentient entities. Moreover, classical education had done little to teach people about the importance of their social bonds. He consequently wrote,

> It is not by learning to appreciate the masterpieces of classical literature that one acquires a feeling for the organic development of society. ... The multiple ties which link us to each other. ... are not so obvious. Having received, therefore, no other education, we are necessarily led to deny their existence.[11]

There was, therefore, a need for a more scientific education to promote the idea of a social bond. However, Durkheim's concern was not with this social bond in the abstract. He was living in a country that had been defeated and humiliated by the rising power of Germany and he wanted to see a national regeneration that would restore France to its worldly status. Moreover, he was deeply concerned about the divisions and instability in French society. Between 1789 and 1880, France had experienced fourteen different constitutions and was haunted by its experience of revolution. Like his fellow republicans, Durkheim believed that a common education system that was grounded in a scientific outlook could help re-awaken French patriotic feelings. The older forms of training in philosophy had to be infused with social science and become part of a strategy of national renewal. What we need now, he wrote,

> is to awaken in ourselves a taste for collective life. What we need to understand above all is the reason for the existence of national feelings and patriotic faith; we need to know if they are grounded in the nature

of things or whether as doctrinaires argue … they are no more than prejudices and barbaric survivals.[12]

A further reason for the emphasis on education was as a means to undermine clericalism. The Catholic Church had consistently opposed the legacy of the French Revolution and wanted a restoration of the old hierarchical alliance of clergy and aristocracy. Even as the Third Republic was born, it was menaced by continual attacks from the Catholic clergy and the royalists. In a major speech in 1900, for example, Waldeck-Rousseau, warned about how church representatives were 'doing their best to make their pupils hostile to the Republic and to republican ideals.'[13] As a defensive measure, the republican government enacted a series of laws to create a more secular society. In 1882, religious education was banned from French schools; in 1886, priests were banned from schools, and in 1905, the formal separation of the church and state was declared in France. These attacks on the church, however, differed from the earlier Jacobin tradition of the French Revolution which sought to destroy religious belief completely. By contrast, the Ferry laws, as they became known, were carried through in the name of a liberal individualism where religion was to be displaced into the private sphere. Even while the state was declared independent of religion, it assumed financial responsibility for the maintenance of church buildings. As they moved against the church, moreover, the republicans felt a certain danger. Traditionally, the church promoted rules of behaviour which helped to create a social solidarity. The republicans believed that this would have to be replaced with a secular morality. Otherwise, the expulsion of the church from the school system might create a vacuum which would encourage a growth of egoism and social disengagement. Two of the key themes of the new secular system, therefore, became moral education and solidarity.

Fournier has pointed out that: 'sociology infiltrated the university via pedagogy'.[14] By this, he meant that the new corps of teachers for secular schools needed to be trained in ways that gave a 'scientific' basis to morality and solidarity. Sociology was tasked with providing this and it is no coincidence that social morality and solidarity became the major themes of Durkheim's sociology. By focusing overwhelmingly on these issues, moreover, Durkheim gave a broader theoretical expression to the burning concerns of the French republicans. In 1869, one of the main intellectual influences on French Republicanism, Charles Renouvier published a book on the 'science of ethics'.[15] Morality, he argued, was not based on religion or metaphysical concepts, but arose from a positive feeling that emerged between two individuals when they realised that duty to the self had also to become duty to the other. 'The moral sense,' he argued, 'is a natural combination of sympathy and benevolence, and the social tendency which is their result, postulates the equal dignity of persons'.[16] Like other republicans, one of Renouvier's key aims was to challenge the ideas of the British utilitarian school which saw individuals as only motivated by self-interest.

SOCIOLOGY AS THE SCIENCE OF MORALITY

Durkheim subsequently took up Renouvier's call for a science of ethics, seeking to root morality in society itself rather than in God or the ruminations of philosophers. He stated that: 'my major concern is to free morality from sentimental subjectivism'.[17] This was code for philosophers who started with an ideal (justice, for example) and tried to deduce their own system of morality for society. As a result, 'they have rather been revolutionaries or iconoclasts', instead of adopting a 'scientific' approach based on an empirical study of moral facts.[18] Rather than seeking abstract ideals, the focus should be on studying what morality actually consisted of and how it evolved in particular societies. In order to understand morality, he argued, 'we must proceed from the moral data of the present and past'.[19] This approach differed both from the revolutionaries, who wanted to develop a moral critique of existing society and the church, who wanted to root an absolute morality in a belief in God. Durkheim's fundamental argument was that morality arose automatically as soon as humans came together as a collective. There was no need for God to hand down morality because 'once a group is formed, nothing can hinder an appropriate moral life from evolving, a life that will carry the mark of the special conditions that brought it into being'.[20] Morality was simply a means by which people learned to adhere to something beyond themselves. It consisted of the rules which promoted the common good of the group over individual interests. But in so doing, it helped to liberate individuals because, as society developed, it 'consecrated the individual and made him pre-eminently worthy of respect'.[21] Once he puts himself under the protection of society, the individual liberates him or herself from blind, unthinking, physical forces. Durkheim concludes therefore that: 'the individual submits to society and this submission is the condition of his liberation'.[22]

The basis for individual respect, however, only arose in advanced societies. Durkheim's emphasis is on a morality that was appropriate to, and shaped by, the special conditions of its own society. Against the absolutist notion of morality that springs from a dialogue between God and the soul, he has a relativist conception that fits morality with the society that gives rise to it. In the case of France, this morality had a specific focus on individual liberty, because it was the French declaration of the *Rights of Man and Citizen* in 1789 that firmly established individual rights. However, Durkheim disputes a revolutionary inter-pretation that people are born with 'inalienable rights'. In particular, he rejects the radical motto of Jean-Jacques Rousseau that 'man is born free, everywhere he is in chains' on the basis that nature does not confer any right to individual freedom. According to Durkheim, 'the rights of the individual are not ipso facto his at birth'.[23] They are not 'inscribed in the nature of things with such certainty as warrants the State endorsing them and promulgating them'.[24] Quite the contrary, it was only the state which was able to create a counterbalance to the close-knit local groups which surround individuals and create the conditions for their own freedom. Were it not for the state, the individual would be 'absorbed' into clans or local groups and would have little concept of their individual rights. Durkheim's conclusion is that:

> Our moral individuality far from being antagonistic to the State, has on the contrary been a product of it. It is the State that sets it free. And this gradual liberation does not simply serve to fend off opposing forces that tend to absorb the individual: it also serves to provide the milieu in which the individual moves, so that he may develop his faculties for freedom.[25]

This argument about how morality, and with it a respect for individual liberty, arose from society and the state had clearly important ideological implications. In particular, it led Durkheim towards a seemingly benign patriotism which expressed itself in a gratitude to *la patrie*. If patriotism is weakened, he argued, where is the individual to find his moral authority? He therefore attacked internationalist beliefs that would undermine this patriotism, arguing that: 'their effect is to disparage the existing moral law, rather than to create others of a higher merit'.[26]

The other major theme in French republican thought that featured highly in Durkheim's sociology was the concept of solidarity. This was also at the core of the new secular system of education. In one of the textbooks used in secondary schools at the time, *Petit Traité de Morale Sociale* by Pierre F. Pécaut, six out of twenty chapters are devoted to this concept. From the very general concept of solidarity were derived various subdivisions such as physical solidarity, based on hereditary; economic solidarity, based on a division of labour; scientific solidarity, based on collective labour; and moral solidarity, based on respect for the rights of others.[27] In fact, the list bears a remarkable similarity to the themes that Durkheim outlined in his first major book, *The Division of Labour in Society*, which we shall examine in Chapter 3.

For the moment, however, let us focus on Durkheim's more general argument. His sociology has a distinctively optimist bent when compared to Marx or Weber. While Marx was damming in his critique of capitalism and Weber offered a bleak defence which characterised it as bureaucratic and disenchanted, Durkheim conceived of modern society as both better and more positive than traditional predecessors because it brought with it newer forms of social solidarity. This approach was evident in an early review he undertook of Tönnies's book on *Gemeinshaft* and *Gesellschaft*. Tönnies was one of the founders of German sociology and his book was an attempt to combine elements of romanticism with the contemporary Marxist critiques of capitalism. The German words *Gemeinschaft* and *Gesellschaft* are normally translated as '*community*', which refers to traditional societies that tend to be culturally homogenous and based on a high degree of common property, and *society* where there is much more diversity based on exchange and contracts. According to Durkheim, Tönnies was too pessimistic because he painted the *Gesellschaft* in sombre colours drawn from Marx.[28] In effect, he was describing it as a cold society based on self-interest and in need of a strong state to hold it together. It was a more artificial society compared to the more natural and organic society of *Gemeinschaft*. This reflected a certain romantic anti-capitalism which contained nostalgia for previous societies where there had been stronger social bonds. Durkheim, by contrast, was far more optimistic. He parted company with Tönnies in suggesting that:

> The life of great social agglomerations is as natural as that of less extended societies of the former days. It is neither less organic nor less internally activated. Beyond purely individual actions, there is in our contemporary societies a type of collective activity which is just

as natural as that of the less extended societies of the former days. It constitutes a different type, but between two species of the same genus, as diverse as they are, there is not a difference in their nature.[29]

This suggests that both modern and traditional societies rested on different forms of social solidarity. The more extended division of labour in modern society meant that people were more interdependent on each other and had to engage in a greater level of social interaction. Modern society, therefore, did not lessen social solidarity but rather created a different form. Durkheim's suggestion was that the modern form was better because it was less all enveloping and claustrophobic than traditional society. It allowed for both strong social bonds and greater individual identities. In *The Division of Labour in Society*, therefore, Durkheim saw solidarity primarily arising from a dependency of each on the other in performing the vital functions of a more complex society. Later, Durkheim was to shift emphasis on what constituted the basis for social solidarity to collective ideas.

From the mid-1890s, he began to assert that the core of society was the collective conscience. This consisted of a distinct psychic life that was common to the members of society combining morality, ideals and generalised ways of thinking. The importance of the collective conscience was evident in the dualist way people conceived their existence – between a body and a soul. The body, he suggested belonged to the material, sensory world while the homeland of the soul lay in a world of the sacred. The simple body–soul polarity was paralleled in thought by the contrast between sensory knowledge and conceptual knowledge. A sense of colour, Durkheim pointed out, varies with each individual but concepts are always common to a plurality of people. Concepts are the means by which we can have an intellectual exchange because they force us to go beyond individual experiences. The dualism in thought therefore expresses itself in terms of both a personal and impersonal psychic life. Durkheim's aim however was to move beyond the religious explanation of this dualism where the soul and the mind were seen as 'a fragment of divinity'. He set out to show that:

Sacred things are simply collective ideals attached on to material objects. The ideas and sentiments developed by a collectivity ... are invested ... with an authority which brings the particular people who think them and believe in them to represent them to themselves under the form of moral forces that rule over and support them. ... They are simply the effects of the ... singularly fertile and creative psychic process called fusion, the communion of a plurality of individual consciousnesses in a common consciousness.[30]

Just as the late French republican tradition tried to displace the church but retain its disciplinary functions, Durkheim sought to demystify religion by attributing to society the location of all things sacred. He thereby reversed the aphorism, 'if God does not exist, it is necessary to invent him' with 'if God exists, it is only because society invented him'. His sociology aimed to show how the collective consciousness gave individuals their morality, their general paradigms of thought and their ideals. The latter category of 'ideals' was particularly important for holding society together. According to Durkheim, it was at moments of collective ferment that the 'great ideals upon which civilisations rest' are born. This refers to periods like the revolutionary epoch in France when there was a more intense form of life with people swept along by an impression that 'the Kingdom of God will be established on earth'.[31] Durkheim believed that such historic moments of great intensity cannot last, but that they leave behind traces that help bind society together. They do, however, have to be periodically revived through rituals and ceremonies. This revivification, he noted, is 'the function of religious or secular feasts and ceremonies, public addresses in churches or schools, plays and exhibitions.' Through these events, people are drawn together in 'an intellectual and moral communion'.[32]

Here Durkheim was giving theoretical expression to the practice of the Third Republic in using social memories to instil loyalty to its state and its value system. The Third Republic was marked by an abundance of secular ceremonies and the erection of monuments which were used as open air classrooms to educate the population in republican virtues. In 1879, La Marseillaise was proclaimed the national anthem. A year later, 14 July – Bastille Day – became a national holiday. From 1880 on, the motto of 'Liberty, Equality and Fraternity' was inscribed on all public buildings by law. Five years later, the Pantheon was taken over by the state and turned into a lay temple. The first of the 'great men' to be buried there was the republican hero Victor Hugo, in monumental ceremony. At local level, the practice of civil burial was encouraged and by 1908, a quarter of burials in Paris were conducted without the church.[33] Durkheim's theory of the importance of ritual in reviving foundational ideals and in displacing the church therefore coincided with quite important political considerations.

THE POLITICAL SOURCES OF DURKHEIM'S OBJECTIVITY

This, however, begs the question as to Durkheim's style of writing because rarely did he focus on the specific events of his own society. Instead, he wrote at a level of theoretical abstraction that only obliquely refers to the trauma of French society at the time. There are a number of important reasons for this. There is, first, the ambiguous legacy left behind by Auguste Comte and his followers. Comte was the first theorist to propose a positive science that would help society overcome the divisions created by the French Revolution. He assumed that society could be studied through the same methods as in the natural sciences. This new *positive* social science would help the regeneration of society after the *negative* critiques of the Enlightenment. This was because social science would have all the authority of the natural sciences and could therefore pronounce on issues in a way that overcame social divisions. Comte's assumption was that positivist intellectuals could help the political elite of society pursue policies that were in the public good. In a period of great social strain, this in turn had a huge attraction for republican politicians. One of Comte's followers, Émile Littré, for example, had a major influence on the republican leaders, Ferry and Gambetta, winning their support for promoting social science in the French education system.[34] Durkheim's own approach was clearly influenced by Comte with his notion of a 'science of ethics' coming from this source as well as from Renouvier.

Despite this, Durkheim had profound misgivings about the mystical elements in Comte's later work. For example, he dismissed Comte's proposal for a new Religion of Humanity to replace Catholicism, complete with its own priests and ceremonies.[35] This was never taken seriously by the new republican elite and Durkheim's aim was to purge from the original positivist project all the messy and rather discredited proposals of Comte. He therefore went to great lengths to stress his strictly academic outlook and took a stance of presenting himself generally as being above politics.

A second reason for Durkheim's more abstract and academic style was that there were already a number of people who referred to themselves as sociologists or social engineers. One example was Émile Cheysson, who had taken up the ideas of the Catholic writer Le Play before modernising them to suit the new republican tradition. Unfortunately, however, his attempts to use 'science' to manage the relations between labour and capital were particularly crude. Cheysson argued, for example, for splitting up the labour movement by forming conciliation boards at the factory level to help cement relationships between individual workers and their employers. This way the masses could be kept away from agitators and revolutionary socialists.[36] The Catholic origins of the social engineering movement meant that it did not advocate greater state intervention, but instead Cheysson urged employers to take a more paternalist role in looking after 'their' workers.

This background meant that sociology – a word that Comte had invented – was generally held in very low esteem. In Durkheim's own words, 'in academic circles, especially, sociology was greatly discredited … the thing itself inspired doubts and revulsion in many people.'[37] He, therefore, consciously adopted a strategy of increasing its academic credentials by creating a journal, L'Année Sociologique, and forming a team around him composed of writers who had academic capital. One element of this strategy was avoiding discussion on current social problems (one exception to this was the Dreyfus affair, where the Durkheimians intervened actively). This enabled the academics to apparently rise above the fray and dispense with any suspicion that they were acting from ulterior motives. In Durkheim's own formulation, 'the lecturer of today must not be seen as the candidate of tomorrow'.[38] This value-free image was a construction that was undertaken by moving away from the realm of the specific and practical to the theoretical.

But, in so doing, Durkheim simply transferred the role of the social engineer to others, whilst he became a sociological ideologue. After all, his project still sought to lay the intellectual foundations for a republican project that was designed to overcome the social divisions in French society by appealing to both a new secular morality and a science which was to be the neutral arbitrator on social issues. His methods were different to Comte's bombastic rhetoric about a new positivist church and Cheysson's crude efforts to manipulate the working classes. Instead, Durkheim set out to develop a wider intellectual framework that would underlie each of the practical interventions of the day. The mere fact that Durkheim repeatedly proclaimed his scientific neutrality, however, should not obscure this ideological role. In fact, his very success in doing so – or to put it differently to translate the concerns of specific social groups into a theoretical outlook – is what guaranteed him his place in the canon of sociology. Three specific issues showed the limits of this proclaimed neutrality: his elitist concept of the state; his embrace of the solidarist strategy for dealing with labour unrest; and his collapse into jingoism with the outbreak of the First World War. Let us examine each in turn.

THE UNDEMOCRATIC STATE

Durkheim's view of the state stands in marked contrast to the critical standpoints taken up by Marx and Weber. Marx did not see the state as a natural institution that humanity was destined to live under. Rather, he saw it as an historic creation that only emerged when society became split along class lines. It was a special organ that both unified the ruling classes and enabled them to exert ideological and physical domination over subordinate groupings. Weber took a more pessimistic stance, suggesting that democracy was fictional because rule by minorities was *always* inevitable. He believed that its control of physical force was at the root of modern state power. States, he argued, were defined by the fact that they exerted a monopoly of violence.

In contrast with both these views, Durkheim advanced an entirely benign and uncritical view of the state. He thought that the state emerged through a smooth process of natural evolution, whereby different groups came into contact with each other and formed a political society. By this, he simply meant an authority that involved some degree of central rule making. Durkheim provides no detailed historical analysis of how this might have occurred. Instead, he simply suggested that in all probability there were 'at the beginning of social evolution',[39] societies where there was not an opposition between the governing and the governed. Durkheim's next distinction is between a political society and the state. The latter is 'a group of officials sui generis, within which the organisation and acts of volition involving the collectivity are worked out, although they are not the product of the collectivity'.[40] In other words, the state is the 'social brain' for the organism that is society.[41] It provides a 'higher, clearer and more vivid' sense of consciousness for the wider society. Somewhat bizarrely, he makes a comparison between the individual personality and the role of the state in society itself. Within individuals there is a host of ideas, tendencies and habits, much of which reside in the realm of the subconscious. But there is also a reflective conscious ego that does not allow the personality to fall prey to its subconscious. This is 'the inner circle upon which we attempt to concentrate light'.[42] The state plays an analogous role to the ego, in that it presents a central and relatively clear consciousness to control the indistinct representations that arise from the rest of society. The state is thus 'the prime mover' in directing society onto a rational path.[43]

This concept of the state as the collective brain for society leads to a particular problem in relation to democracy. Namely, if the mass of people are subject to minority control by the prime mover how can republican governments claim to act in their name? Durkheim understands this contradiction and resolves it decidedly in favour of the state. 'We must not,' he writes, 'declare that democracy is the political form of government, in which the government is spread throughout the *milieu* of society.'[44] Accepting such a definition of democracy would represent a return to more primitive and inferior societies wherein the clan chieftain did not have much power, being subject to the will of the majority. Compared to these crude early forms of social organisation, Durkheim asserts, monarchy is more democratic.[45] This is a strange twist in logic arising from Durkheim's peculiar method of argumentation. He normally starts with a somewhat tedious discussion of definitions before using the latter to set up the structure of the subsequent argument. In this case, as democracy is defined as a form of government *over the governed* – rather than rule by the people – societies with weaker governments are less democratic.

Durkheim's ideological project becomes clearer in his discussion of the radical Enlightenment figure, Jean-Jacques Rousseau. Durkheim blamed Rousseau for the idea that government must only be the 'transmitter of the general will'.[46] This theory of democracy was extremely popular in France and, according to Durkheim, was at the root of the chaos in French political life. By asserting the right of the people to govern themselves, Rousseau was undermining the ability of the state to rule. Change followed on change because the 'driving force of the state came from a multitude of individuals who regulated its course with almost a supreme power.'[47] According to Durkheim, however, such changes were merely superficial and underneath lay a regime of 'habitual stagnation'.[48] Although the reference here is to the manner in which French society was unable to deal with the unresolved legacies of its major revolution, Durkheim transmutes his concern into a wider theoretical framework. Namely, the masses, who are prisoners of their own unconscious vagueness, can never direct society in any positive fashion. Progress demands a strong and centralised minority of republican officials to steer the ship in a positive direction. The logic of Durkheim's position is therefore to challenge the idea that the people should directly control their own governments. He writes,

> As long as the political order brings deputies in immediate contact with the unorganised mass of individuals, it is inevitable that the latter should make the laws. This direct contact does not allow the state to be itself.[49]

Durkheim's solution is that a host of intermediary bodies should be set up between individuals and their government. These would then become the natural and normal organs of the social body. Their purpose would be twofold. First, they would help limit the power of the state by reminding it of its duty to promote individual rights. In other words, they act as a counter-force to the state. But second, as the state expands into many diverse areas of social life, it needs to communicate with and become aware of the sentiments of the wider society. This is subsequently presented as a type of balanced arrangement for everyone's benefit, but there is no doubting Durkheim's focus on the guiding role of the (elitist) state. For example, the state has to 'permeate all those secondary groups of family, trade and professional association, Church, regional areas and so on.'[50] Moreover, he warns that if the state is 'not sufficiently in touch with the individuals in the mass to be able to mould them inwardly, so that they can readily accepts its pressure on them,' it will face all kinds of resistance and distressing conflict.[51]

Here Durkheim was replacing the radical Jacobin concept of democracy that arose from the ideals of the French Revolution with a more truncated form of liberal democracy. For the Jacobins – in theory, at least – the people were sovereign and their will was to be exercised through universal (albeit male) suffrage. The executive was to be subordinated to a legislature that was to be elected for periods and answerable to their constituents. There was to be only one chamber and, in some instances, state officials should also be subjected to election.[52] By contrast, in Durkheim's proposal for a guided democracy, the state apparatus has maximum autonomy and educates the citizens in its values. It permeates all aspect of their lives under the guise of creating a space for individuality. But in so doing, it grants itself an efficient mechanism of communication that allows it to reach all areas of society. This particular notion of democracy suited the elite of the Third Republic who were anxious to move beyond the turmoil left behind by the French Revolution and create a strong state more suited to the Imperial age. And coincidentally, the same concepts are even more prevalent in our post-democratic age.[53]

REPRESSING LABOUR

The second area where Durkheim's direct ideological project was evident was in his approach to the labour movement. During the 1890s and 1900s, there was a considerable upsurge in labour unrest in France. From an average of 100 strikes per year in the 1880s, the norm rose to over 1,000 per year in 1900. In 1906, there were 9 million days lost in 1,309 strikes.[54] Alongside this strike wave, there was a growth in Marxist and anarcho-syndicalist ideas. Marxists made their strongest gains among textiles towns in the north of France, especially after the shooting of workers in Fourmies in 1891. Anarcho-Syndicalism drew on earlier artisanal traditions but eventually captured the leadership of the General Confederation of Labor (CGT) in 1900. In 1906, Marxist and anarchist tendencies came together to help foment a general strike to demand the eight-hour day. The response of the radical republican, Clemenceau, was to instigate a policy of brutal repression. Paris was flooded with troops and the CGT leaders were arrested on the pretext that they were plotting with anarchists and royalists to overthrow the state. In the following two years, Clemenceau, now dubbed 'France's number one cop', responded to further strikes with great brutality, resulting in 19 workers being killed, 700 injured and jail sentences totalling 104 years being handed out.[55] These events marked a fundamental breach between the workers' movement and French republicanism. Prior to this, the republicans had sought to integrate the workers' movement into the organs of the state by proclaiming their opposition to free market liberalism and developing an ideology of Solidarisme.

Durkheim was centrally involved in this project and this is why it makes little sense to categorise him as a conservative. His nephew, Marcel Mauss, with whom he worked very closely, claimed that he was sympathetic to the version of socialism promoted by his college friend, Jean Jaurès.[56] The context here is all important, however. Before 1906, the republican tradition – particularly its radical variants – had sought to identify with workers' aspirations as a means of winning them over to their cause. They had legalised unions in 1894 to help foster moderate unions and, in 1892, inaugurated industrial arbitration procedures which employers were reluctantly forced to participate in.[57] However, as these measures seemed to embolden the workers' movement, writers such as Durkheim responded by attacking the concept of class struggle in the name of social partnership. This is most clear in his arguments about socialism which he regarded 'as a cry of pain and anger uttered by men who feel acutely our collective malaise.'[58] The metaphor of sickness was by no means accidental. Durkheim's strategy was to dismiss socialist doctrines as responding to momentary sicknesses that needed to be cured. Piecemeal reforms were the way forward rather than any half-baked schema for social revolution. This approach allowed Durkheim to position himself as a social doctor, diverting socialist workers from the mistaken paths they were being led down by Marxists and anarchists. He wrote,

> To the facts that arouse it [socialism], it is comparable to the groaning of the sick person to the illness from which he is suffering and to the needs that torment him. But then what would we say of a doctor who took the replies or desires of his patient for scientific aphorisms?[59]

Part of this strategy meant disputing the socialist claims to being 'scientific' while elevating his own sociology to precisely this scientific status. However, despite his own strictures that doing battle with socialist doctrines was like 'the labour of Penelope'[60] – the faithful wife of Odysseus, who keeps suitors at bay – he was invariably drawn into these same battles. In a review of the writings of the Italian Marxist, Antonio Labriola, he acknowledged that both he and Labriola shared the same 'fertile idea' whereby history was not explained by the consciousness of those participating in events, but by deeper causes that arise from their social group. However, he denied that the determining factor in these social groups was economic relations and suggested instead that it was religious belief systems.[61] His main criticism of Labriola and Marxism more generally was the prime importance assigned to class struggle and hostility to the state that characterised both Marxist and anarcho-syndicalist views. In a review of a book by the Italian anarchist, Merlino, Durkheim praised his attempts to move beyond 'doctrinaire' positions whilst attacking Merlino's identification of socialism with class struggle. The malaise which gave rise to socialism 'is not rooted in any particular class ... it attacks employers as well as workers, although it manifests itself in different forms in both.' The employers suffered from 'disturbing, painful agitation' while workers experienced 'discontent and irritation'.[62] Against this class-based politics, Durkheim proposed a refashioning of the moral composition of society. This, however, suggested an alliance with the state rather than a strategy of overthrowing it. The state, according to Durkheim, was not a repressive institution, still less an instrument of class rule, but an institution that runs parallel to the growth of civilisation.

Instead of analysing society in terms of class conflict, therefore, Durkheim conceptualised it as a division of labour, where each had a function to play for the common good. This schema enabled him to suggest that 'solidarity' was the most appropriate and normal relation between social groups. Discontent or agitation were symptoms of a malaise that occurred in an otherwise healthy body. They arose from a lack of regulatory cover over the evolving and complex forms of the division of labour. This approach dovetailed neatly with the republican strategy of developing industrial relations machinery that would end agitation through greater regulation. Durkheim articulated the same view very clearly when he stated that:

> We aspire to a time when strikes in industry would be rare, and even one when they would be compulsorily referred to arbitration tribunals, when wages would be more stable and less dependent on bargaining, capriciousness and circumstances.[63]

However, alongside greater state initiatives to regulate 'industrial relations', Durkheim wanted to form corporate bodies that developed moral rules to 'overcome the amoral character of economic life'.[64] In *The Division of Labour in Society*, this was to some extent presented as a regeneration of the older guild system but, equally, there was an understanding that there might have to be separate guilds for workers and employers. The main thing for Durkheim is that they both be bound by precise moral rules which spelled out how their relations of solidarity were to be organised. The focus on solidarity – or in modern parlance, social partnership – was at the core of republican politics at the time. Solidarisme was virtually the official doctrine of the Third Republic. It presented itself as a midway position between the rampant individualism of the laissez-faire economists and the 'collectivism' of the Marxists. The theory of mutual interdependence of social strata was outlined by the radical republican politician, Léon Bourgeois, in his book *La Solidarité*. Like Durkheim, Bourgeois also described himself as a socialist, but this was more by way of a strategy to forge an alliance with more moderate elements of the labour movement such as Millerand and, at one point, Jaurès.

The main themes of the solidarisme philosophy find a more abstract theoretical expression in Durkheim's work. There is a focus on moral reform and a need to develop an awareness of the mutual obligations between social classes. There is a reduction of social class to a functional unit in the division of labour. There is a call to supplement legislative reform, which regulates economic relations, with corporate organisation that provided mutual aid to each other. And finally, there is an advocacy of private property as a condition for individuality.[65] In Durkheim's case, however, these themes are elevated beyond the arena of practical politics to a more general and abstract theory where they enter the canon of sociology. In reality, however, they merely articulate an alternative strategy for how capitalist social relations might be managed. Instead of a gung-ho celebration of market competition, there is a strategy of seeking to incorporate subordinate groups through social partnership.

NATIONALIST JINGOISM

The final area of Durkheim's direct ideological intervention may be dealt with as briefly as it is ignominious. Throughout his life, Durkheim advocated a benign form of patriotism that stressed moral cohesion rather than military prowess. The role that the higher command of the French army played during the Dreyfus affair was enough to immunise him against overtly chauvinist interpretations of nationality. But while adopting this more liberal position, Durkheim was equally appalled by the internationalist ethos of sections of the socialist movement. In 1914, however, his liberal patriotism became a savage form of warmongering. In the same manner as some of his left-wing opponents collapsed into a *union sacrée* with the French military machine, so too did Durkheim join the war effort – not just as a citizen but as a prominent intellectual. He offered his considerable academic prestige to a virulent propaganda campaign that demonised his opponents. He joined a committee to do propaganda work for the French government and helped to write pamphlets and nationalistic articles. He regularly refused to write articles or cooperate with German academics. He celebrated the 'moral greatness of France' because it had overcome 'a chaotic and mediocre public life' of the pre-war years.[66] And he even claimed that sociology was 'essentially a French science'.[67] Truly, the ideological mask of scientific, academic neutrality had slipped to reveal the nasty nationalism of French republicanism.

3
The Division of Labour

The Division of Labour in Society was Durkheim's first major work. Published as part of his PhD thesis, the book carves out a distinctly republican position in a long-standing debate about employment relations in a modern economy. According to the liberal perspective, capitalist free markets were the pinnacle of human achievement. Unlike government planning or feudal monopolies, capitalism allowed the highest level of individual initiative, freed from the deadening grip of regulation. Writing during the 1770s, Adam Smith famously captured this position with his iconic vision of the Invisible Hand.[1] Taking the example of producing pins, Smith explained how the emerging capitalist division of labour was increasing output from 10–20 units per day to over 40,000.[2] Underpinning this process was a virtuous cycle of natural self-interest and a certain form of economic freedom. Instead of worrying about the well-being of others, Smith argued that producers should act solely on the basis of their own interests. In this way, the laws of the market could take their course, reducing costs and making society ever more productive. This was music to the ears of Britain's industrialists, who used Smith's ideas to justify their treatment of the working classes. More than this, they adopted laissez-faire economics as the official creed of the British establishment.

From the other side of the political spectrum, a growing band of socialist writers were focusing on the class dimensions of the capitalist division of labour. Instead of glorifying the extra freedom for the owners of capital, these writers highlighted the extreme exploitation associated with factory labour. The working classes were undoubtedly churning out great quantities of new output, but all of the profits, and the political power, immediately went to the top of society. For revolutionaries like Karl Marx and Friedrich Engels, this explained the massive rise in class conflict associated with industrial capitalism.[3] Conflict and struggle were written into the very DNA of capitalist society and the only long-term solution was a revolution by the toiling classes.

Neither of these positions were particularly attractive to the young Durkheim. Having watched his own society continually plunged into social conflict, Durkheim could not accept the overwhelmingly optimistic views of the British liberals. After the disaster of the Paris Commune, moreover, he was painfully aware that the Invisible Hand of the capitalist market was often supported by the visible fist of absolutist government. He also freely acknowledged the inequality and social conflict that emerge within capitalist societies, but felt that these were transitory problems that could successfully be eradicated. By temperament, training and class perspective, Durkheim was a firm supporter of the 'progressive bourgeoisie'. This ensured that he viewed capitalism not as an inherently progressive system, nor as a deeply exploitative one, but as a complex whole constantly in need of enlightened forms of regulation.

This belief was evident in two key strands of Durkheim's thesis in *The Division of Labour in Society*. First, Durkheim insists that it is not the place of the working classes to organise their own forms of resistance. Socialist revolution was little more than a dangerous utopia that would only make life worse for the working classes. Instead, state planners should create the institutional environment to allow the capitalistic division of labour to grow and flourish. In order to support this process, scientifically trained intellectuals should investigate the types of moral forces binding people together under capitalism, whilst the school system should disseminate these virtues to the next generation. In this way, Durkheim wanted to combine science and education with social reform and gradual progress. At the outset of *The Division of Labour in Society*, he lays out his vision in the following terms,

> This book is above all an attempt to treat the facts of moral life according to the methods of the positive sciences ... Yet because what we propose to study is above all reality, it does not follow that we should give up the idea of improving it. We should esteem our research not worth the labour of a single hour if its interest were merely speculative. If we distinguish carefully between theoretical and practical problems it is not in order to neglect the latter category. On the contrary, it is in order to put ourselves in a position where we can better resolve them.[4]

Second, Durkheim insists that new forms of social solidarity would soon replace the economic conflicts currently threatening the social order.[5]

Against the prevailing view of the French intelligentsia, Durkheim felt that the division of labour was the very thing that would prevent society from being ripped asunder. From the time of its great revolution (1789), France had been wracked with the kinds of social conflict that made it difficult for the elites to sustain any optimism. Reflecting on the revolutionary wave of 1848, for example, Alexis de Tocqueville, famously denounced the 'illness' and 'disease' that continually beset his mother country.[6] Auguste Comte was, if anything, even more despondent, arguing that the self-interest underpinning capitalist relations was tearing French society apart. Comte, like many of his disciples, particularly feared the breakdown in the 'moral consensus', but Durkheim insisted that new forms of solidarity were necessarily emerging, even if they inevitably took time to fully develop.[7]

The division of labour separated workers in terms of their occupations, but it also meant that they needed each other to meet the majority of their daily needs. Taken together, 'the butcher, the baker and the candlestick maker' formed a complex patchwork of complementary economic occupations. Like the various organs in the human body, the economy was increasingly characterised by an interconnectedness that would eventually generate new forms of social solidarity. This sense of *functional interdependence* became the organising category of Durkheim's entire analysis, as he counter-posed the 'mechanical solidarity' of traditional societies to an 'organic solidarity' born of complementary occupations.

In this way, Durkheim was able to develop an innovative take on the division of labour that flowed seamlessly from his republican ideals. Against the unbridled optimism of liberal individualism, Durkheim acknowledged that capitalist social relations were often chaotic, divisive and unequal. In the hands of the revolutionary socialists, these attributes were enough to condemn capitalism completely, but for Durkheim they were merely transitory problems capable of eradication through proper regulation. Left to its own devices, capitalism was destructive, but this needn't be the outcome if the right regulations were put into action. In place of classical liberalism, Durkheim developed a conception of the solidarity associated with economic interdependency; in place of right-wing authoritarianism, he posited the enlightened governance of elite intellectuals; in place of revolutionary socialism, he looked to the liberty, equality and fraternity of the French Third Republic.

SOLIDARITY IN 'PRIMITIVE' SOCIETIES

Durkheim's formative years coincided with France becoming the world's second great colonial power. In their official rhetoric, many republicans opposed colonialism, but the foreign policy of consecutive governments was staunchly imperialist. The French Prime Minister, Jules Ferry, was a living embodiment of this contradiction. At home, Ferry was a staunch republican who insisted on separating the church from the state, but when it came to France's colonial possessions, he suddenly spoke in terms of the white man's burden. According to Ferry, France had a moral imperative to 'civilise the lesser nations of the world', particularly as Britain and Germany were similarly motivated.[8] This was the 'Realpolitik' of imperialist rivalry, as the French elite sought national regeneration through colonial expansion. From their base in Cochinchina, the French colonised much of modern Vietnam in 1884–1885. Together with Cambodia, this area soon formed the bulk of French Indochina, with Laos added in 1893 and Guangzhouwan in 1900. In 1881, France also began the continent wide 'Scramble for Africa', going on to colonise the bulk of the territory north of the Sahara. The French Empire eventually occupied an area of 5 million square miles, containing some 110 million people in total.[9]

This background is important in order to understand the central dichotomy set up in *The Division of Labour in Society*. This is between primitive societies which have *mechanical solidarity* and modern societies which have *organic solidarity*. Although Durkheim was rarely overtly racist, his work did reflect the basic prejudices of the colonial era. Like Ferdinand Tönnies (*Gemeinshaft/Gesellshaft*) and Herbert Spencer (*Military* versus *Industrial Societies*), Durkheim's central categories neatly separate the world into the 'primitive societies' of the colonial periphery and the 'advanced societies' of the capitalist core. Without any field research or first-hand experience, he also argues as if the entirety of human history can be understood in terms of these two mutually exclusive social categories. When one thinks of the different societies that have actually existed (city states, castes systems, slave economies, capitalist nation states, etc.), this claim seems completely outlandish. However, it has to be understood in terms of the prejudices of Durkheim's historical era.

The simple division between traditional and modern societies is also a reflection of his scientific method. At the outset of *The Division of*

Labour in Society, Durkheim makes it clear that he wants to examine different types of solidarity in a way that matches the empirical standards of the natural sciences.[10] This is a most ambitious task, however, as he is trying to assert that economic specialisation is the modern cause of organic solidarity. Yet how is he to find observable evidence? To make this task more manageable, Durkheim uses proxy variables to stand in for social solidarity and argues in terms of simple contrasts.[11] He argues that the law is an observable indicator of solidarity in a given society and legal rules can therefore function as meaningful substitutes for social solidarity. They can then be compared and contrasted in different social settings. By dividing his analysis into two mutually exclusive categories of traditional and modern societies, Durkheim believes he can mimic the conditions of experimentation. He explains this method in the following way,

> How does one proceed with verification? We have not merely to investigate whether in societies there exists a solidarity arising from the division of labour … We must compare this social bond to others, in order to measure what share in the total effect must be attributed to it. To do this it is indispensable to begin by classifying the different species of social solidarity. However, social solidarity is a wholly moral phenomenon which by itself is not amenable to exact observation and measurement. To arrive at this classification, as well as this comparison, we must therefore substitute for this internal datum, which escapes us, an external one which symbolises it, and then study the former through the latter. That visible symbol is the law.[12]

Primitive societies are effectively Durkheim's experimental control group to enable him to examine the solidarity of modern societies. Based on almost total homogeneity, primitive societies are characterised by low levels of social density, low levels of social interaction and extreme simplicity in the division of labour. The basic unit of a primitive society is the tribal-clan group. In Durkheim's estimation, each member of these clans is identical to the others so that they become interchangeable in terms of their social functions.[13] Blood ties notwithstanding, he therefore characterises each clan as being capable of losing members and gaining them without any difficulty, 'since each one contains within himself the whole of social life, he may remove himself elsewhere … [And] because labour in society is not greatly divided, it does not come out strongly against such reductions in its numbers.'[14] This is a strange claim that we will come back to later. For now, it is important to understand how these individual clan groups are brought into association.

According to Durkheim, primitive societies are made up of the replication of these identical clan groups throughout a given geographical area.[15] Invoking a biological metaphor, he likens the social structures of primitive societies to the segmental rings of an Annelid worm.[16] A more accessible modern example might be the segments of an orange. For Durkheim, segments are the appropriate metaphor as they are 'absolutely homogenous ... and consequently not ... arranged in any order in relation to each other.'[17] Internally, tribal groups lack any form of economic specialisation between their members. Externally, primitive societies are made up of a series of these identical tribes and so lack any form of macroeconomic differentiation. In all of this, it is essential to keep Durkheim's central thesis firmly in mind. He wants to argue that the division of labour is the primary driver of modern solidarity and so he needs to assume that primitive societies are without any kind of specialisation. Tribes, and the individuals within them, are consequently defined as being totally interchangeable. This lack of economic inter-dependency means that the ties that bind individuals to each other in primitive societies are fewer in number. A form of social solidarity does nevertheless still exist and he labels this *mechanical solidarity.*

According to Durkheim, the moment individuals come together in any form of social interaction they are immediately subject to the disciplinary force of social rules.[18] In modern societies, these rules are generally embodied in the legal framework, whilst in primitive clans, they are overwhelmingly religious in nature.[19] In a theme that was to become increasingly important in his later writings, Durkheim suggests that religious beliefs help to construct meaning for tribal participants in everything from law and ethics to political organisation and family relations. In primitive societies, moral rules thereby function as the glue that binds individuals *directly* to their social surroundings. Solidarity *between* particular individuals is deemed to be relatively weak, but the collective mores that bind the group together are exceedingly strong. To defend this conception, Durkheim argues that each one of us is made up of 'two consciousnesses ... the one comprises only states that are personal ...whilst the other comprises states that are common to the whole of society.'[20]

In primitive societies, collective mores and behaviours totally predominate, being universal in nature, permanent through time and exceptionally strong.[21] Unlike modern societies, moreover, there is a strongly inverse relationship between social solidarity and individuality.[22] The individual ego is virtually nil, with Durkheim insisting that: 'in societies where this solidarity is highly developed the individual does not belong to himself; he is literally a thing at the disposal of society.'[23] Participation in tribal life, therefore, necessitates the complete internalisation of these collective ideas. People act predictably and uniformly when under the control of the *collective consciousness*, leading to *mechanical* forms of social solidarity. This regularity in people's collective reactions is captured in the statement below,

> Since such collective motives are the same everywhere, they produce everywhere the same effects. Consequently whenever they are brought into play all wills spontaneously move as one in the same direction.[24]

It is this sense of regularity and resemblance that leads to fellow feeling among tribal members. According to Durkheim, 'members of the group are not only ... attracted to each other because they resemble each other', they are also linked together through their collective belief system.'[25] This also explains why any act that challenges these values is particularly dangerous. Referencing the rules against eating beef in the Indian caste system, Durkheim notes that once this rule has become embedded, anyone who decides to eat this meat is committing a crime against deeply held collective beliefs (the collective consciousness). If left unchecked, a series of these acts would loosen the bonds of social solidarity and in order to defend itself, society creates a body of repressive laws. Criminal acts are defined as those that transgress the sacred rules of tribal behaviour, whilst punishment is a mechanical response to any attack on collective moral values. Because of this, Durkheim argues that the law in primitive society is entirely repressive, with legal sanctions designed to punish acts that undermine the community's sense of collective well-being. It is essential that criminals be made to suffer, not as gratuitous acts of cruelty, but in order that the 'community of minds' remain protected.[26]

Durkheim's model of primitive society is now complete. Starting from an assumption of low population density, Durkheim has argued that primitive societies are characterised by a virtual absence of economic specialisation. The different tribes covering a geographical area are also mirror images of each other. Within them, each member of a tribal community works together and are interchangeable. The form of social solidarity reflects this lack of a division of labour. In particular, tribal society is characterised by mechanical solidarity which works through resemblance and deeply embedded social rules. The observable evidence of this form of solidarity is the repressive nature of the legal sanction. Constructed in this way, primitive society becomes the perfect test case for Durkheim's thesis. They are societies *without* any division of labour and are characterised by a mechanical form of solidarity manifest in a repressive form of social sanction. It remains to investigate whether *changes in the division of labour* lead to changes in the forms of social solidarity manifested in changes in legal sanctions. This task is achieved through Durkheim's analysis of advanced societies.

SOLIDARITY IN 'ADVANCED' SOCIETIES

To develop his analysis of modern society, Durkheim engages in a polemic with the work of Herbert Spencer.[27] Spencer was an English philosopher who married aspects of Social Darwinism with the utilitarianism of Jeremy Bentham.[28] As part of the liberal tradition, utilitarianism assumes that society results from the freely made choices of its individual members. Thomas Hobbes helped to found this tradition with his seventeenth-century book – *Leviathan*. According to Hobbes, civil society was preceded by a *state of nature* in which everyone was continually at war with each other. This made life nasty, brutish, solitary and short.[29] It also compelled men to enter into a *social contract* to found society in the place of anarchy. Society is therefore conceived as little more than a useful agreement rooted within rational self-interest. Utilitarians assume that a division of labour emerges more or less spontaneously within this new civil society. Safe in the knowledge that their property will be protected, individuals exhibit a natural desire to increase their utility through market exchanges. Specialisation also makes economic sense, as individuals become vastly more productive. For these reasons, private property becomes a sacred right that should only be transferred through mutually beneficial contractual agreements.[30] Society, on the other hand, adds little utility beyond protection and has no right to infringe on the property of sovereign individuals.

As a republican scientist, Durkheim disagreed strongly with all aspects of utilitarianism. In his view, people are inherently social beings born into a nexus of pre-existing social relationships. Everything from our ability to speak to our ability to make contracts is determined within the confines of our particular social settings. To live at all, is to live in society, meaning that utilitarianism had gotten matters completely back to front. He lays out this view in the following way,

> Utilitarians … suppose that originally there were isolated and independent individuals who thus could only enter into relationships with one another in order to co-operate … But this theory which is so widely held, postulates a veritable creation *ex nihilo*. It consists, in fact, of deducing society from the individual. But we possess no … grounds for believing in the possibility of such a spontaneous generation.[31]

Alongside these philosophical concerns, Durkheim understood that such extreme individualism leaves little room for genuine solidarity. If society rested on the shaky foundations of individual contracts, then in the infamous phrase of Margaret Thatcher, 'there would be no such thing as society'.[32] If every person is out for themselves, then the Hobbesian *state of nature* is effectively brought back in through the back door. The result would not be harmony and cooperation but chaos and repeated social conflict. Durkheim disputed these utilitarian assumptions on two main grounds. First, he argued that naked self-serving could never be strong enough to bind individuals sufficiently together. Self-interest is, for Durkheim, 'the least constant thing in the world. Today it is useful for me to unite with you; tomorrow the same reason will make me your enemy'.[33] Without trust and solidarity, there could be no sense of society persisting for any period of time. In place of the pure self-interest of utilitarianism, Durkheim therefore posits a level of social solidarity which underpins capitalist markets, allowing them to function. There had to be a social element that stood behind individual contracts consisting of 'common sets of rules, of moral obligations, [and] of institutions, governing the actions of men in the community'.[34] Durkheim summed up his position by remarking that: 'if a contract has any force at all, it is society which confers that force'.[35] Social solidarity is the moral glue that binds individuals to their places in modern society rather than naked self-interest.

Durkheim's second argument against utilitarianism disputed the idea of a state of nature. Rather than starting within a hypothetical thought experiment, Durkheim insists on empirical evidence that can link the development of modern society to its primitive predecessor. To build up this picture, *The Division of Labour in Society* argues that it was population growth that initially gave rise to changes in tribal social structures which, in turn, led to modern forms of economic specialisation. Population growth is a natural phenomenon that historically brought people closer together. Once this process was sufficiently developed, it began to have important social effects, as the rigid structures that characterise tribal societies came under pressure. Durkheim points to the rapid increase in communications and the emergence of towns as key signposts on the way to modern forms of social interaction.[36] In part, the division of labour was due to the fact that previously independent social segments were brought into closer alignment. In part, it was due to the struggle for survival that simultaneously ensued. In low density environments, tribal members could live hand to mouth, without any need for economic specialisation.

Productivity levels were generally low, but the population was also sufficiently low for everyone to survive relatively easily. As populations increased, the struggle for resources inevitably intensified. People eventually came under intolerable pressure and the only solution was to differentiate themselves into various economic specialisms. Charles Darwin had shown that within nature animals live better side by side the more they differ and Durkheim argued that the same law supposedly applies in modern societies. He makes this explicitly Darwinian argument in the following way,

If labour becomes increasingly divided as societies become more voluminous and concentrated … it is because the struggle for survival becomes more strenuous … In the same town different occupations can coexist without being forced into a position where they harm one another, [only if] they are pursuing different objectives.[37]

Without a functioning division of labour, society would degenerate into all-out warfare, but once the latter has been established, it provides the basis for genuine solidarity. People in modern societies have significantly more dealings with each other than their tribal counterparts. More importantly, they come to rely on each other to meet the bulk of their material needs.

Take the example of producing food. In modern societies, agriculture has become the economic specialism of no more than a small subset of the workforce. Farmers now make up less than 10 per cent of the modern economy, selling their produce to massive corporations, who redistribute it to wholesalers and retailers. As this process unfolds, it creates a chain of interdependent professional relationships that have the potential to engender social solidarity. If farmers get ill, they rely on doctors to know how to treat them. If they have young children, they rely on teachers to know how to teach them. Society must therefore ensure that subgroups of the population also go into medicine and education, respectively. Doctors and teachers rely on farmers in order to eat, and so a whole patchwork of interdependent professional relationships begins to emerge. Through their market interactions, working people come to realise that they need each other in order to survive. This brings forth a sense of solidarity that is actually stronger than that which binds people in tribal communities.[38]

To reinforce his central idea, Durkheim likens modern societies to complex organisms with various parts working in unison. Brains, hearts and lungs achieve very different tasks within the body's division of labour, but each is needed to make up the whole. Organic solidarity presupposes individuality and difference as opposed to similarly and resemblance. Yet it also presupposes interdependency. What are the effects of this new-found economic specialisation on mechanical forms of solidarity? In general, Durkheim argues that collective belief systems lose their intensity as the division of labour develops. Specifically, he argues that the collective consciousness becomes more abstract and imprecise. Religion in particular loses much of its previous moral authority with Durkheim insisting that: 'there is a constantly decreasing number of beliefs … that are both sufficiently collective and strong to assume a religious character.'[39] Each peer group has its own beliefs and code of conduct that undermine the universalism of tribal sentiments. Society, therefore, loses its grip on the ego and individuals begin to form their strongest bonds with their fellow professionals. These societies generally rely on more secular morals, but there is one area in which the collective consciousness actually grows stronger. While many collective beliefs are losing their purchase, modern society reinforces a collective respect for the dignity of the human being.[40] Individualism becomes the moral creed *par excellence*, thus bringing Durkheim to the brink of answering his foundational question, namely, 'How … the individual, whilst becoming more autonomous depends ever more closely on society.'[41]

Durkheim's answer is the keystone of his entire investigation. He insists that respect for the self and respect for the other have identical roots in the social division of labour. In modern societies, individualism and organic solidarity are two sides of the same coin. On the one hand, 'each one of us depends more intimately upon society the more labour is divided up', on the other hand, 'the activity of each one of us is correspondingly more specialised, the more personal it becomes'.[42] We learn to appreciate the dignity of the individual through our participation in market society, whilst the latter also provides the social conditions for a rise in organic solidarity. The two, therefore, have the potential to grow side by side in perfect harmony. With this explanation in place, Durkheim feels he can refute Spencer's defence of laissez-faire markets, without thereby conceding ground to revolutionary socialism. Contra Spencer, modern society is not a utopian collection of self-interested atoms, but a vast organic tapestry in which cooperation is not only possible but necessary.[43] Contra the socialists, this tapestry is not underpinned by alienation and exploitation but by a genuine level of social solidarity.

Durkheim's evidence for all of this flows from the nature of modern legal rules. As in his earlier model, he presents the penal code as the most observable indicator of solidarity, arguing that restitutive law (law of redress) predominates in modern society. In order to function, this society insists that individuals respect the rights of private property, but infringement of these rules doesn't threaten the underlying social fabric. For this reason, the sanction attached is restitutive rather than repressive. The idea is not to punish the transgressor, but to make them cover losses to the injured party. Restitutory law is the law of contract and Durkheim makes it abundantly clear that whilst 'repressive law is losing ground, restitutory law, which in the beginning did not exist at all, is continually growing.'[44] He also suggests that: 'one need only cast an eye over our legal system to confirm the much diminished position ... occupied by repressive law in comparison with co-operative law.'[45]

Durkheim now has the empirical evidence needed to defend his primary thesis. Starting from increases in population density, Durkheim argues that a division of labour necessarily emerges equipped with its very own form of social solidarity. Organic solidarity underpins fellow feeling in market societies and its emergence is captured by the rapidly growing body of restitutive or contract law. In each of his models, Durkheim shows how the social system is connected up to the forms of solidarity embodied in the legal code. Yet, right at the end of his work, he also felt compelled to address the 'abnormal forms of specialisation'. Perhaps the struggles raging in France gave Durkheim cause to doubt his republican optimism. Either way, it is to the pathological forms of divided labour that we must now turn.

THE ABNORMAL FORMS OF SPECIALISATION

Like any complex biological system, Durkheim accepts that capitalism is capable of pathological abnormalities wherein the various parts become ill adjusted to one another.[46] In this context, he references three main dysfunctional forms: anomie, inequality and insufficient organisation. Instead of social harmony, these pathological strains cause conflict that can only be eradicated through enlightened reforms.

Anomie emerges when the pace of economic change outstrips the moral regulation that usually accompanies it. In normal circumstances, Durkheim insists that new regulations emerge in the course of social interaction. As part of a long-term process, manners turn into social rules and eventually into legal codes.[47] Unfortunately, however, the pace and scale of industrialisation has meant that many of these legal rules have not had time to properly develop. Durkheim argues that unlike any previous era, companies produce for customers who are dispersed across the entire country or even the world. This undermines the sense of local familiarity that normally nourishes organic solidarity. More importantly, it leaves society ill prepared to regulate the relationships between production and consumption.[48] According to Durkheim, as labour becomes more divided, economic crises regularly emerge, as there is nothing to regulate the anarchy of the private market. Added to this problem, there is increased hostility between capital and wage labour.[49] In the guild era, employers usually had personal relationships with many of their employees. Workers also generally took pride in their roles, as they experienced the functional interdependency of the working environment. In capitalist mega-corporations on the other hand, work is often menial and unrewarding. Durkheim writes, 'if every day he repeats the same movements with monotonous regularity. He is no longer a living cell in a living organism … He is no more than a lifeless cog.'[50]

Looking at the nature of modern employment, Durkheim worried that many people actually seemed insufficiently integrated into their allotted role in the capitalist economy. Major employers seemed remote and uncaring about the workers on their payroll. Workers likewise seemed demotivated and angry about their dehumanisation. Without proper rules in place, Durkheim believed that the hostility between the classes would become intolerable. His solution was to look to a series of corporate organisations that could reinvigorate the morality of employment relations.

In their working lives, men and women relied on codes of conduct that could be specifically redesigned to engender solidarity. Employment associations should convince workers that their particular roles had meaning in the overall functioning of their society. In addition, corporate associations should offer workers real protection through codifying the rights and regulations of employment. Durkheim felt that a whole series of corporate bodies should play this integrating role between the state and the individual. If properly developed, such institutions would exert a moral force 'capable of curbing individual egoism, nurturing among workers a more invigorated feeling of their common solidarity and preventing the law of the strongest from applying too brutally in industrial and commercial relationships.'[51] Accordingly, 'the corporation will be called upon to become ... one of the essential foundations of our political organisation.'[52]

Turning next to *inequality*, Durkheim worried that inherited privileges would undermine the proper allocation of roles in society. Here it is not a lack of regulation that causes the problem but the nature of the rules themselves. In the ideal scenario, market competition should ensure that those best suited to any particular role are best able to fill it. Social roles and natural talents should be perfectly aligned to allow everyone to do the tasks most suited to their abilities. Social solidarity necessarily implies equality of opportunity, whereas in class societies, elite groups get to monopolise high status professions for themselves. If the working class is shut out of these professions, there is likely to be conflict. Durkheim argues that any constraint on the spontaneous division of labour will generate 'miserable squabbling rather than ... solidarity.'[53] Allocating roles on the basis of status is antithetical to the proper functioning of market societies and government, regulation should therefore aim to reduce unearned sources of wealth and privilege. Durkheim is not, however, arguing that the role of government is to eradicate competition, but to make it more equal. He was never a supporter of equality of outcomes within society, but of 'fairness' when it comes to the struggle for the best opportunities,

> If nothing hampers or favours unduly rivals who are disputing the tasks they perform, inevitably only those most fitted for each type of activity will succeed in obtaining it. ... Thus a harmony is automatically realised between the constitution of each individual and his condition.[54]

Having dealt with inequality in social functions, Durkheim turns his attention to inequalities in market transactions. Here it is not the ability of elites to monopolise the best occupations that concerns him, but their ability to gain disproportionally through contractual exchanges. In the Marxist paradigm, ruling-class ownership of the means of production ensures that exchanges between capital and labour are inherently unequal. The formal equality of the employment contract masks the exploitation of the working class at the point of production. Sometimes Durkheim seems close to conceding this point. His starting position is that justice must underpin the fair exchange of equivalent values. As long as there is equality in the external conditions of struggle, contracts become a means for obtaining a just reward for one's individual labour. This results in a form of contractual solidarity that pushes society towards a balanced equilibrium. If, on the other hand, elites use their power to tilt the scales in their own favour, they automatically undermine the moral conditions of economic exchange,

> If one class in society is obliged in order to live, to secure acceptance by others of its services, whilst another class can do without them, because of the resources already at its disposal, resources that, however, are not necessarily the result of some social superiority, the latter group can lord it over the former. In other words there can be no rich or poor by birth without there being unjust contracts.[55]

There seems to be a major fault line in Durkheim's argument here, however. He claims that organic solidarity relies on the just and free exchange of market equivalents, but the power of the capitalist classes immediately undermines the idea of a just exchange. Capitalism is a system that relies on people who have nothing to sell but their labour power, and people who necessarily have the means to employ them. Stated differently, the existence of workers and bosses, the rich and the poor is written into the DNA of the capitalist system. If pushed too hard, this would spell disaster for Durkheim's entire thesis and so he retreats and claims that modern society will witness an increasing preponderance of economic equality. As capitalism develops, the public increasingly demand exact reciprocity in services exchanged. Despite the contemporary evidence of widespread inequality, Durkheim therefore argues that the history of market contracts confirms that situations where 'one party gains the lion's share of the spoils are on the wane'. It is always necessary to inject 'greater equity into our social relationships',[56] but over time the justice of contractual solidarity will almost certainly prevail.

Finally, we come to the dysfunction caused by *insufficient co-ordination*. Durkheim devotes less space to this form of pathology which arises most often *inside* capitalist organisations. Within a highly developed division of labour (an assembly line, for example), any lack of coordination can spell disaster for the total process. Inside modern factories, each worker relies on the skills and co-ordination of her colleagues, if she is to accomplish her own tasks efficiently. As soon as one worker fails to keep up with the pace, a whole series of repercussions may be felt throughout the rest of the system. Drawing yet another biological analogy, Durkheim explains how the human body relies on a constant flow of oxygen from the respiratory system, if it is to avoid death in the rest of the organism. Managing the parts of a complex corporation consequently needs intelligent and experienced leadership. Alongside this, the pace of the work has to be sufficiently brisk to keep the workers on their toes. Interdependent functions can obviously get out of kilter, but Durkheim believes that modern forms of specialisation are making this eventuality far less likely. Remaining competitive in modern markets necessitates being willing to work more or less continuously. There is simply no room for bouts of lethargy, ensuring that this form of pathology is really exceptional. Like the cases of anomie and inequality, Durkheim assumes inadequate organisation will eventually be eradicated through the normal workings of the division of labour. In critical periods, the social system is prone to disorder, but Durkheim insisted that the pathologies he referenced at the end of his thesis were exclusively transitional. Social conflict was neither fundamental nor endemic to the capitalist system. Modern societies were merely trapped in transitional crises that called for enlightened forms of (republican) regulation. Given time and the right interventions, organic solidarity would inevitably become the predominant morality underpinning market societies.

PROBLEMS WITH DURKHEIM'S THEORETICAL MODEL

The problems with Durkheim's thesis can be broken into two main categories: problems with his model building and problems with his conception of capitalism. Durkheim's model is designed to be watertight theoretically and empirically. In order to meet the standards of positivist science, he works with two basic social types, each with a clearly defined set of causal relations. In primitive societies, the lack of economic specialisation means that solidarity flows exclusively from identity and resemblance. This leads to a mechanical form of solidarity observable in repressive laws. In advanced societies, the existence of economic specialisation means that solidarity flows from difference and interdependency. This leads to an organic form of solidarity observable in restitutive laws.

The symmetry developed between these two ideal types offers Durkheim three methodological advantages. First, it allows him to argue that the way labour is organised in each society *explains* the form of social solidarity alongside its attendant rules. This means there is a fundamental cause, an unobservable effect and an observable piece of empirical evidence. Second, it provides him with what seems like scientific rigour, as primitive society acts as an experimental control group. Finally, it allows Durkheim to argue that the division of labour is a crucial variable in the move from primitive to advanced societies. Table 3.1 shows the main cause and effect relations defended in his primary thesis.

Table 3.1   The Structure of Durkheim's Scientific Argument

Social Type	Cause	Effect	Observable Evidence
Primitive Society	Economic Homogenisation	Mechanical Solidarity	Repressive Law
Advanced Society	Economic Specialisation	Organic Solidarity	Restitutive Law

To give his model its maximum purchase, Durkheim argues in more or less exclusive categories. On the one hand, there is *no* division of labour in primitive societies; there is *only* mechanical solidarity in primitive societies; there are *only* repressive laws in primitive societies. On the other hand, each of these attributes have been altered significantly by economic specialisation. His problems begin with this style of absolute either/or argumentation. Like many other nineteenth-century thinkers, Durkheim claimed the mantle of the natural sciences, whilst propagating basic prejudices of the colonial era.[57] Indeed, his entire thesis relies on a number of crude stereotypes about what life was like in primitive societies. Without any first-hand experience whatsoever, Durkheim assumed that so-called 'primitive people' associated with each other for exclusively non-rational reasons. Thus, everyone mechanically reproduced collective mores without reflecting on them; religion was the only social institution created by primitive cultures and even a division of labour amongst the sexes was absent.

Criticising Durkheim's basic argument, Kemper argues that there would be little reason for blood ties to unite people into tribal groups unless their relationships were also useful economically.[58] For people to live together over an extended period of time, they must be gaining something beyond sets of collective ideas. To take the two most obvious examples, finding food and building shelter surely relied on tribal collaborations that were far more than exclusively moral. Without sustained cooperation amongst the members of a group, it would have been extremely difficult to meet their basic survival needs. Working collectively was essential to their material survival, meaning that an economic logic would always have been part of the reason for uniting.[59] Stated differently, economic interdependence is basic to all forms of human society, regardless of whether they are 'primitive' or 'advanced'.

Empirically, this has indeed been born out in numerous ethnographic studies conducted since Durkheim's death. Research by Schnore (1958);[60] Schwartz and Miller (1964);[61] Fortes (1969)[62] and Bendix and Roth (1971)[63] has confirmed that in societies with high levels of mechanical solidarity, there is always fellow feeling resulting from economic interdependency. Malinowski has also shown that 'primitive societies' often contained a body of restitutive laws involving rights and duties amongst the various members.[64] This undermines the two fundamental casual hypotheses put forward in Durkheim's model of 'primitive' societies: that there was no division of labour; and that there was no body of restitutive laws.

In many ways, it was his determination to appear scientific that caused Durkheim's difficulties. Instead of seeing his conceptions as 'ideal types' that needed adjustment in concrete circumstances, he posited them as historical societies with empirically verifiable relations. Arguing that there is *no* division of labour is important if one wants to use primitive society as an experimental test case, but it sets the bar intolerably high in terms of empirical evidence. After all, it only takes minimal forms of economic cooperation to falsify Durkheim's central thesis.

Meanwhile, Durkheim's difficulties were significantly increased as he expected his evidence to reach the standards of positivist laws which assert that there are constant conjunctions, so that whenever x occurs y occurs. This is most evident in his claim that the legal code is a perfect index of underlying forms of social solidarity. To prove this, the legal code would have to change in perfect harmony with the different types of solidarity much like water turning to steam when it reaches 100 degrees. But instead, as Merton points out, 'it is precisely this sort of relationship that Durkheim fails to demonstrate'.[65] Taking stock, we can see that much of Durkheim's model of primitive society has been falsified. His central claim can't even be investigated, as it turns out there is a significant division of labour in primitive societies. Added to this, are the existence of organic solidarity and bodies of restitutive laws in traditional societies that Durkheim had expressly denied. His form of empirical evidence is also deeply suspect, as noted by even his own PhD inspectors.[66]

Turning briefly to Durkheim's theory of transition, many thinkers have objected to the vague, transhistorical nature in which this shift is developed.[67] Formally, Durkheim builds an evolutionary bridge between primitive and modern societies on the basis of a Darwinian struggle for resources, but in reality, he argues in strictly dichotomous terms.[68] According to Barnes, for example, Durkheim 'does little to demonstrate that there are any intermediate societies along the scale.'[69] Merton fundamentally agrees, arguing that Durkheim would be better off dropping his 'unilinear development thesis' in favour of two societies taken as heuristic fictions.[70] Without a theory of primitive society or a defensible theory of evolutionary transition, Durkheim's case is decisively weakened. His claims to scientific analysis relied upon contrasts between key variables in primitive society which have not stood up to critical scrutiny. This decisively undermines his overall thesis, but perhaps his theory of modern society can still be salvaged? Unfortunately, Durkheim's problems in this regard are, if anything, even greater.

The most obvious problem with regard to modern societies is the inherent implausibility of organic solidarity (in other words, cooperation because of economic dependence) emerging in conditions of capitalist competition. The logic of a capitalist society is naked self-interest, making it difficult to see how solidarity would become the natural reaction of market participants. Firms compete with each other for a share of the profits, holding down wages and working conditions in order to achieve this. In these circumstances, it is far more likely that strife and conflict would be the dominant characteristics rather than fellow feeling or solidarity. Indeed, strife and conflict is exactly what was occurring. From the 1890s onwards, the level of class struggle in particular was intensifying. From an average of 100 strikes per year in the 1880s, the norm rose to over 1,000 by 1900. The workers movement was also becoming increasingly Marxist, leading to a growing sense of working-class militancy. Given the logic of capitalism and the evidence that Durkheim was confronting, his basic thesis seems highly improbable. Added to this, there is a fundamental conceptual problem in his cause and effect relationships.

Durkheim's whole project seeks to attribute the two forms of social solidarity to differences in the division of labour. In primitive societies, the lack of any division of labour causes mechanical forms of solidarity, so that people are bound together by a uniform and somewhat oppressive collective conscience. In modern societies, the existence of a division of labour causes an organic form of solidarity, so that the basis of the social bond is a cooperation based on economic interdependence. Yet he also insists that in modern societies a particular form of the collective conscience becomes stronger. This is called the cult of individualism. This has nothing to do with the division of labour and once Durkheim acknowledges that an element of mechanical solidarity – the collective consciousness – is growing stronger, it muddies the waters in terms of the respective influences of collective values and economic interdependency on modern solidarity. Pope and Johnson capture this latter difficulty here,

> How is organic solidarity different from mechanical solidarity? Perhaps more than any other, this [question] encapsulates [Durkheim's] theoretical difficulty. He is trying to distinguish between mechanical and organic solidarity. He acknowledges 'a place where' the common

conscience 'is strengthened', namely, the cult of personal dignity. To acknowledge, however, that an element of the common conscience is growing stronger and, therefore increasingly important as a bond of solidarity ... undermines his thesis that mechanical solidarity and the collective conscience grow weaker and are increasingly replaced by a different kind of solidarity ... At best we reach a paradoxical result. The greater individuality is, the stronger is solidarity; conversely the stronger solidarity, the less extensive is individuality.[71]

This shows that Durkheim's model is trying to have it both ways. He wants to prove that the division of labour causes a shift from mechanical solidarity based on a strong collective conscience to organic solidarity based on economic dependence. But he simultaneously introduced a novel form of mechanical solidarity, which binds people through an alternative process. What is more, it is generally these supposedly secondary – mechanical – forms of fellow feeling that prove decisive.

His analysis of occupational groups is a case in point. These groups most certainly emerge as part of the division of labour, and yet, the forms of solidarity associated with them are entirely mechanical. According to Durkheim, professional institutions bind workers to their colleagues through 'shared beliefs and codes of conduct'.[72] Corporations are therefore moral institutions par excellence, regulating the life of their members through shared experience and similarity. This is also true of the norms undergirding the school system and the republican polity. Officially, Durkheim insists that organic solidarity is replacing outmoded social bonds, whilst his political prescriptions reveal that it is mechanical solidarity that really counts. After all, by his own admission, it was the pathological forms of divided labour – rather than organic solidarity – that was currently dominating the French Third Republic.[73] If Durkheim was hopeful that this situation would soon be transformed, he never returned to the concept of organic solidarity in any of his published writings. Instead, he increasingly put his faith in collective belief systems and moral regulations to bind individuals to their roles in society. All told, Durkheim's analysis of advanced society is no more successful than his earlier analysis of primitive society. In both cases, theoretical inconsistencies interact with empirical weaknesses to undermine his central theses.

PROBLEMS IN DURKHEIM'S CONCEPTION OF CAPITALISM

Durkheim's conception of capitalism rested on a biological metaphor which immediately biased his work in favour of the status quo. Just like the human body, capitalism supposedly has various parts brought into harmony through the normal operations of the division of labour. In its natural state, capitalism was therefore healthy and harmonious. Unlike the general public, moreover, social scientists also had the ability to spot any problems and alleviate 'disease'. This vision of diagnostic social science dovetailed perfectly with Durkheim's republicanism, but there are obvious problems in equating the organs of the human body with the individual units of a capitalist economy.

Bodily organs evolved in tandem to work as part of an integrated biological organism. The normal functioning of these organs is as Durkheim described, but this in no way makes human physiology an appropriate metaphor for capitalist society. In the latter, economic interactions are overwhelmingly competitive rather than cooperative. The entire logic of the system is naked self-interest, with corporations competing with each other to monopolise market share and profit- ability. Their central task is to expand aggressively making them akin to cancerous growths in the human body, rather than healthy forms of mutual interdependency.

To see this more clearly, think about how he marshals the evidence. In *The Rules of Sociological Method*, Durkheim insists that the job of sociology is to observe reality as it actually exists, rather than adding any subjective interpretation. He writes that the 'mind must always be prepared to go outside itself',[74] but in this case, Durkheim refuses to accept what reality is telling him. Throughout the nineteenth century, French society was wracked by conflicts that were clearly rooted in the capitalist economy, yet rather than accepting this observable evidence, Durkheim engaged in an ideological sleight of hand. He defined it as a transitory problem that would soon give way to organic solidarity. Unfortunately, however, Durkheim's ability to make this claim is left entirely unjustified. The evidence was saying one thing, his interpre- tation was saying another. Accepting the observable pathologies of capitalism would have been the scientifically legitimate step to take, but it would also have compromised Durkheim's underlying republican- ism. To defend his own society, therefore, Durkheim had to believe that organic solidarity was just around the corner. Steven Lukes accurately labels this aspect of Durkheim's thesis as wishful thinking designed to equate the 'normal, the ideal and the about to happen'.[75] But the future of capitalism in the twentieth century was to completely disprove him.

Reflecting on a rise in economic crises from the mid-nineteenth century onwards, Durkheim was convinced that a regulatory state coupled with corporatist workplace relations could eradicate the instability that capitalism was exhibiting. Following the Great Depression of the 1930s, Durkheim's prescriptions were largely enacted, but the instability largely remained. After a period of relative stability following the Second World War, capitalism once again fell into a period of crisis in 1973. It then entered a period where economic recessions became more frequent. Neoliberalism became the dominant discourse and social partnership only a fig leaf for a reassertion of power of capital. By 2008, the system was facing an even deeper economic crisis. The cause of these crises can be variously attributed to the relationship between levels of profitability and investment and financial speculation. This suggests that it is the continual search for profit that drives the dynamics of the capitalist system, not the regulation of economic relations. The concept of organic solidarity is ill equipped to bring out this instability of the capitalist economy, undermining one of Durkheim's central categories.

His optimism, meanwhile, proved no less misplaced when it came to the workplace. Although Durkheim recognised the hostility between workers and employers, he fervently believed that enlightened regulation could make the labour process function harmoniously. On the one hand, corporate associations would help workers to appreciate their roles in the wider society. On the other hand, new employment legislation would protect these workers from the most brutal forms of commercial oppression. Harry Braverman's study of workplace practices in capitalist organisations tells a very different story. In *Labour and Monopoly Capital*, he demonstrates that the conflict set up between workers and their bosses has been the determining feature of employment relations in the twentieth century.[76] After Durkheim' death, Taylorist time and motion studies became firmly embedded in factory labour as work became further atomised and further intensified. Labour unions were also assaulted, partly to reduce the cost of wages and partly to make workers feel more precarious. Instead of work becoming more harmonious as Durkheim had predicted, it moved in the opposite direction.

Finally, we turn to Durkheim's hope that market inequality would soon become a thing of the past. In Durkheim's opinion, capitalist markets work best when social talents and natural talents are closely aligned. Market societies supposedly rely on 'equality of opportunity', meaning that reductions in inequality and privilege should have accompanied capitalist development in the twentieth century. Unfortunately, Thomas Piketty's monumental data analysis from *Capital in the 21st Century* shows no such reduction in inequality. According to Piketty, the upper decile of the income distribution in most market economies takes around 30 per cent of the national income, whilst owning between 50 per cent and 95 per cent of the accumulated wealth. In comparison, the bottom 50 per cent of the population always own less than 10 per cent and usually less than 5 per cent of the accumulated wealth.[77] In France, the richest 10 per cent commands 62 per cent of total wealth – the poorest 50 per cent commands 4 per cent.

These levels of inequality are comparable to the Belle Époque, showing that there has been no reduction in class-based privileges over the very long term. What makes these statistics all the more shocking, moreover, is that much of this inequality stems from wealth that is completely unearned. Piketty picks up the story below,

> Global inequality in wealth in the early 2010s appears to be comparable in magnitude to that observed in Europe in 1900–1910 [Durkheim's era]. The top thousandth seems to own nearly 20 percent of total global wealth today, the top centile about 50% and the top decile somewhere between 80–90%. The bottom half of the global wealth distribution undoubtedly owns less than 5% of total global wealth … [Moreover], all large fortunes whether inherited or entrepreneurial in origin, grow at extremely high rates, regardless of whether the owner of the fortune works or not.[78]

Oxfam, the British-based charity, have recently reinforced this pessimistic picture, arguing that just 1 per cent of the world's population now holds more wealth than the bottom 99 per cent combined.[79]

How could Durkheim have gotten it so wrong? In essence, it is because he fails to acknowledge the primary dividing lines within a capitalist economy which separate the owners of capital from the working population. Although he doesn't make this point explicitly, Durkheim's entire thesis presupposes small tradespeople working alongside each other in relatively limited geographical areas. It is an idealised model drawn from nineteenth-century France with everyone trading on the basis of their mutual advantage. The problem is that 'actually existing capitalism' never looked anything remotely like this model. From the outset, class power was used to systematically monopolise productive assets and reinforce political privileges. Working people had to be deprived of all productive property so that the owners of capital could exploit them at the point of production. Employment contracts are therefore rooted in class conflict and exploitation regardless of whether workers can be integrated into the system through regulations or not. To put this point slightly differently, Durkheim bemoans the dangers of class-based inequalities without investigating their fundamental causes. Like every other form of abnormality, he assumed that class divisions were merely transitory, when in fact they were part of the DNA of his beloved republic. Organic solidarity was always likely to be a pipe dream within the structural conditions of capitalist society. Indeed, the reality of the twentieth century was class struggle and imperialist warfare that led to the collapse of the Third Republic in 1940.

4

Durkheim's Method of Scientific Inquiry

Durkheim's *The Rules of Sociological Method* was published in 1895. Having turned the most important part of his PhD thesis into *The Division of Labour in Society*, Durkheim wanted to lay down the necessary methodological procedures to transform sociology into a genuine science. In Durkheim's mind, most of the work that had previously claimed the title of 'scientific sociology' was badly flawed when benchmarked against the natural sciences.[1] Unlike physics or chemistry, much of what passed as sociology was speculative and ideological. Instead of patiently observing the phenomena of the social world, philosophers like Auguste Comte and Herbert Spencer imposed abstract philosophical principles onto their subject matter. This forced sociology into ready-made formulas and prevented the facts from 'speaking for themselves'.

To avoid this deficiency, Durkheim laid down a number of rules for the observation, description, classification and explanation of social facts. This process immediately involved him in a delicate balancing act vis-à-vis the other sciences. On the one hand, Durkheim wants to draw on the authority of the established sciences, adopting key analogies and reworking their concepts to suit his own purposes. On the other hand, he needed to present sociology as a completely autonomous discipline, investigating a set of phenomena that could only be studied through his new methodology. In general, Durkheim achieves this balance by drawing positively on the natural sciences and keeping his distance from philosophy, psychology and the various human sciences. In this sense, the *Rules* can be read as a manifesto for sociology in general and the burgeoning Durkheimian School in particular.[2]

Durkheim's second aim is to use his *Rules* to clarify some of the more difficult arguments from *The Division of Labour in Society*. In the Introduction he writes that,

The results of our work ... are undoubtedly implicit in our recently published *La Division du Travail Social*. But it seems to us to have some advantage to single them out here, formulate them separately and accompany them with proofs, illustrating them with examples culled from that book or taken from work as yet unpublished.[3]

Reflecting on the relationship between the two texts, Warren Schmaus notes that Durkheim was disappointed with the reception of *The Division of Labour in Society* in terms of its key relationships of cause and effect.[4] Instead of keeping to exclusively sociological variables, many commentators accused Durkheim of rooting the modern division of labour in a physical increase in population. This is an understandable view given what Durkheim says, but it undermines his claim to explain social facts exclusively through sociological variables. To guard against any further misconceptions, Durkheim uses his *The Rules of Sociological Method* to clarify crucial methodological variables such as cause, effect and social function.[5] Whether he achieves this or not is, of course, a separate matter.

Durkheim's final aim was to construct a sociology capable of rein-vigorating the French Third Republic. As we have repeatedly argued, Durkheim's work was overwhelmingly concerned with the potential sources of secular morality in his own society. Religion bound the masses together in traditional societies, but the 'cult of individualism' now meant that the previous 'Gods are growing old or are already dead, but others are yet to be truly born'.[6] As an Enlightenment rationalist, Durkheim welcomed the decline in religious influence, but he also worried about the disintegrative effects of rampant individualism. To create new 'Gods' on a firmly rational and secular basis, Durkheim turned to scientific sociology.[7] Although the latter had its start in France, Durkheim was increasingly worried that the empirically grounded analysis of the German tradition was stealing a march on its more speculative neighbour. Institutionally, the German system emphasised detailed analysis of concrete scientific problems through a highly integrated division of labour. This contrasted with a French system that still relied on the folklore of the individual scientific genius. The effects of this contrast were extremely important, moreover, as the superiority of German science was widely credited with underpinning their military successes in the Franco-Prussian War.[8]

In his writings between 1885 and 1890, Durkheim repeatedly warned that sociology was rapidly becoming a German science, imploring his colleagues to follow the example of the experimental and empirical bent of Wilhelm Wundt's *Psychologisches Institut* in Leipzig.[9] In this context, it was clearly essential to lay down the correct procedures that such a science would subsequently take. In his own estimation, Durkheim was to be the founder of an empirical sociology that was not only capable of investigating the sources of modern solidarity, but also of adding to them via the education of republican citizens. In this sense, *The Rules of Sociological Method* becomes multi-layered and significant. At one and the same time, Durkheim is laying claim to the scientific credentials of a newly formed theoretical discipline; laying out its methodological procedures and helping to (re)form its very subject matter. Unlike physics or chemistry, sociology has the ability to influence the forces that it objectively studies, and everything from Durkheim's choice of problems, to the way he addresses them, equips his sociology to become the living embodiment of French Republicanism.

SOCIAL FACTS AND THE RULES FOR OBSERVING THEM

Developing a new science is extremely difficult. Pioneers are not merely taking up problems and investigating them from within the categories of a pre-established scientific community, they are attempting to create an entirely new field of analysis. This is a challenging task that generally begins by identifying phenomena that can only be studied through the methods of a newly emerging scientific discipline. When physics first broke from natural philosophy, for example, it did so by selecting the forces of matter-in-motion such as inertia and gravity as a unique area of investigation.[10] Coming later, biology laid claim to its scientific originality by selecting those physical processes that lead to life in organic matter. For psychology, the key was pinpointing the unique capabilities of the human mind – but how was sociology to follow suit? During the late nineteenth century, many thinkers completely discounted 'society' as an object that was capable of scientific enquiry.

In the estimation of liberals and utilitarians, society was merely the unintentional consequence of individual decisions, which must take precedence in any sociological investigation. Durkheim fundamentally disagreed with this position. For him, society had to be considered a living force in its own right, completely separate from the human beings that make it up. Social forces may emerge from the interactions of people in association, but their origins, their nature and their social functions are completely distinct. Throughout his writings, Durkheim never tired of telling his readers that society was a reality *sui generis*, capable and worthy of scientific investigation. This is the founding principle of his entire sociology, captured admirably in the following remarks,

> Social facts differ not only in quality from psychical facts; they have a different substratum, they do not evolve in the same environment or depend on the same conditions. This does not mean that they are not in some sense psychical, since they all consist of ways of thinking and acting. But the states of the collective consciousness are of a different nature to the states of the individual consciousness. They are representations of another kind. The mentality of groups is not that of individuals: it has its own laws. The two sciences [psychology/ sociology] are therefore as sharply distinct as two sciences can be ... In order to understand the way in which society conceives of itself ... it is the nature of society and not that of individuals that must be considered.[11]

To substantiate this claim, Durkheim points to the qualitative differences between our physical attributes and our creativity. Just as it would be absurd to suggest that our creativity could be reduced to the oxygen, hydrogen, carbon and nitrogen atoms that make us up, so it is absurd to suggest that societies can be reduced to their individual constituent members. Social forces are therefore real in the same way as gravity and electromagnetism are. Like these physical forces, they act on individuals from the outside, helping to determine their behaviour in scientifically discernible ways. Holding this position makes Durkheim into a scientific realist – although his is a realism of a particular type, being mostly focused on the mind, independent of the reality of collective *ideas*. Be that as it may, the opening chapter of *The Rules of Sociological Method* lists everything from the structural make-up of society to the momentary influences of mob psychology as social facts with causal significance. Some of the many examples he gives in the book are listed in Table 4.1.

In *The Division of Labour in Society*, Durkheim emphasised the importance of the variables in the left-hand column. Recall that population growth and moral density determined the different forms of social solidarity in a basic cause and effect relationship.

Table 4.1   Examples of Social Facts in Durkheim's *The Rules of Sociological Method*

Infrastructural Social Facts	Physical/Practice-Based Social Facts	Ideal/Representational Social Facts	Subjective/Momentary Social Facts
Distribution of Population (Social Density) Number of Genuine Social Interactions (Moral Density) Political Divisions, Networks of Communications	Religious and Social Rituals, (Marriages, Funerals, Criminal Trials) Familial Relations Financial Systems	Language, Moral Rules, Legal Rules, Aphorisms, Popular Beliefs and Sayings, Customs	Social Ways of Thinking and Feeling that don't Persist (for example, a Momentary Group Psychology)

From 1895 onwards, however, it is the nature of collective belief systems that begin to take centre stage in his writings. This, in turn, presents Durkheim with an important methodological conundrum rooted in the links between social ideas and individual ideas. On the one hand, Durkheim must draw a clear distinction between these two sets of phenomena. On the other hand, Durkheim cannot allow social ideas to be studied as a completely mind-independent reality. Positive science would never accept the idea of a social consciousness existing outside of human minds – and so he needs to find a way to study the *social ideas* in people's heads in a way that separates them out from their other, more subjective, *ideas*. To put this slightly differently, he needs to *distinguish collective ideas from other thoughts in our minds, without thereby transforming society into a free-standing personality*. To achieve this rather difficult balancing act, Durkheim developed a number of arguments.

First off, he emphasises the pre-existing nature of society for newly born individuals. When people first come into the world, they find a whole series of social institutions already in place. Reflecting on the fact that religious beliefs are passed down through the generations, for example, Durkheim writes that: 'the believer has discovered from birth, the beliefs and practices of his religious life [and] if they existed before he did, it follows that they *exist outside* him.'[12] The legal framework and the financial system also share this pre-existent quality, proving that they too, must be located *outside* the mind of any individual. Turning next to the national language, Durkheim insists that whilst we are not, strictly speaking, forced to communicate in our mother tongue, life in society would become almost impossible without its support. On the positive side, social institutions enable individuals to achieve many of their most important goals. On the negative side, they provide powerful external constraints as soon as we try to move our will against them. To live in a society is to be moulded and shaped by its dominant ideas. Whether one accepts the superiority of collective ideas or whether one rejects them, the *coercive nature* of society's principle institutions cannot be doubted. Contrary to popular opinion, this suggests that there are, in fact,

> Ways of acting, thinking and feeling which possess the remarkable property of existing outside the consciousness of the individual. Moreover, not only are these types of behaviour external to the individual, they are endued with a compelling and coercive power by virtue of which whether he wishes it or not, they impose themselves upon him.[13]

Having established criteria of pre-existence, externality and coercion as the basis for identifying social facts, Durkheim argues that the latter must necessarily be studied as 'objective things'.[14] This means observing facts as they actually are, before classifying them in such a way that they can become scientifically intelligible. For Durkheim, the mark of genuine science is its ability to make discoveries that are not amenable either to common sense or speculative philosophy. Being too close to the facts, lay people 'can hardly glimpse, save in the most imprecise way the real reasons which impel them to act'.[15] To achieve success, the sociologist must consequently discard all common sense preconceptions and free themselves from the prejudices of popular opinion.[16] This is a demanding task which can only be achieved by feeling oneself in the presence of facts, which, contrary to all expectations, are governed by objective laws.

Indeed, sociologists must be prepared to make discoveries that surprise and disconcert the public. For example, many people would surely be surprised to discover that there are social forces pushing them towards their choice of marriage partner and even towards suicide. Yet this is exactly what sociologists have found. From the other side, Durkheim bemoans the fact that philosophers generally *treat ideas about reality as if they were reality itself.* In this context, he notes that: 'up to now sociology has dealt more or less exclusively not with things, but with concepts.'[17] Philosophical thought must now be discarded if sociology is to transition onto a proper scientific footing. This effectively means replacing idle speculation with observation, classification and scientific conceptualisation. Durkheim explains the essence of his view in the following remarks,

> To treat facts of a certain order as things, is therefore not to place them in this category or that, it is to observe towards them a certain attitude of mind. It is to embark on the study of them by adopting the principle that one is entirely ignorant of what they are, that their characteristic properties, like the unknown causes upon which they depend cannot be discovered by even the most careful introspection ... Science implies no metaphysical conception, no speculation about the innermost depth of being. What it demands is that the sociologist should assume the state of mind of physicists, chemists and biologists when they venture into an as yet unexplored area of the scientific field.[18]

Treating phenomena as 'objective things' constitutes the starting point for a science that moves from the most visible external characteristics to those which are often hidden, but more essential. Disposing of speculative frameworks allows the sociologist to classify facts in such a way that every phenomenon possessing the same external marks is brought under the same definition. This classificatory stage is crucial if social science is to become objective, methodical and specific. The sociologist begins with observations of objective things, before proceeding to classify them according to characteristics that are the most visible amongst them. Durkheim writes that: 'the subject matter of research must only include a group of phenomena defined beforehand by certain common characteristics and all phenomena which correspond to this definition must be included.'[19]

As an example, he argues that the true nature of crime is revealed through forms of punishment. The sociologist must therefore gather data on all phenomena that involve punishment and then classify them in a certain order. Moreover, to make the selection as objective as possible, the scientist must strive to consider facts in general, rather than homing in on their particular manifestations. It is preferable to study how punishment is enshrined in legal codes rather than selecting particular criminal acts which may be coloured by unconscious bias. Having laid out the rules for observing and classifying social facts, Durkheim's next task is to separate pathological from normal facts in every particular social type.

PATHOLOGIES AND THE RULES FOR CLASSIFYING SOCIAL TYPES

Although Durkheim is now satisfied that he has general rules for initiating sociological investigation, he immediately declares that there are two orders of facts that must be kept separate.[20] One can distinguish those traits which are good for society from those that are pathological or dysfunctional. He consequently writes that: 'at the very beginning of our research it is important to be able to classify facts as normal or abnormal ... in order to assign physiology and pathology each to its proper domain.'[21] We previously witnessed this distinction in relation to the *abnormal forms of the division of labour*. Here the idea is to generalise that model by cultivating 'normal' phenomena, whilst eradicating abnormalities. Defining facts as 'pathological' might seem to contradict Durkheim's earlier call to let the 'facts speak for themselves'. However, he assures us that it is possible to find objective criteria upon which to make our distinction.[22]

Drawing a biological analogy, he argues that health is associated with: (1) the perfect adaptation of an organism to its wider environment; and (2) the normal state of an organism when looked upon in general. In contrast, sickness is anything which upsets the balance between the organism and its environment or is unusual when compared to the normal functioning of the organism. Health, Durkheim declares, is intrinsic to the constitution of an organism in a way that sickness isn't. He concludes that those facts which appear in the most common forms of the organism are normal, whilst the rest are morbid or pathological.[23] Having made these claims about *biology* moreover, Durkheim immediately applies them to *sociology*,

Every sociological phenomenon, just as every biological phenomenon, although remaining essentially the same can assume a different form for each particular case. The first are common to the whole species [whilst] other forms exist which are exceptional/pathological ... The physiologist studies the functions of the average organism; the same is true of the sociologist.[24]

By proceeding in this manner, Durkheim believes he is meeting all of the standards of objective classification. Because health is the sign of affinity between an organism and its environment, it is inconceivable that those traits that are common and persistent would not also be the most advantageous. Once social facts become generalised throughout society, it therefore becomes permissible to accept them as normal. Conversely, those facts which are fleeting or unusual can safely be defined as abnormalities. That said, normality and abnormality are never absolute characteristics, but are relative to a particular society at a particular stage of its development. Cut throat behaviour may be perfectly adapted to a financial district for example, but it would be pathologically dysfunctional within a cooperative community. The cooperative behaviour of an Amish family would conversely be pathological within the social rules of the City of London. In 'normal periods', what matters is the fit between the sociological phenomenon in question and the general conditions of the wider environment. The more prevalent a social fact is amongst the population, the more likely it is to be normal and healthy. But in what Durkheim defines as 'transitionary periods', everything can be dramatically turned on its head.

During these periods of upheaval, 'The only normal type extant at the time and grounded in the facts is one that relates to the past but no longer corresponds to the new conditions of existence.'[25] Unlike in normal periods, the dominant social facts may be momentarily dysfunctional – such as anomie or inequality. In these circumstances, Durkheim worries that a purely empirical search for the most general traits would lead to confusion. To avoid this eventuality, the sociologist must consistently determine whether the social conditions which gave rise to a fact still pertain or whether they are no longer present. If a social fact is currently linked to the wider conditions of social living, it can be admitted as normal. If not, even the most general traits must be considered pathological. Returning again to a theme from *The Division of Labour in Society*, Durkheim insists that the economic chaos that is currently in evidence is an example of a generalised trait that is nevertheless rooted in a previous set of social conditions. He therefore writes,

> To know whether the present economic state of the peoples of Europe, with the lack of organisation that characterises it, is normal or not, we must investigate what in the past gave rise to it. If the conditions are still those appertaining to our societies, it is because the situation is normal

despite the protest it stirs up. If, on the other hand, it is linked to that old social structure which elsewhere we have termed segmentary, and which, after providing the essential skeletal framework of societies is now dying out, we shall be forced to conclude that this now constitutes a morbid state, however universal it may be.[26]

For Durkheim, therefore, normality and abnormality always relate to a given context. Everything turns on the links between: (1) *a particular social fact*, (2) *a particular social type, and,* (3) *a particular stage of its evolution.* This necessitates laying out the rules for classifying social types. Charting a course between what he defines as the extremely specific analysis of historians and the universal principles of philosophers, Durkheim argues that sociology must combine the patient accumulation of diverse social facts with a scientific quest for universal explanations. *Prima facie,* the only way to achieve this task is to study each society in meticulous detail, searching out the relevant factors that underpin their structure. As a first principle, Durkheim sees nothing wrong with detailed statistical and descriptive analysis, although he recognises the impossibility of cataloguing every aspect of a given society. To make this task a bit more manageable, Durkheim advocates looking for those *decisive or crucial facts* which are capable of explaining other facts.

The way to do this is to resolve a system into its component parts before isolating those that hold the system together. In *The Division of Labour in Society,* for example, it is the moral density of a given social formation that provides the crucial facts of the investigation. Once we know the nature, the number and relations of the parts, it is theoretically possible to work our way right back to the simplest societies that have ever existed. From here, we can add various layers of social complexity, working our way towards the most advanced social types that have ever existed. Durkheim explains,

> We shall begin by classifying societies according to the degree of organisation they manifest, taking as a base the perfectly simple or the single segment society. Within these classes different varieties will then be distinguished, according to whether a complete coalescence of the initial segments takes place.[27]

Starting with the basic clan group, every society can be properly classified according to its subsequent level of social complexity. Sociological phenomena must always be investigated within the context in which they arise and the result will be a detailed taxonomy of social types – including the normal and abnormal phenomena residing within them.

EXPLAINING SOCIAL FACTS AND SOCIOLOGICAL PROOFS

Observing social facts is the starting point of any investigation, but the crucial task is explanation. To explain 'why' something is the way that it is means searching out the *causal roots* of visible phenomena. Durkheim's interest in social integration meant that he has often been labelled as a structural-functionalist, because he is supposed to have suggested that if society has a need for a particular institution, this will cause it to exist. Durkheim however denies this and suggests that the function of a social fact is never its cause. To confuse the causes and functions is to slip into *teleology*, which Durkheim rejects in the strongest possible terms.

Teleology means explaining phenomena by the functions or purposes that they serve. It was a feature of Aristotelian philosophy that the *final cause* of processes and phenomena was equally as important as their *efficient cause*. To take an example, an acorn was assumed to *purposely* grow into an oak tree as this was the most natural state for it to achieve.[28] Heavy objects were likewise assumed to *purposely* return to earth, as this was their most natural resting place. In natural science, this sense of purposes for natural forces was eradicated during the scientific revolution, but for Durkheim, much of it was still at play in sociology. Assessing his contemporaries, Durkheim bemoans the fact that: 'most sociologists believe they have accounted for phenomena once they have demonstrated the purpose they serve and the role they play.'[29] This form of reasoning not only adds purposes to inanimate social forces, it also opens up a series of other abuses that undermine the objective nature of sociological investigation.

The first of these is 'metaphysical speculation'. Comte, for example, squeezed social facts into a universal schema based on human progress. Everything from modern science to the nuclear family is 'explained' on the basis of their 'metaphysical purpose', thereby leaving their causal origins out of the picture. It is as if these institutions were consciously created to serve particular human purposes rather than emerging spontaneously though objective forms of social interaction. In a similar vein, Spencer accounts for the wide diversity of social facts by linking them all to individual happiness. Here a second problem comes into play, as psychological motives sneak into sociology through the back door. In Durkheim's estimation, most teleological explanations assume that the purposes of given social institutions are ultimately found in the desires of the individuals who 'create' them. In the orthodox school of economics, for example, 'the whole of economic life … hangs in the end upon a purely individual factor, the desire for wealth.' This is also true in those sociological explanations where society is conceived as a system of means set up by humans to achieve certain ends.[30]

To guard against this form of psychological reductionism, Durkheim once again reiterates the fact that social forces are a reality *sui generis* (in their own right). The power of society is evident in its ability to constrain individual behaviour and it is ludicrous to assume that just because people desire a given social institution that they can magically create it. The social world is just as objective and factual as the world of physics. We may want world peace or endless wealth, but we cannot create these ends out of our own heads. This suggests two important rules about sociological explanations. First, when the sociologist 'undertakes to explain a social phenomenon the efficient cause which produces it and the function it fulfills must be investigated separately.'[31] Second, they must feel themselves in the presence of forces that have a nature completely independent of the individual and their psychological consciousness,

> There is between psychology and sociology the same break in continuity as there is between biology and the physical and chemical sciences. Consequently every time a social phenomenon is directly explained by a psychological phenomenon, we may rest assured that that explanation is false.[32]

Durkheim then argues, somewhat repetitively, that the importance of group association means that the sociologist must begin their explanation with an assessment of the internal structure of a particular society. In *The Division of Labour in Society*, Durkheim sought to show how an increase in the volume and character of social interactions profoundly transformed group solidarity. Here he once again argues that: 'the primary origin of social processes must be sought in the constitution of the inner social environment.'[33] Indeed, 'this conception of the social environment as the determining factor in collective evolution is of the greatest importance. For if it is discarded sociology is powerless to establish any causal relationship.'[34] With these – admittedly scant – *rules of explanation* established, Durkheim turns to his rules for *sociological proof*.

Assessing John Stuart Mill's work on scientific logic, he argues that the only way to prove that one phenomena is the cause of another is to compare those cases where the two factors are present (or absent) and ask whether the variations they display in these different circumstances suggest that one might be the cause of the other.[35] This is the classic technique used in natural scientific experimentation. To establish that heat is the cause of water changing from a liquid into a gas, for example, a researcher will initially put these two phenomena into a relationship and then study the water without any heat. Alternatively, if she wants to explain the cause of biological disease, she can study the body in the absence of a virus and then again when the virus is present. Although Mill himself doubted whether this method could be successfully applied to social phenomena, Durkheim insists that the greater complexity of the social environment does not exclude it from experimentation. All the investigator needs to ensure is that one unique and identifiable cause is tied to one unique and identifiable effect.[36] Put slightly differently, 'to the same effect there always corresponds the same cause.'[37]

Durkheim demonstrates this with another look at the nature of crime.[38] Superficially, it might appear that there are as many causes of crime as there are criminal acts, but for Durkheim this surface diversity masks an inner uniformity. If there seems to be a variety of causes, it is because there are multiple *species* of different crimes, each one brought about by its own unique and identifiable cause. This is equally true in the biological world, where different species of fevers exist, each with their own unique and identifiable biological cause. Durkheim is confident that as soon as two phenomena are seen to vary together in a sufficient number of cases, their *constant concomitance* can be taken as akin to a law of nature.[39] We must still remain vigilant, however, as constant concomitance can occur, not because one of the phenomena is the cause of the other, but because they are both effects of the same cause. Likewise, a cause may be impeded from delivering its effects, whilst effects can frequently be distorted by other factors in the social environment. To cope with the reality that society cannot be turned into a perfectly closed experimental environment, Durkheim lays out the following proof procedure,

First we shall discover, with the help of deduction, how one of the two terms was capable of producing the other; then we shall attempt to verify the result of this induction with the aid of experiments, i.e. by making fresh comparisons. If the deduction proves possible and the verification is successful, we can therefore regard the proof as having been demonstrated, If, on the other hand, no direct link between the facts is perceived ... we must set about finding a third phenomenon on which the two others equally depend or which may have served as an intermediary between the two.[40]

Suicide rates consistently increase with education, for example, but for Durkheim it would be wrong to conclude that merely having more years of schooling increased the chances of individuals ending their own lives. In reality, there is a third determining factor which is the weakening of religious traditionalism that causes both the desire for knowledge and the tendency towards suicide.[41] It is wrong to suggest that sociology is inferior to the natural sciences because social life is bursting full of variations. What must be done is to examine series of concomitant variations residing in the statistical records of crime, suicide, births, deaths, marriages and savings etc. When dealing with general facts such as these, it is permissible to study them in any one society. However, it is always preferable to compare and contrast series of statistics across different societies at the same stage of their social development. In this way, the investigator can ascertain whether or not the same phenomenon evolved in the same way over time in the same conditions. Indeed, the best strategy is to follow a particular social institution through all of the variety it has hitherto exhibited, with Durkheim insisting that to 'explain a social fact of any complexity one must follow its entire development through all social species'.[42]

This so-called 'genetic method' is the high point of a sociological method which can be summarised as follows. The first task is to view social facts as objective things. This means adopting the perspective of natural scientists, like geologists when observing a rock. Next the scientist must reject all forms of common sense preconceptions in order to view the facts as they actually are. This allows for the classi-fication of all those phenomena that have the same external marks or empirical characteristics. Once this classificatory phase is completed, the scientist moves from surface descriptions to genuine explanations. This represents the most profound phase of the investigation, as the causes of sociological phenomena are revealed. To test the validity of its explanations, sociology relies on forms of proof that also mirror those in natural scientific experimentation. Two or more phenomena are initially put into sequence with each other, before one of them is either held in check or totally eliminated. If there is a constant concomitance – of the form *whenever A occurs B occurs* – in the first case and no such concomitance in the second, we can be sure that there are genuine and objective forces causing the sequence that is being recorded. At the end of the book, Durkheim insists on three final rules.

First, sociology must be independent of all philosophical and practical ideologies. Sociology can neither be positivist, evolutionist or spiritualist, nor individualist, communist or socialist.[43] Instead, it must seek to strictly apply the logic of causality to the natural variety of social phenomena. This leads to Durkheim's second key principle, which insists that because social facts are 'external things' the sociological method must be both objective and specific. Finally, because social things are often immaterial, collective belief systems and representations must be explained by tracing out their social roots in the inner social environment.

Once these scientific methods have been applied, sociology can be used as a sophisticated form of social engineering to better society. Table 4.2 is a summary of the scientific and engineering phases of Durkheim's method.

This concludes Durkheim's summary of his *The Rules of Sociological Method*, but it remains to assess his scientific method for its cogency and consistency.

PROBLEMS IN DURKHEIM'S CONCEPTION OF THE SCIENTIFIC ENTERPRISE

In all of its essential features, Durkheim's method is the positivist approach made popular by the successes of the natural sciences from the late seventeenth until the early twentieth centuries. In positivism, investigators supposedly raise themselves above their own society in a way that allows them to examine external phenomena in a rigorous and objective manner. Information flows one way from an external object towards an enquiring subject who merely describes and explains a mind independent reality. Having revealed the true nature of society's institutions, positivism shifts towards the model of the engineer. In the social context, the most important task is to distinguish those forces which are functional for the wider society from those which are pathological. This gives Durkheimian sociology an important role in

Table 4.2 Summary of Durkheim's Key Methodological Procedures

Phases in Scientific Investigation	Phases in Scientific Engineering
Observation Social facts as objective things – identified on the basis of their: (1) externality, and (2) ability to constrain	*Scientific Analysis 1* Investigate the nature of social forces and moral norms
Classification 1 Classify social phenomena on the basis of similar external marks	*Classification and Selection* Identify those moral norms most suited to the requirements of a given society
Classification 2 Separate those facts suspected of being healthy from those deemed to be pathological	*Policy Formation* Provide information for republican forms of enlightened governance
Classification 3 Define various social types in order to definitively classify individual phenomena into healthy/pathological	*Educational Programmes* Develop scientific education to pass the spirit of scientific sociology to the next generation.
Explanation Move from classifying to explanation by moving from surface phenomena to their underlying causes	*Analysis of Outcomes* Empirical assessment of the outcomes of policy and educational initiatives
Proof Put phenomena into a suspected causal sequence; remove the cause and observe the result. If there is no 'effect', the method has proved the underlying cause.	*Scientific Analysis 2* Ongoing sociological analysis to determine the evolving structure of society and the nature of the morality needed to cohere it.

the wider society as it imparts objective knowledge to policy makers that can only be discovered through their scientific investigations. In this way, the positive and normative aspects of the methodology are kept radically distinct, with sociology providing neutral information to be acted upon only after it has been revealed. Although this method has a certain plausibility when applied to physics, it has been utterly demolished by philosophers of science since at least the middle of the twentieth century.[44]

Today we realise that all knowledge is the product of theories that are developed within scientific communities, themselves embedded within the wider society.[45] Gravity is a force with objective and measurable effects, but *our knowledge of gravity* had to be painstakingly constructed by scientists who themselves were trained and influenced by the society around them. Isaac Newton's scientific theories were influenced by the commercial needs of industrialisation, for example, whilst his atomistic philosophy reflected the increasing atomisation of human beings in early capitalism.[46] Charles Darwin's theory of the 'survival of the fittest' was similarly influenced by his own society, accurately depicting the increasingly competitive relations of the early capitalist-industrial economy.

Durkheimian sociology was no different in this regard, privileging the kinds of categories that helped the French republic to cohere its citizens. Recall that the late nineteenth century was a period in which the morality of the church had waned at the same time as the class struggle was intensifying. In these conditions, the burning issue for policy elites was whether they could generate new forms of cohesion to stop society descending into anarchy. Rather than merely observing the facts, Durkheim's central categories reflect these concerns, emphasising order over conflict, integration as inherently healthy and morality as the most important explanatory variable. According to Robert Alun Jones, Durkheim's 'entire social science, including choice and formulation of problems, definitions of terms, classification of social types, methods of proof – indeed, even the denial of all philosophical and political commitments – was deeply political.'[47] Steven Lukes fundamentally agrees, arguing that: 'Durkheim's social science did not merely serve political purposes: It is itself inherently political, in its very formulation of problems, in its proposed explanations and in its very conception of what is to be explained.'[48] Rather than objective science patiently allowing the 'facts to speak for themselves', Durkheim's categories were deeply moulded by the object he was purporting to investigate. To a point, this problem is common to all of the sciences influenced by positivism, but there can be little doubt that Durkheim's difficulties are more severe given the fact that his objects of investigation are predominantly thoughts, ideas, feelings and actions. This leads to a second problem, centred on the relations between sociology and the other sciences.

Throughout his writings, Durkheim displayed an almost fanatical need to tie sociology to the natural sciences, whilst separating it completely from the humanities. This is evident in his frequent use of analogies from physics and chemistry, which Lukes has correctly identified as part of a wider attempt to gain legitimacy and respect.[49] In Durkheim's estimation the all-important factor in legitimising sociology is to have an object of investigation that is qualitatively distinct from the individual psyche. For this reason, he defines social facts as modes of thinking and acting that are both external to individuals and imposed upon them by virtue of their coercive power. For Durkheim, society is an inherently novel phenomenon emerging in much the same way as new substances emerge through chemical synthesis in nature. Just as hydrogen and oxygen combine to make water (H_2O) for example, so two individuals brought into association combine to create social forces that exist outside their individual minds. According to Durkheim, 'in order for a social fact to exist, several individuals ... must have interacted together [creating a] synthesis outside each one, which [is] independent of their particular wills considered separately.'[50]

This analogy has a certain plausibility when Durkheim references language and culture, but it ultimately fails for two interrelated reasons. First, every synthesis that takes place in nature involves the combination of substances that are themselves already qualitatively distinct. One can't bring hydrogen together with hydrogen for example, and expect to produce a new combination. Yet human beings, while they may have individual personalities, are not qualitatively distinct in the same way as hydrogen and oxygen. It was Durkheim himself who emphasised how social forces often led to a conformity of beliefs. But if there is a high level of conformity, then individual minds are not qualitatively different. Gisbert takes up this point in the following way,

> By synthesis, especially creative synthesis we mean a combination or putting together of elements out of which a new being results specifically distinct from them. Chemical combinations like OH_2 or H_2SO_4 are outstanding examples of synthesis freely used by Durkheim. Yet we do not know of any synthesis (creative) in which components are homogenous ... Individual minds are homogenous and, no matter how they may combine ... no true synthesis appears possible.[51]

Second, Durkheim actually requires the social forces he identifies to *interact uniformly* with each of the individuals under their control. This is a prerequisite for a science based on one unique cause and one unique effect, but it creates an obvious problem for Durkheim's sociology. Either people have diverse reactions to social forces, in which case it is hard to defend them as natural laws, or individuals are homogenously socialised, in which case the idea of synthesis or emergence must be rejected.

Durkheim's use of physical analogies is no more successful. Throughout *The Rules of Sociological Method*, he defines social facts as real world forces with all the power of their natural counterparts, but this impales his sociology on the horns of a dilemma. On the one hand, social forces must be readily distinguishable from the minds of individuals, if sociology is to have a proper object of investigation. This is the reason for Durkheim's repeated assertion that social facts be treated as objective things. On the other hand, Durkheim needs to tie social facts *into the minds* of individuals, if he is to avoid the charge of social reification – treating society as a thing in itself. This explains why he also defines social phenomena as becoming observable through the acts of socialised individuals. At one and the same time, Durkheim needs to argue that social ideas are external to the individual and yet can only be investigated through their effects on behaviour. This results in repeated equivocation as the proper distinction between social ideas and individual ideas becomes difficult to disentangle. In particular, how can the investigator be sure that what she is observing is a uniquely sociological phenomenon?

Pushed too far in one direction, society is in danger of becoming a free-standing consciousness. Pushed too far in the other direction, Durkheim loses the ability to defend his conception of objective science. Reflecting on these issues, Takla and Pope argue that Durkheim's whole conception of 'social forces' relies on an illegitimate comparison with natural phenomena.[52] Physical forces are neither dependent on the mind nor changed fundamentally by our learning about them. In the case of sociology, however, ideas themselves become the primary object of investigation making it impossible to stand outside these facts in the way that Durkheim ultimately wants to. Whether it be religious beliefs or modern-day nationalism, social forces can only be reproduced through the meaningful actions of intelligent human beings. This should have been apparent to Durkheim by the fact that the religion was losing its grip on the mass of people but he acted as if social forces were natural and immutable.

Added to these general problems, Durkheim regularly broke many of his own rules. To see this, consider the rules laid down for observation and classification. According to Durkheim, the scientist must initially discard all common sense preconceptions in favour of observations rooted in 'objective criteria'. Yet he himself immediately imposes his own subjective evaluations on the data, rather than investigating facts as they actually appear. Gisbert takes up the story below,

> For the categories of common sense he would substitute arbitrary definitions. But how are the classes chosen that are to be defined? Durkheim ... admits that even an external mark, when belonging to all members of a class ... must be closely connected with the more essential features of a class. But from this it is clear that the class defined is not determined by the definition. ... The class is chosen in advance, and the definition is contrived to square with it ... he has [consequently] substituted for common sense his own intuition; which may be an improvement but hardly constitutes a rational method.[53]

Although Durkheim insists that his classifications are in line with objective reality, this is never (nor can it be) demonstrated. Instead, he imposes a set of arbitrary classifications on facts which are made to square with the wider aims of Durkheimian sociology. Take the distinction between normal and pathological phenomena as a case in point. Durkheim insists that those facts which appear most regularly in society must generally be regarded as 'normal' and 'healthy'. So far so good one might think, except that this rule must periodically be jettisoned in cases where the most observable traits are out of line with the wider needs of the social system. Deciding between periods of normality and periods of transition is crucial for Durkheimian social engineering, but this task seems impossible to achieve. The sociologist has to somehow link social facts to the wider conditions that initially gave rise to them, before further investigating whether these social conditions still pertain.[54] In addition, sociologists must be able to achieve this feat whilst deciding what stage of its evolution a society has reached. Unsurprisingly, Durkheim lays down absolutely no rules that can actually achieve this. After all, how is the empirical scientist to link what they see in front of them to the wider needs of the social totality? More to the point, are sociologists supposed to record individual phenomena as they observe them or rank them in terms of their ability to aid with social reproduction? None of these questions are satisfactorily answered beyond the claim that each society must be investigated in terms of its own specificity.

Turning to Durkheim's model of explanation, there is no clear pathway developed between the external mark of classification and the underlying causes that must be discovered. Durkheim officially insists on the importance of causal analyses, without thereby giving any sense of how to achieve it. Indeed, his chapter on causation never once tells us what Durkheim means 'by a cause, other than it is not a function'.[55] His analysis of sociological proofs is also riddled with internal contradictions. Recall that for Durkheim the method of concomitant variations relies on *one unique cause leading to one unique effect*. This is supposedly the proof procedure for objective sociology and yet it is completely at odds with Durkheim's social rules and his earlier sociological practice. In *The Division of Labour in Society*, Durkheim insists that during normal periods, the division of labour necessarily causes an increase in organic solidarity. The cause (division of labour) and effect (organic solidarity) relationship is therefore extremely transparent, except that it breaks down completely during periods of transition. Instead of specialisation leading to increased solidarity, periods of transition are characterised by social dislocation, anomie and class conflict. *Here the same cause is leading to completely different effects, thereby undermining one of the central strictures of Durkheim's methodology.*

Taken together these various difficulties have served to undermine the standing of *The Rules of Sociological Method* in most secondary assessments. According to Stephen Turner, for example, the text has a 'problematic and ambiguous status', being a poor guide to Durkheim's practice.[56] Charles Lemert is even more scathing, arguing that: 'Durkheim was so intent on writing the canonical text of sociology's methods that he stipulated rules that even he could not use'.[57] The end result was not a set of rules for genuine scientific investigation but a deeply ideological system built to achieve an aim that was itself overtly political.

PROBLEMS IN DURKHEIM'S CONCEPTION OF SOCIAL ENGINEERING

Durkheim's desire for social engineering added a second conservative element to his thinking.[58] By taking the health of the French republic as his primary concern, Durkheim allowed the normative aspects of his theory to completely undermine its scientific potential. This, in turn, was manifest in three supplementary weaknesses.

First, Durkheim allowed his preference for social stability to take precedence over the observed realities of French society. In Chapter 3, we noted the class conflict, inequality and social dislocation that Durkheim recorded in *The Division of Labour in Society*. Class power necessarily creates deep divisions within capitalist society, but Durkheim's republicanism meant that he was prepared to assume these problems were 'pathological abnormalities' soon to be eradicated. The fact that French society had been riven apart for over a century was consequently minimised, as Durkheim attempted to convince his readers of the basic desirability of republican institutions. Indeed, following Renouvier's lead, he constructed a theoretical framework that was tailor-made to the needs of the republican elite.[59]

This led to his second key weakness, as Durkheim's normative concerns deprived his sociology of crucial social scientific categories such as power, ideology, exploitation and structural conflict. By focusing overwhelmingly on social cohesion, Durkheim was left with little option but to see the horrors unfolding around him as fleeting challenges unworthy of detailed investigation.[60] Had he chosen to investigate them, Durkheim might have uncovered the class-based exploitation causing the problems that so worried many of his contemporaries. He may also have realised that republicanism relied on the successful integration of very different classes of people into society. For the ruling classes, Durkheim's sociology promised institutions that would increase their power and allow them to rule. For the working classes, these same institutions constituted a major block to their genuine emancipation. This shows the importance of investigating the nature of the social relationships *within a society* rather than merely the functional needs of *society as a whole*. Insofar as Durkheim refused to look at the different ways that workers and their employers were integrated into society, he became an apologist for class exploitation. Put in slightly different terms, what is functional for the overall stability of society may be deeply dysfunctional for large classes of its members.

The events surrounding the Paris Commune are once again a case in point. By virtue of the fact that the commune was defeated, the workers of Paris were successfully reintegrated into French society. For thousands of Parisians, this process was synonymous with violent oppression, but insofar as it led to social cohesion, the needs of 'society' were greatly enhanced. As in the colonies, the elites proved themselves more than willing to engage in repression, but Durkheim's categories couldn't reflect this. His unwavering loyalty to republican values therefore constitutes the third and final weakness in Durkheim's normative position. In place of genuine scientific investigation, he developed a set of ideological categories designed around the needs of the French elite. Positively, his methodological rules proved basically unworkable. Normatively, they lead to the kind of social engineering that is readily compatible with class-based oppression. For these reasons amongst many others, Durkheim's *The Rules of Sociological Method* proved a failure.

5
Suicide

Durkheim's first major work after his *The Rules of Sociological Method* was a study on *Suicide*. Published in 1897, it grew to become his best known publication. Almost everyone who studies sociology today has encountered it. It is seen as a classic because it proves there can be a science of society. Durkheim had taken the most individual action – the decision to end one's life – and shown that there were social patterns which required a social explanation. The book therefore helped to found sociology as a genuine scientific discipline. As Charles Lemert put it, Durkheim 'was able to invent sociology in France out of nearly nothing because he wrote two texts, Rules [of Sociological Method] and Suicide, which are canonical to the empirical sociologist.'[1]

If this was indeed Durkheim's motive, it was a relative failure in his own lifetime. Only about 1,000 copies of the book were printed and it went unrecognised for decades after publication. It was not until the 1930s when US sociologists like Elton Mayo, the founder of the human relations approach to workplace management, and Talcott Parsons, the main theoretician of conventional sociology, gave it a positive evaluation that it started on the road to becoming a classic.[2] By that stage, however, the particular social and political context that Durkheim was addressing had long been forgotten.

Durkheim had lectured on the subject of suicide for ten years before the book's publication. His first public intervention came with a paper published in 1888, *Suicide and Fertility: A Study of Moral Statistics*. This looked at the statistical correlation between birth rates and suicide rates and claimed that they varied inversely. A high birth rate was linked to a low rate of suicide and a low birth rate to the higher rate of suicide. Durkheim suggested that suicide was 'a sign of social malaise' and was linked to declining birth rates because it arose from a similar source. This was a fall in family size, which was producing a lack of 'domestic solidarity'. Instead of gaining joy from domestic life, men were becoming more concerned about their material well-being. He concluded that:

'where families are smaller, weaker, less fertile, individuals being less close to each other, leave gaps between them through which blow the icy blast of egoism, chilling the heart and breaking the spirit.'[3]

The tone of the article was pessimistic and highly moralistic. By implication, it was suggesting that French people were not doing their duty by creating large families. Durkheim regarded this as a danger to the nation and to individuals themselves. He thought that France would be less capable of 'holding its own against rival societies' and individuals would become less resilient because of declining birth rates. These had indeed fallen dramatically because the working class had begun to limit their families. On the eve of the First World War, for example, the average family size was just two.[4] In the aftermath of the defeat by Prussia in 1870, this was viewed as an existential threat with writers such as Émile Cheysson, for example, calling it a 'national peril'.[5] A strong pro-natalist movement had emerged which drew strength from both Catholic and republican ideologies. It spoke of the weakening of the social body and, in the case of the republicans, called for a social science to tackle the signs of social decay. Durkheim was strongly influenced by these concerns and so he focused on suicide primarily as an indicator of a social disease striking at the vital elements of the French nation.

This framing of the issue of suicide and use of statistical sources was comparatively recent. There was a much longer history whereby the meaning of suicide shifted and changed according to the world-view of the various elites. It was by no means a natural or obvious way of viewing suicide but reflected a particular context shaped by dominant powers.

SUICIDE – FROM SIN TO ILLNESS

In his book, Durkheim provides a brief sketch of how suicide has been perceived throughout the course of human history. But behind the narrative lies a suggestion that 'with the progress of history, the prohibition [on suicide] instead of being relaxed only became more strict'.[6] He suggests that among 'primitive peoples' it is probable that suicide was not formally forbidden. In Greece and Rome, it was generally forbidden but the state could permit it under certain circumstances. Suicide was, therefore, only immoral when conducted in private and without the state's permission. This changed with Christianity which introduced an absolute and universal prohibition. Durkheim suggests that behind a mystical reasoning about life being a gift from God, lay an important progressive development. Christianity introduced a new conception of the human personality that, in a more secular age, became the cult of human dignity. In this context, any attempt on man's own life was viewed as a 'sacrilege'. Prohibitions on suicide, he argued, were not simply to be regarded as survivals from the past, but as a reflection of society's more progressive morality today. As a corollary, rising suicide rates should be taken as evidence of a social disease. This narrative, however, glosses over key developments in order to present a more simple evolutionary pattern.

In the classical world, there appears to have been a plurality of opinions on suicide. In Ancient Greece, a distinction was often made between cowardly suicides and those caused by shame or honour.[7] Different philosophical schools held opposing views with the Pythagoreans condemning it absolutely and the Epicureans and Stoics approving of it.[8] In Rome, free citizens had a right to commit suicide, provided it was not done through hanging and there were acceptable reasons for doing so. These included defeat in battles, rape, or painful suffering. Life was not considered a gift of the Gods and so writers like Seneca argued that individuals had a right to dispose of themselves, if old age became too burdensome. The story of how Lucretia killed herself after being raped was popular in Roman folklore. This qualified right was not extended to slaves however. A slave was defined as the property of his or her master and so their suicide represented a form of theft. Soldiers who took an oath of loyalty to the state were also forbidden to commit suicide and anyone who attempted it was punished for trying to rob that state.[9]

Early Christianity had an ambiguous attitude towards suicide. It defined the earthly world as a vale of tears and urged its followers to aspire to being close to God's presence. This led to an undercurrent of support for martyrdom, especially when Christians faced persecution. However, the figure of Judas was also held up as an example of a shameful suicide that resulted from despair. This changed dramatically in the early fifth century and Durkheim gives no hint of the cause, assuming instead that there was a smooth cultural evolution. In reality, the context was shaped by the fact that Christianity became the official state religion of Rome after a decree by Theodosius the Great in AD 280. The integration of the Christian Church leaders into Rome's power structures coincided with the empire's decline as it was being attacked by barbarian tribes. When expansion ceased, the supply of captured slaves also dried up. This in turn led to a major change in the status of Roman citizens when new systems of agricultural exploitation emerged. During the rule of Diocletian, there was a change in the taxation system which effectively led to the coloni – Roman tenant farmers – sinking into greater debt. Instead of a more equal relationship with their landlords, they became tied to the land and fell into a status somewhere between freemen and serfs. Previous injunctions against suicide which were considered a theft on the landlord's 'property' now came into play. As Minois put it, 'an acute shortage of manpower dictated the requisitioning of all human lives for the service of the economy and the defence of empire. One result was harsher legislation which replaced the Roman world's traditional indulgence towards suicide.'[10]

Christian Church leaders began to articulate a strong absolute condemnation of suicide and challenged those inside their own ranks who glorified martyrdom. In 452, the Council of Arles condemned the suicide of family slaves or servants, who killed themselves 'in prey to a diabolical fury' as it was detrimental to their masters' interests.[11] One of those masters was none other than the church itself, which was becoming a large landowner. In the councils of Braga in 563 and Auxerre in 578, all forms of suicide were condemned and rulings were issued that there should be no commemorative offering of Mass for suicides. Augustine and later, Thomas Aquinas, formulated a set of ethics which defined the act as self-murder and a 'detestable crime' that offended laws of God, nature and society. Increasingly, suicide was viewed as the work of Satan, the devil being able to twist an individual's consciousness to create terrible despair. It is simplistic, therefore, to claim that cardinals and leaders of the Christian Church were motivated by a desire to promote individual dignity. They had initially wanted to assert power over their servants on the land. Later they wanted to strengthen their claim to be a spiritual force that could ward off diabolical interventions.

The shift in Christianity helps to explain the extraordinarily harsh prohibitions on suicide throughout the middle ages. Suicide came to be regarded as a more wicked crime than even murder itself. The corpses were put on trial in many European countries and in cases where 'self-murder' was decreed, the body was subject to a variety of ritualised violations. It was often tied to a horse and dragged through streets with a rope. In some instances, it was decapitated or hung for days on gallows. In Germany, there developed a practice of *rinnen* whereby the body of a suicide was placed in a barrel and cast into the Rhine. Suicides were forbidden to be buried in consecrated ground and, in some cases, a stake was driven through the heart and burial took place at crossroads, apparently to confuse the evil spirits. Acts from the thirteenth century in England led to the confiscation of goods belonging to those who committed suicide, which in effect became a punishment on surviving families. In France, there was a practice known as ravages where the homes of suicides' were attacked by crowds, property stolen and the house destroyed. Most of these extreme punishments arose from an outlook that linked suicide to an act of the devil. Both Luther and Calvin, for example, defined suicide as self-murder that arose from 'demonic possession'.[12] The ritualised practices that followed were believed to protect the surviving community from evil spirits.

However, this outlook changed from the early seventeenth century onwards as feudal society broke up and there was a growing intrusion of the market into everyday life. Production for exchange and the money economy became more common. With it came a new image of society as a social contract forged between individuals rather than a pre-ordained order created by God and interpreted by his church. Alongside a greater quest for individual freedom, came a scientific revolution which sought natural causes for observable phenomena. This shift in culture – often associated with the Enlightenment – led to an attack on superstitious ideas about magic, diabolical possession or witchcraft. In their place came a desire for rational explanations. Suicide was re-conceived as an illness – the result of individuals suffering from melancholy. A plea of insanity was increasingly used in coroners' courts to stop the confiscation of family property. But later there was a full-blown shift to either psychologise the victim or to assert that suicide was an undesirable but necessary element of a new society based on individual liberty. An early representative of the latter change was the poet John Donne who used his own understanding of theology to dispute traditional interpretations. Shakespeare also tackled the issue in thirty-two of his plays in a factual manner, without extreme condemnation.

These wider shifts in society led to the creation of a new word – 'suicide'– in place of the more moralistic 'self-murder'.[13] In 1701, Pennsylvania and Delaware did away with laws confiscating the property of suicide victims. Thomas Jefferson later explained that: 'Suicide is not to incur Forfeiture, but considered as a disease'.[14] Influenced by Enlightenment beliefs, the Prussian king Frederick I decriminalised suicide and identified its cause as 'madness', 'dementia' or 'melancholy'.[15] Subsequently, the French Revolution swept away the laws against suicide, many of whom had already fallen into disuse. Other countries followed suit, although it was not until 1993 that Ireland decriminalised suicide. Underlying this shift was a re-conception of suicide as an individual tragedy that resulted from a deranged psychological state.

FROM ILLNESS TO SOCIAL PATHOLOGY

By the mid-nineteenth century, however, there was a further shift in the understanding of suicide. Once again, this did not arise from a teleological progress towards respect for human dignity. Rather, nine-teenth-century Europe was a place in which early proclamations about 'liberty' and 'fraternity' were being replaced by growing social conflict. We saw earlier how sociologists like Auguste Comte and Claude Henri de Saint-Simon reflected these new concerns with their calls for a 'positive' science to replace the 'negative' critiques of the Enlightenment.[16] Both felt that an understanding of scientific laws could help experts to manage the new conflicts and recreate integration and harmony. Their followers were assisted by an explosion of social statistics which provided the raw material for a new science of society. Within this framework, suicide came to be viewed as an indicator of deeper social problems. These problems did not result from society itself or its unequal structures, but rather from undercurrents within that society or, crucially, the lack of 'social integration'. The republican milieu from which Durkheim sprang was particularly enthusiastic about this use of social science to promote better integration. *Suicide* was therefore Durkheim's first application of a diagnostic social science capable of examining the symptoms of underlying disease and helping society to heal itself.

He was not the first to use suicide statistics as an indicator of moral distress, however. From the early nineteenth century, there had developed a tradition of examining figures on birth rates, murders and suicides as indicators of the moral health of the nation. In 1833, André-Michel Guerry published an essay on the 'moral statistics' of France, noting that amongst this data, suicide attracted the most attention. The Belgian writer, Adolphe Quetelet, believed that moral statistics revealed 'the anatomy' of the social body. The awesome regularity in figures on crime, suicide or murder implied that they resulted from social rather than individual causes.[17] He claimed to have discovered 'laws' of social behaviour through such an examination. In Germany, the use of moral statistics to examine the health of society was even more developed.

Wagner discovered that Protestants were more likely to commit suicide than Catholics. He implied, however, that this was due to the superiority of Protestant culture because of its greater emphasis on reason and freedom. Enrico Morselli in Italy produced the most comprehensive data on suicide statistics, from which Durkheim drew some of his material. Morselli titled his book, *Suicide: An Essay on Comparative Moral Statistics* and argued that the regular but progressive increase in suicide rates was linked to civilisation. Suicide represented a form of natural selection whereby weaker elements, who did not gain the benefits of civilisation, were removed. Douglas is therefore correct to assert that Durkheim's own book *Suicide: A Study in Sociology* was 'an attempt to synthesize the better principles, methods of analysis, and empirical findings of the moral statisticians' who preceded him.'[18]

However, Durkheim also differed from this tradition of viewing suicide as an indicator of social distress in two key ways.

First, Durkheim approached the subject with greater theoretical vigour and this led to a different method of viewing social statistics. Previous moral statisticians had been content to find an association between observable variables – for example, climate and suicide rates – and to assert some causal influence. Durkheim, however, demanded a more strict parallelism and an examination of whether or not the relationship had been contaminated by the intrusion of other factors. Thus, whereas Morselli had claimed that climate temperature had an influence on suicide rates, when Durkheim looked at the figures more closely he found that the 'parallelism' did not always apply. In various countries with the same temperature, there were different rates of suicide. Instead of looking at superficial factors which appear to be associated, Durkheim was looking for deeper, basic causes that were not immediately observable. As Turner put it, his goal was getting 'past this level of surface manifestation to the basic level of causality'.[19] The causes that Durkheim focused on arose from his own theoretical framework and were based on concepts such as integration, anomie or regulation. He thought of these not only as theoretical constructs but also as real underlying factors which produced the regularity in both suicide figures and the association between different variables.

Later US sociologists, who held to a more positivist approach, would have difficulties in using Durkheim's schema because they sought to confine research to the level of observable variables. However, that was for the future and the immediate impact of Durkheim's approach was an opposition to common sense explanations. Common sense operated at the level of immediate observation or anecdotes handed down through the generations. Durkheim's great contribution – and it was a genuinely progressive one – was to challenge these perceptions in the name of a deeper scientific reality.

Second, Durkheim was far more determined than his predecessors to root explanations of suicide rates in exclusively social causes. He rejected explanations based on climate or race and showed the limitations of focusing on individual psychology. He was 'non-reductionist' when it came to society, believing that once people formed groups they generated a separate and distinct reality, a moral order. Ironically, however, Durkheim's own concept of society was limited. As he had no interest in fundamental change, he looked at social psychological 'undercurrents' within society – rather than the wider structure of society itself. He wanted to examine moods, values and morality rather than the unequal nature of the social relations. He disdained any examination of the economic relationships which underpinned particular societies. He therefore assumed that the basic structures of society were fine but wanted to focus on the relationship of individuals to that society. His purpose was 'discovering through science the moral restraints which can regulate economic life and by this regulation contain egoism.'[20] In other words, he accepted the fundamental structure of economic life but wanted to superimpose moral regulation on to them.

This meant that his key categories were the *integration* of the individual into social groups; and the *regulation* of the individual by social norms. Durkheim could do this because he made the correct assumption that human beings need a social existence. But instead of examining the specific nature of the society they lived in, he summed it all up in the category Society and divided that into traditional and modern forms. Although he made a strong case for the social nature of suicide rates, his analysis was limited by this concern to promote the stability of the French Republic.

COMMON SENSE EXPLANATIONS

Durkheim begins *Suicide* by outlining his dual purpose. He wants to, first, move beyond metaphysical or very generalised speculations and arrive at 'real laws' which demonstrate a link between suicide and other social phenomena such as marriage, religion and family life. His material for study will be 'social facts' which will be studied as objectively as a biologist or psychologist studies their respective material. Second, he aimed to produce suggestions about the causes of the 'general contemporary maladjustment being undergone by European societies.'[21] In other words, he will treat suicide as an indicator of ill health and, like a good doctor, will seek remedies.

Durkheim then adopts his familiar procedure by providing a definition of suicide. He states, 'the term suicide is applied to all cases of death resulting directly or indirectly from a positive or negative act of the victim himself, which he knows will produce this result.'[22] One problem he will face is whether this definition is the one used by the state officials who gather the data that he uses. However, he ignores this issue and suggests that the official statistics show there is a definite pattern to suicide rates.

Broadly speaking, suicide figures generally vary within a narrow range on a year-to-year basis. In the 1840s, in France, for example, the number of suicides ranged between 2,814 and 3,583. This was a very stable pattern that could not have arisen solely from the accidental decisions made by individuals. If suicide results from purely individual decision-making, there would be a random sequence. Numbers might jump, for example, from 16 to 587 to 133 to 1,600. Yet in all the countries Durkheim examined, this was not the case. The pattern was so stable that there was less variation in the numbers of suicides each year than there was in the general death rate.

There were, however, two important qualifications. First, there were sometimes abrupt changes. In one particular year, there might be a sudden increase or decrease and the variation then starts again on a narrow range. Second, there was a general progressive increase in suicide in all countries. In France, England, Saxony, Bavaria, Prussia and Denmark, the numbers of suicides grew considerably, sometimes doubling or trebling over a long time frame. But once again, the figures did not display a random sequence but rather there was a gradual rise, sometimes punctured by abrupt shifts.

If this is the general pattern for suicides, there are differences between individual countries. All countries display a stable pattern but they will have different rates. Durkheim measures these rates in terms of suicides per million of the population and finds that Italy, for example, had 30 suicides per million whereas France had 135 in the period 1866–70. But while suicide was increasing in each country, the ratio remained constant. In other words, if France had four times the Italian suicide rate, it maintained this ratio even as the numbers of suicides grew. This pattern lent further support to the argument that suicides could not result purely from individual decisions. Using a somewhat ominous expression, Durkheim claimed that: 'each society is pre-disposed to contribute a definite quota of voluntary deaths' and this pre-disposition could only be studied sociologically.[23]

Before advancing his own theory, Durkheim tackled common sense explanations. His method is to show there is no statistical parallelism between these purported causes and suicide rates. Let's look briefly at how Durkheim carries out this exercise.

Insanity: This was the dominant pre-nineteenth-century explanation of suicide. But Durkheim claims that most suicides are carried out by people who had not previously been certified as insane. 'Many suicides,' Durkheim states, 'are completely indistinguishable from other men ... and there is no reason to impute a general delirium to them.'[24] Statistics from every country show that there are more women than men in insane asylums – yet for every female suicide there are on average four male suicides. There are higher rates of insanity among Jews – but lower rates of suicides. More generally, there is no strong co-relationship between insanity rates in different countries and suicide rates.

Alcoholism: This is another psychological state used to explain suicide. But there is no co-relation between the figures for prosecutions for drunkenness and suicide rates. Nor is there a relationship between a country's suicide rate and its level of alcohol consumption. Thus, whereas France consumed 2.84 litres of alcohol per person per week, Russia consumed 10.69 litres. Yet Russia had a lower rate of suicide.

Race: Durkheim expresses doubt that race corresponds to anything definite but settles for three main types: Germanic peoples, Celto-Romans and Slavs. He disputes the biological theory by showing that there are different rates of suicide among Germanic or Slav peoples. Moreover, when Slavs and Germans live in the same environment, their suicide rates also tend to converge.

Hereditary: This was a piece of common folklore, but Durkheim challenged anecdotal evidence about particular families. There is no large-scale evidence to support the theory. Moreover, if hereditary was a major cause, it should have equal effects on women as well as men. But, as we have seen, women commit less suicide. The hereditary effect should also 'kick in' at any age, yet suicide is extremely rare among children.

Climate: Sometimes it is thought that cold, dark or wet climates increase the rate of suicide. But Durkheim found no evidence of this. Suicide rates were, in fact, higher in spring and summer. Daylight hours rather than night-time were also more favourable to suicide. Moreover, countries that had similar climates had different rates of suicides.

Imitation: Durkheim takes issue with this argument from his rival for sociological expertise, Gabriel Tarde. He does so by making a distinction between individuals being affected by broader currents of public opinion and imitation proper, which he sees as unthinking repetition. If imitation were the main cause of suicide, there would be a geographical pattern of strong clusters in particular areas which become weaker as they radiate out from a central point. Durkheim claims that there is no such pattern in the official figures.

Before embarking on his own theory of suicide, Durkheim spells out his approach to suicide rates. He will not examine the declared motivations of the suicide as these can only be imputed by officials subsequently. Even where a suicide leaves a note, Durkheim believes that the declared motives may not be the real motives. Instead of starting with intentions, therefore, Durkheim wishes to examine the social causes which produce them. His aim is to draw up a list of these causes by working back from official suicide rates and analysing the social environment that can lead to suicide. From this method, arises his famous three plus typology.

EGOISTIC SUICIDE

In examining the official figures, Durkheim highlights a number of major relationships. Suicide rates vary, first, with religious affiliation, with Catholics committing less suicide than Protestants and with Jews, in general, having lower rates again. In the Swiss cantons, for example, Catholics show four or five times less suicide than Protestants.

Durkheim does not attribute the different rates to the particular religious doctrines because all equally condemn suicide. The issue was rather that Protestants permit free inquiry to a greater degree than Catholics. Catholicism is a more hierarchical system where traditional beliefs are often unquestioned and these differences have a pronounced social effect. Protestantism tends to have less collective beliefs and sentiments which means that its adherents are a less integrated social group. Jewish people face anti-Semitic prejudice and so they form small, compact and coherent communities which are also highly integrated.

It could also be suggested that the more educated a social group, the less integrated it will be because there is more questioning and free inquiry. Durkheim, however, resists any attempt to impute blame. Indeed, he asserts that: 'far from knowledge being the source of evil, it is its remedy.'[25] Older established religious beliefs are being swept away and cannot be artificially recovered. The advantages that Catholicism provides arose only from its ability to create a community based on shared beliefs. Durkheim suggests that this social dividend can be created again with science and intelligence.[26]

The second stand-out relationship that he examines is between suicide and marriage, but here he finds some complications. In general, marriage provides a higher 'coefficient of preservation' against suicide than non-marriage. By this, Durkheim means the numbers showing less frequent suicide than the wider population or a comparable group. From the age of 20, married persons are likely to commit 1.6 times less suicide than single people. Even though widowhood may reduce this ratio, it does not entirely eliminate it. Strangely, however, below the age of 20, marriage increases the possibility of suicide, especially for men. Durkheim does not explore his discrepancy at this point, merely stating that: 'premature marriage brings about a harmful moral state.'[27]

The one area, however, that causes a huge discrepancy is gender. Durkheim notes that marriage is far more beneficial for men than women. To examine why, Durkheim distinguishes between two aspects – the 'conjugal element', which refers to the marriage contract between two individuals and a 'family element', which consists in the creation of children. There is an advantage for men in the conjugal element but it is relatively slight. The greater advantages comes with the presence of children and the larger the family, the greater the benefits. For women, it is quite different. Marriage alone, without children, actually increases the likelihood of suicide for women. As he puts it: 'conjugal society is harmful to the woman and aggravates her tendency to suicide.'[28] However, with the presence of children, there is also greater immunity for women.

Durkheim's essential point is that large families increase the level of collective interaction and shared memories. They are more likely to create stronger collective sentiments and so are more stable and long lasting. In other words, large families form a more compact social group into which the individual is integrated. Durkheim turns his polemical pen on Malthusian advocates of birth control and asserts that far from large families bringing greater burdens, it diminishes them. Large families are not just 'an unnecessary luxury appropriate only to the rich, they are actually the indispensable stuff of daily life.'[29]

Durkheim also discovers that suicide rates decline in times of war, great social disturbances and even in times of election crisis. During these periods, there is a rise in collective spirit and a stimulation of passions. These force people to close ranks and confront common dangers and so 'the individual thinks less of himself and more of a common cause.'[30] Once again, persons become more integrated into a social group.

From these three key relationships – between suicide and religious affiliation, family life and political cohesion – Durkheim suggests that there is a distinct cause of *egoistic* suicide. In simple terms, suicide varies inversely with the degree of integration. Where an individual is detached from social bonds and focuses exclusively on his own goals rather than the larger society, he is vulnerable to egoistic suicide. By contrast, 'when society is strongly integrated, it holds individuals under its control, considers them at its service and forbids them to dispose wilfully of themselves.'[31] Durkheim also believes that there is a feedback effect from a loosening of the social bonds. The growth of an 'excessive individualism' creates 'currents of depression and disillusionment' that express 'society's state of disintegration.'[32] With the decline in religion and the decrease in family size – all features of what Durkheim terms civilisation – there will be an increase in suicide rates. Or rather, this will continue until social science can propose new methods for restoring the proper social bonds.

ALTRUISTIC SUICIDE

As in *The Division of Labour in Society*, Durkheim limits the pattern of historical change to a simple dichotomy between traditional and modern. Whereas modern society suffers from an excess of individualism, traditional society places little value on the individual personality. In traditional societies, altruistic suicide is the main form, caused by the weight of society bearing down on individuals.

Several examples are given. In Visigoth society, there was a Rock of the Forefather where older people would throw themselves off. In Indian society, widows were sometimes encouraged to kill themselves after the death of their husbands. In Ashanti society, the officers of a King had to die after his death. In all of these examples, individuals were made to feel duty bound to kill themselves. The individual was so highly integrated into society that they barely thought of their own desires, committing suicide for the greater good.

These societies tended to be small and to share many beliefs and practices. The individual was under a high degree of surveillance from the social group. Sometimes there was an obligation to commit suicide and a failure to do so invoked negative sanctions. Among the ancient Goths, for example, it was believed to be a disgrace to die of natural causes. In other cases, the altruistic suicide was optional in the sense of being supported by wider public opinion. In North America, for example, the Dakotas and Crees would commit suicide over disappointment in love.[33] In both types of case, there was a benefit to society – either a material benefit insofar as the elderly ceased to be a burden for the Goth or a moral benefit in that social norms were reinforced. The suicide victim also carried out the act with some enthusiasm as opposed to the sad state that often accompanied egoistic suicide.

This form of suicide mainly belongs to the past but Durkheim finds one exception: the modern army. As an institution, the army trains the soldier to accept a high degree of impersonality. The soldier is encouraged to place little value on himself and to carry out orders without any thinking. In elite troops, the suicide rate is even higher precisely because the individual suffers a more excessive 'spirit of abnegation'.[34] However, Durkheim – possibly out of deference to French patriotism – plays this pattern down. He suggests that it is decreasing because of the wider questioning of blind obedience in society.

ANOMIC SUICIDE

Egoistic and altruistic suicides are linked to the degree of integration in society. In his third major category, however, Durkheim turns to the regulation of the moral order and looks at how it affects individuals.

In periods of economic distress, the rate of suicide increases and an obvious explanation might be that the ensuing poverty leads to despair. But Durkheim rejects this, claiming that 'poverty protects against suicide' in countries like Ireland where the peasantry leads a wretched life.[35] Suicides also rise in periods of economic boom and therefore the economic factor could not be the primary cause. It is rather that booms and slumps create disturbances in the moral order and this lack of social equilibrium disorientates individuals.

Durkheim resorts to a philosophical theory about the nature of humanity to explain this. In the natural world, he suggests, animals automatically establish equilibrium between their needs and their means. Amongst humanity, however, the power of reflection means that new and unlimited needs can be imagined. Our capacity for feeling, Durkheim warns, 'is ... an insatiable and bottomless abyss' and pursuing such unattainable goals is a recipe for unhappiness.[36] Individuals, therefore, require regulation and being unable to provide it themselves, need to be subject to the moral regulation of society. The right to restraint is a fundamental requirement for human beings.

Here Durkheim is drawing on a conservative tradition that speaks of the weakness of individuals. His emphasis is on how individuals should internalise limits on their aspirations. Where this does not occur due to a weakening of moral regulation, *anomic* suicide develops. Durkheim's real target in this context is the growing class aspirations in French society. He wants an 'upper limit to which a workman may aspire in his efforts to improve his existence.'[37] If this limit is too low, little effort would be made for improvement, but if the aspirations are too high, class conflict and social problems emerge. Society therefore needs 'a regime which fixes with relative precision the maximum degree of ease to which each class may legitimately aspire.'[38] If such exists and if each person 'respects regulations and is docile to collective authority and a wholesome moral constitution' they will not ask for more.[39] This relative limitation, Durkheim suggests, will make men contented with their lot and so the rate of suicide decreases. But when society is disturbed by painful crises, this regulation breaks down and 'all classes contend among themselves because no established classification any longer exists.'[40] Society then moves to a state of anomie where suicide rates increase.

While Durkheim initially conceives of anomie as occurring during periods of economic turbulence, he adds – almost as an afterthought – a further notion of *chronic anomie*. This arises primarily from the lack of regulation in the market and in the sphere of industrial relations. In a traditional society, the relations between workers and their masters was regulated by customary prices which were promoted by occupational groups. In a modern society, this breaks down and wages are set by a struggle between the social classes. Moreover, as the doctrine of economic materialism grips society, appetites are excited. The very freedom of markets – especially where the government is weak – leads to a longing for the infinite. Even the modern belief in social progress carries with it a danger of anomie as people constantly long for better. While Durkheim is offering a critique here of market forces, it is coming from a conservative direction aimed at getting each social class to know its proper place.

This conservatism comes even more to the fore when he discusses the other source of anomie in modern society: divorce. Figures demonstrate, he claims, that divorced persons kill themselves between three and four times as often as married people.[41] Moreover, the provision for divorce weakens the institution of marriage itself and so general suicide rates increase. As the primary function of marriage is to regulate sexual desire and establish a code of monogamy, its weakening has a similar effect to economic distress. Lacking regulation, the passions of men stray and there is little restriction on their desires and so rates of suicide increase. However, Durkheim has to acknowledge one difficulty in this argument, namely, that women benefit from divorce. The higher the rate of divorce, the lower the rate of suicide in women.

Durkheim's explanation for this anomaly is extraordinary. A woman's sexual needs, he claims have 'less of a mental character because … her mental life is less developed.'[42] Because she is a more instinctive creature, she only has to follow those instincts to find calmness. She does not require the strict regulations that are part of the marriage contract and may even find them burdensome. By contrast, men have a more active mental life and a larger imaginative aspect to their sexuality. They can always envisage new forms of sexual enjoyment and an infinite horizon of pleasure. This, however, is unattainable and will only lead to despair and a higher rate of anomic suicide. Hence, men benefit from marriage where 'enjoyment though it is restricted is assured'.[43]

In another surprising move, Durkheim adds a footnote to his discussion on anomic suicide. Just as altruistic suicide with its excessive regulation was the opposite of egoistic suicide on the axis of integration, so he equally creates a foil for anomic suicide. This is defined as *'fatalistic suicide'* and results from the over-regulation of individuals. However, Durkheim asserts that this is of so little importance in modern times that it requires only a cursory treatment. The only contemporary examples are very young husbands (those aged under 20) and childless married women – the two groups who might find the regulation of marriage over-burdensome. In the past, suicide among slaves might also have fitted this pattern.

Table 5.1   The Four Main Types of Suicide in Durkheim's Theory

Causes of Suicide	Too Little	Too Much
Integration of Individual into Society	Egoistic Suicide	Altruistic Suicide
Regulation of Society's Morality	Anomic Suicide	Fatalistic Suicide

SOLUTIONS

Through this examination, Durkheim concludes that there are social currents and collective tendencies which lead people to commit suicide. There is no other explanation for why unconnected individuals who do not communicate with each other produce definite and specific rates of suicides in different countries. These tendencies are 'as real as cosmic forces'[44] and only sociology can establish the laws which govern them. But what solutions does it propose?

Durkheim's argument is that a certain amount of individualism and belief in progress is necessary. He is not proposing a return to a religious culture or the semi-feudal structures of pre-revolutionary France. He does not want 'to restore, artificially, social forms which are outworn'.[45] Rather, he wants to retain the cult of human dignity, but surround it with a secular morality that gives individuals moral restraints as well as rights. Thus, he warns that: 'too cheerful a morality is a loose morality [and] it is appropriate only to a decadent people.'[46]

The growth of suicide is an indicator that there is 'a state of crisis and perturbation [which] will not be prolonged with impunity.'[47] The first step in his solution, therefore, is to retain certain sanctions against suicide in order to define it as an offence against the moral order. The suicide should be refused the honour of a regular burial and those found attempting it should not be eligible for public office or – and it is not clear what exactly is meant – 'certain attributes of paternal power'.[48] However, sanctions alone or even sanctions when combined with formal education will not solve the wider issue. Durkheim, therefore, proposes three specific measures to increase the integration and regulation in society.

First, he suggests the re-creation of corporatist occupational groups which are able to get a firm grip over individuals and imbue them with moral restraint. This echoes his call in the second edition of *The Division of Labour in Society*, which argued that occupational groups should bring everyone who works on specific tasks together. They should also stress solidarity and a common interest which cuts across distinct class interests. In order to limit 'excited appetites', the corporations would 'decide the share that should equitably revert to each part'.[49] As they have the necessary authority, they could 'demand indispensable sacrifices and concessions' from their members.[50]

Second, Durkheim suggests that the gap between the modern state and atomised individuals must be narrowed. This can be done by giving corporations a legal existence so that they become a part of the body politic. Although it is not spelled out in *Suicide*, Durkheim is proposing a fundamental re-ordering of state institutions. Parliament should not derive its mandate from the votes of individual citizens but from the corporate bodies. The problem with the existing form of democracy, he claims, was that as 'each man makes his choice in isolation, it is virtually impossible for such votes to be inspired by anything other than personal and egoistical preoccupations.'[51] This system should be gradually brought to an end as corporations become responsible for electing delegates to parliament.

Third, Durkheim wanted to strengthen the institution of marriage by opposing divorce. The only way to reduce the numbers of suicides due to conjugal anomie is to make marriage more indissoluble, he asserts.[52] This proposal is made despite his own data that point to a divergent gender interest in marriage. Durkheim is simply and unequivocally on the side of men, claiming that women will never play the same role in society. He attacks feminists who champion equal rights because they try to abolish 'the practice of centuries'. He bluntly declares that: 'juridical equality cannot be legitimate so long as psychological inequality is so flagrant.'[53]

When Durkheim joined the canon of official sociology, these solutions were mainly ignored. His remarks on corporatist groups, his critique of parliamentary democracy and his attack on divorce were an embarrassment to his American sponsors. Yet they should be read in the context of French republican society facing growing challenges from a workers movement and a struggle for women's rights. Durkheim's sociology was deeply political and despite its abstract form was an intervention in those debates. He saw suicide as an indicator of a social malaise and under the guise of a social scientist wanted to assume a role that was above the conflict. But like many who claim such a spurious objectivity, he was taking a distinct position by making proposals to strengthen the existing order.

CRITICISMS

Thus far we have provided an accurate summary of Durkheim's theory. But what of criticisms of this classic text? More importantly, how does it stand up as a theory about suicide today?

The most common argument levelled against *Suicide* is that Durkheim relied too closely on official statistics. His main accuser, Jack Douglas, insisted on distinguishing between a real rate of suicide and one that is socially constructed by officials. Thus, for example, Durkheim's finding that social integration leads to less suicide could be fictitious. The more integrated a person is, the more likely they are to have 'significant others' who ensure that their death is not classified as suicide.[54] According to Cicourel, official statistics are a social construct produced by officials who deploy their own 'folk sociology' to classify cases.[55]

This, however, is the weakest criticism of Durkheim and represents a step backwards from attempts to grapple with wider social explanations. The real distinction should be between *inaccuracy* in statistics and *systematic distortion* caused by officials and other agents. Current research indicates that there is a greater likelihood of underestimating suicides of women because they are inclined to overdose; the elderly or the chronically ill because their deaths are less likely to be investigated; and teenagers because they often do not express suicidal intent.[56] However, one study found that this type of inaccuracy does not necessarily impact on Durkheim's wider theory because the discrepancies are not so large as to overthrow his analysis.[57] Thus, even if women's suicide rates are higher than reported, it does not negate the overall finding that men commit more suicide. Evidence for *systematic distortion* by officials is therefore negligible. General claims are often made about attitudes but they do not show exactly how officials actually distort figures in a specific and systematic fashion. Bias in the categorisation of death is more likely to be random. In modern society, where there is a greater reliance on medical examiners rather than untrained coroners, the criticism is even weaker. One French study found that while official statistics may under-estimate the suicide rate by about 20 per cent, this does little to change the socio-demographic profile.[58] However, if one recognises Durkheim's adherence to French republicanism, more substantial criticism can be made.

The first glaring omission in his theory is the denial of the effects of economic factors on suicide. As suicide rates increase in periods of both economic boom and slump, Durkheim suggests that the impact of poverty must be minimal. He also claims a 'poverty protection' against suicide by looking at just two cases, Ireland and Calabria. However, Durkheim's supporting evidence is faulty. His uses macro level figures for the economic cycle but does not break them down into richer or poorer areas. The figures from Ireland –which Durkheim did not produce – actually show a doubling of the rate of suicide from 1864 (the first year statistics on suicide were gathered) to 1892.[59]

Durkheim may be correct to assert that there are low rates of suicide when people live in poor, tightly knit communities. But being poor in a poor society is different to being poor in a rich society. In the former, the individuals are not excluded from social activities whereas in the latter they are. The key issue is not poverty in general but *relative poverty* or sudden *impoverishment*. Relative poverty occurs when income drops significantly below the national average. This can happen during both an economic boom and a slump. Impoverishment occurs when there are sudden drops in customary living standards. The French sociologist, Serge Paugam, has drawn a useful distinction between *integrated poverty* where poor people are not stigmatised because they are part of a poor society with high levels of solidarity and *disqualifying poverty* where people are excluded from social life because of low pay, precarious employment or living in poor housing in outer suburbs. Durkheim ignored this distinction because his concern was with social order and not inequality. He only focused on whether social groups enveloped the individual and did not examine the quality of integration or how economic factors created involuntary exclusions.

Subsequent research has found complex but important links between poverty and suicide. The links are not automatic but there are some general trends. Baudelot and Establet have compiled evidence from different studies in the USA, France and Britain. They found that, in the USA, suicide rates were lowest in the richest and most modern states and highest in areas more distant from the centre of political life. In France, suicide was lowest in the richest, most modern and most urbanised departments and highest in the poorest departments. In Britain, suicide was highest in de-industrialised cities with high rates of social deprivation. Suicide rates also tended to be higher among those who were economically inactive, the unemployed, disabled, housewives or the retired. While there was no automatic link between unemployment rates and suicide, there was a strong co-relationship for men under 25 and particularly for those aged between 25 and 29.[60] The wealthy suffered lower rates of suicide because, Baudelot and Establet claimed, they are less exposed to insecurity or the harshness of life; they live in big cities with better social conditions; they have access to stronger networks and are better at consulting doctors before they lapse into depression and despair. One area that Durkheim neglected to examine was the effect of the workplace on an individual's life. While he suggested that upper professionals were more detached from social groups, he neglected to look at how their actual labour process involves a high degree of autonomy and empowerment. The work satisfaction they gain might counteract their lack of integration into social groups. Contrary to Durkheim, Jean-Claude Chesnais suggests that: 'the hierarchy of unhappiness is indeed the negative of the hierarchy of social status.'[61]

In the nineteenth century, suicide increased with age and the young had low rates of suicide. In the 1970s, however, this pattern was reversed. In the United States, the suicide rate for young people aged between 15 and 24 trebled while the rate for adults and the old fell. This pattern of increased suicide among the young was repeated in many OECD countries, with some exceptions. One explanation was the rapid drop in customary living standards. The mid-1970s marked the end of the golden age of modern capitalism and the growth of more precarious and insecure work. The changed pattern suggests a sensitivity of suicide rates to economic downturns. The case of the USSR provides even more stark evidence. One hundred years ago, the suicide rate in Russia was at the bottom of the international table, but at the end of the twentieth century, it was at the top. This reflected a more general pattern in the countries of the former Soviet Bloc. With the fall of communism, these countries experienced a 'shock therapy' that led to considerable inequality and deprivation. By 1995, the six countries with the highest rate of suicide in the world – Lithuania, Russia, Estonia, Kazakhstan, Hungary and Belarus – were all former members of this block. It is to Durkheim's credit that he drew out the link between suicide and social cohesion. His political project, however, prevented him from questioning the economic relations which underpinned his society. This meant that his theory could not anticipate the changes we have discussed above.

One of the master concepts that Durkheim uses to explain rising rates of suicide is anomie. This had originally appeared in *The Division of Labour in Society* and in *Suicide*, it is put to use as an explanatory cause. When the concept of anomie is unpacked, however, it reveals a deeply pessimistic view of human beings and an enthusiasm for a repressive social order. As Horton puts it, anomie is a 'utopian concept of the political right' that is deployed as a critique of liberalism.[62] Durkheim was not an adherent of the traditionalist right, but his use of anomie reveals a hankering for social control that existed during the *ancien régime*. He welcomes a modern secular, market economy but wants the social benefits of religion. There are two key elements to the concept.

It relies on a conservative view of human nature. This tradition of pointing to human weakness stretches back to Thomas Hobbes, who thought that humanity had been engaged in a war of 'all against all', and even further back to the doctrine of 'original sin'. It sees the human being as a bundle of desires with infinite appetites that need to be tamed. Far from requiring freedom or liberation, humanity needs more restraint. The contrast with Marx's category of alienation is illuminating. Marx saw the defining feature of human life as production to meet needs and this, he thought, led to an ability to reshape both the natural world and human sensibility itself. Humanity was, therefore, defined by its potentiality and individuals by their need for self-realization. This, however, was thwarted by the existing form of society.

In Durkheim, society appears as an abstract force which towers above individuals, granting them the gift of moral restraint. Unequal social relations are of no relevance whatsoever – society is simply a force for good. When Durkheim speaks of morality arising from social relations, he never asks: whose morality? Or who does this morality serve? The category of Society instead becomes a reified power with an existence independent of the individuals who compose it. To put this slightly differently, it has become 'thing-like', with a power to shape the people who create it. The contrast with Marx could not be greater. In his *Economic and Philosophical Manuscripts*, Marx explicitly warned that: 'it is above all necessary to avoid postulating "society" once more as an abstraction confronting man.'[63] Society, he thought, should be seen as an extension of peoples' real world struggles with each other, thereby making it capable of being reshaped in the interests of the working classes. By portraying society as a power that is transcendent and external to individuals, Durkheim is engaged in a type of alienated thinking that promotes the powerlessness of the masses.

Durkheim's use of anomie suggests that social malaise is caused by the *time lag* between moral regulation and the market. It emerges because the rapid growth of industry has brought 'changes (that) have been accomplished with extreme rapidity (and so) the interests in conflict have not yet had time to be equilibrated.'[64] The present 'morbid disturbance', he suggests, is the result of the institutions of the past being uprooted and not replaced. Durkheim hopes that this is a temporary state of affairs that arises because 'the work of centuries cannot be remade in a few years.'[65] But if the key problem is a time lag, there is no need to question fundamentals. Adjustment rather than fundamental change is required. Even when Durkheim makes a passing reference to inequalities, he suggests they can be remedied by better regulation. He is, therefore, a defender of the new republican and capitalist order, unlike he says, 'the anarchist, the aesthete, the mystic, the socialist revolutionary ... who have in common ... a single sentiment of hatred and disgust for the existing order.'[66]

Durkheim's chosen role as a social doctor for the existing order leads him to a theoretical sleight of hand. His two key dimensions of analysis are integration and regulation and each comes with two polar opposites. Thus, egoistic suicide and altruistic suicide arise from either insufficient or excessive integration, while anomic suicide and fatalistic suicide result from insufficient or excessive regulation. Yet, strangely, Durkheim, deals with fatalistic suicide only in a footnote. It affects 'persons with futures pitilessly blocked and passions violently checked or choked by oppressive discipline', but he claims this is of such little contemporary importance that examples are hard to find.[67] It is, therefore, mainly of historic interest.

This is an extraordinary claim. In effect, Durkheim is suggesting that there are hardly any suicides resulting from excessive regulation. Yet he has already noted that some women may find there is over-burdensome regulation in marriage and, if they are childless, may be more disposed to fatalistic suicide. If he had looked a little further, he might have found other examples of excessive and unjust regulation. They could be found in the colonies where oppression might drive some to despair; or in the prisons where some might not cope with confinement; or even in factories where harsh discipline was too much to bear. These could be multiplied many times over, but the more interesting question is: why did Durkheim not look? Besnard suggests that Durkheim was obsessed with the problem of divorce and this was 'largely instrumental in his sociological treatment of social constraint.'[68] He did not want to give succour to its advocates by focusing on excessive regulation and so he relegated fatalistic self-destruction to an historic interest. While this explanation is accurate, it is also limited. Durkheim was not just an opponent of divorce, he was also an ardent defender of the republican order in a French society facing a series of revolts. This more general orientation prevented him from examining excessive and unjust regulation.

The most glaring problem with *Suicide* for the modern reader is gender. Durkheim's views are not just anachronistic, they were distinctly anti-feminist, even by the standards of his own time. The demand for greater equality for women in France was made at a series of feminist conferences in 1878, 1889, 1896 and 1900 and this had led to 'a full scale national debate'.[69] In 1884, the Naquet Law was passed which allowed for divorce under certain circumstances including adultery, some criminal convictions and domestic violence. Durkheim did not oppose restricted divorce but he vigorously rejected a move towards no fault or divorce by mutual consent. He tried to frame his opposition as coming from an authoritative social science position. His own research, however, produced an inconvenient truth: that women were more likely to benefit from divorce than men and so he disposed of this by a number of spurious strategies. He produced a narrative which justified inequality; then he defined women by biology; and, lastly, he rejected his own evidence.

Sexual similarity and equality in public life, Durkheim argued, belonged to a primitive society. 'The privileged situation of women, far from being a sure index of progress, is sometimes caused by still rudimentary domestic organisation,' he declared.[70] As society evolved, women withdrew from participation in war and public affairs and concentrated instead on the interior of the family. Among civilised people, he claimed, women lead an existence entirely different to men. She monopolises the 'affective functions' and he the 'intellectual functions'.[71] This story of gender differentiation was a common Victorian perspective on the evolution from savagery to civilisation.[72]

However, Durkheim's spurious narrative was also supplemented by a crude biological reductionism. As women took up their role inside the family, they withdrew from social life. As Lehmann points out, Durkheim believes that women are not full participants in civilisation, making them more instinctive creatures than men. This explains why he sees female sexuality as natural and physical, rather than social or mental. It is more limited and satisfied because women are more lacking in an intellectual outlook that might open up more infinite desire.[73] Moreover, as women are less immersed in collective existence, they do not experience harmful social currents as much. The reason why women do not benefit from the protection of marriage is that it is not 'useful for limiting her desires, which are naturally limited'.[74]

Durkheim's final stratagem is to deny his own evidence. In *Suicide*, he posed the rhetorical question about whether one of the sexes be sacrificed because they have opposing interests within marriage. The man required more regulation because of his intellectual life; the woman does not need it because she is instinctive. But as the debate on divorce heated up, he found this assertion embarrassing and so in a subsequent article, 'Divorce by Mutual Consent', published in 1906, he revised his own position. He revisited his finding that had found advantages that Paris women gained from the presence of divorce. He now claimed this was only apparent because he had misread the figures, concluding that: 'it does not seem that the practice of divorce affects female suicide rate appreciably'.[75] As marriage did not detrimentally affect women, there was no real advantage to be gained from divorce. It was therefore best to focus on men's needs. Hence, any legal measure that weakened that institution should be opposed.

On this issue, Durkheim was positioned on the right of the republican spectrum. The French Revolution had granted divorce on request, but after the restoration of the monarchy, it was banned once more. Many French republicans saw the introduction of divorce as a revenge against clerical influence and supported it. Durkheim, however, embraced some of the ideas of the clerical faction in his defence of marriage.

His solution for rising suicide rates also combines a strange nostalgia for the corporations of feudal Europe with a gesture towards 'guild socialism'. Syndicalism was popular in the French labour movement at the time. It suggested the possibility of bypassing parliamentary democracy and reorganising society based on workers control of industry. Sometimes this philosophy shaded off into a desire to create cooperatives within capitalism; on other occasions, it spilled over into anti-capitalist and revolutionary ideas. Durkheim took up some of the more moderate ideas of the syndicalists but gave them a peculiarly conservative twist. Instead of class-based organs of struggle, he proposed an older version of the medieval corporation. He was perceptive to focus on the workplace as an arena where future forms of social solidarity could be recreated. The breakdown of close-knit local communities left the workplace as a neglected, but key area where social bonds could be forged.

But Durkheim's project was doomed from the very start because the workplace is also the point where conflicts of interests between workers and employers are at their most obvious and intense. His advocacy of joint employer–workers corporations to generate new forms of solidarity was therefore a non-runner. On one level, it appeared simply as a utopian ideal, which subsequent sociologists quietly dropped. But at another level, it was a reflection of Durkheim's wider project: how to divert labour away from militancy and incorporate it into the republic.

6

The Elementary Forms of Religious Life

The Elementary Forms of Religious Life was Durkheim's last major work. Written more than a decade after *Suicide*, it is generally regarded as his greatest achievement.[1] Pared down to its essential characteristics, the text represents the culmination of a professional career dedicated to two central objectives: a defence of the scientific credentials of sociological investigation and a defence of republican forms of social integration. By taking religion as his object of investigation, Durkheim was once again challenging common sense understanding in the interests of science. In *Suicide*, Durkheim set out to challenge common sense notions about the motivations underpinning self-destruction. For most people, the act of suicide seemed to be the very essence of individualistic decision-making. By pointing to the social forces underpinning observable differences in suicide rates, Durkheim simultaneously disrupted the dogmas of common sense and furthered the claims of his 'science of society'. Durkheim's investigation of the social forces underpinning primitive religions rested on similar considerations.

From the time of the Enlightenment, religion was increasingly viewed as an antiquated force with little relevance to modern understanding.[2] For many positivist scientists, in particular, the use of reason and experimental evidence were directly counterposed to the perceived ignorance and superstition of religion. This was especially true in liberal circles which equated religion with the boorish and uneducated masses. From a position of overwhelming dominance, religion had been continually battered by evidence flowing from the natural sciences.

To take one important example, the Catholic Church had always taught its followers that the earth was at the centre of the universe. Indeed, God had made it so, in order to place humanity at the heart of creation. This made sense to the pre-scientific mind of the Middle Ages as the earth *appeared to be* flat, eternal and unchanging. However, the publication of Copernicus' *On the Revolutions of the Heavenly Spheres* (1543) turned this Christian world-view on its head. Over the next two centuries, the idea of a static and unchanging earth, was replaced with the idea of a solar system containing earth as merely one of its many satellite planets. This seriously undermined the credentials of a Christian cosmology that had reigned basically unchallenged for nearly a millennium.

As an atheist himself, Durkheim had little time for the truth claims of the established churches. Yet rather than dismissing religion in the way that so many of his contemporaries had done, he perceived in it, a truth that went to the very heart of the human condition.[3] Put simply, Durkheim insisted that religious beliefs and practices were the lens through which human life in society has always been mediated. Stripped of their supernatural shells, religious beliefs were revealed to be nothing more than social forces that had been reified, and often deified, by the social groups who had created them.

This narrative had a number of similarities with the German philosopher, Ludwig Feuerbach, whose *The Essence of Christianity* (1841) developed an overtly anthropological account of the roots of religion. In Feuerbach's estimation, human beings created their Gods as the highest expression of their human nature, only to mistake their own creations as all-powerful, supernatural creators. For Feuerbach, this made religion a significant source of social disempowerment as the masses bowed down to forces they had actually created. This also informed Karl Marx's view of religion a year or two later.[4]

Although he agreed with Feuerbach that humans had created god, Durkheim disagreed with his negative assessment. Religion, he asserted, was the source of everything worthwhile in human history. It was originally responsible for our shared identities, our sense of community and even the categories through which we came to understand the world.[5] Everything from art and science to literature and culture had been born through religion, making it an institution eminently worthy of genuine respect.[6] To defend this claim, Durkheim wanted to explain the rationality of the seemingly most primitive of religions – that of the Australian Aborigine. For Durkheim, the rituals and practices of these 'primitive' men necessarily contained a rational kernel. Society itself was the real source of their admiration, reified and turned into the kind of force that the 'primitive' mind could more readily conceive. Understood in this way, religious forces become existentially real and worthy of scientific investigation. More than this, Durkheim regarded religious practices as particularly useful in the context of his overall sociological objectives. This was true in at least three important respects.

First, Durkheim's insistence that religion is the social institution par excellence was designed to dispute the growing influence of historical materialism.[7] If religion – as opposed to economic production – could be shown to be the foundation of human societies, then the scientific pretensions of Marx's revolutionary socialism could potentially be weakened. Second, Durkheim perceived his investigation as being capable of offering sociological answers to the most intractable philosophical questions. By successfully explaining the social roots of the foundational categories of our understanding (time, space, causation, force, class, etc.), Durkheim assumed that the reputation of his sociology in the Western Academy would be assured forever.[8] He therefore weaves a form of social-Kantianism into his primary investigation in order to dispute the epistemological claims of both rationalism and empiricism.[9] Finally, Durkheim makes it clear that religious beliefs and ritual practices are the glue that binds tribal participants to their social environment. If Durkheim could uncover the essential traits of this primitive form of solidarity, he could potentially utilise his scientific findings to promote greater social integration in the French Republic.[10] For these reasons, amongst many others, Durkheim regards *The Elementary Forms of Religious Life* as the highest point of his theoretical output.

A SIMPLE EXPERIMENT IN SOCIAL INTEGRATION

The central thesis in *The Elementary Forms of Religious Life* is that religion is the institution through which human beings initially became socialised. This was true in two interrelated senses. On the one hand, it was through their participation in religious beliefs and practices that human beings first gained a sense of their common identity. By acting in identical ways and believing in identical things, humans formed around themselves the social bonds of their tribal communities. On the other hand, religion helped to systematise and classify the most important human experiences. Religious ideas were at the base of all our early communication systems – language, myths and abstract thinking – making them an indispensable guide to practical life in the natural environment. In marked contrast to many of his contemporaries, Durkheim insisted that nothing as essential as this could rest entirely on falsehood.[11] Regardless of the obvious flaws in the truth claims of the established churches, religion remained an essential object for a positivistic-scientific investigation. To understand it properly, however, sociologists had to free their minds of preconceived ideas and put aside their modern prejudices.[12]

One way to achieve this task was to take on the seemingly most irrational form of religion – that of the Aborigines of Central Australia. The temptation of many ethnographers in the early twentieth century was to use their studies of 'primitive people' to further the claims of Western Imperialism. On the surface, tribal beliefs and practices seemed so outlandish that many ethnographers immediately dismissed them. The idea of dancing around totem poles seemed utterly ignorant and superstitious. For Durkheim, however, there were deeper meanings to these outward appearances that had to be appreciated. The reasons given by tribal people for their religious activities were invariably mistaken, but the activities themselves were essential insofar as they met vital human needs that are both 'fundamental and permanent'.[13] In this sense, Aborigines are 'as rationally constituted as are their Parisian contemporaries. There is no question of one being civilised and the other not, or of the two groups having different mental constitutions.'[14] Establishing this continuity across different societies is crucial for Durkheim, as he wants the results of his study to apply to modern forms of social integration. For this reason, Karen Fields argues that *The Elementary Forms of Religious Life* 'exemplifies a single well conducted experiment whose results may be put forward as *holding for all cases that can be shown to be of the same kind*.'[15]

Like any experimenter, Durkheim wants to isolate the forces he is investigating in order to make the most important information easier to detect. Natural science has the luxury of creating these conditions through artificial means, but the sheer complexity of social institutions makes these forms of scientific closure impossible to achieve. To compensate, Durkheim suggests that focusing on a simple society with uniform beliefs and practices is the best way to approximate a natural scientific experiment. He captures this thinking in the following way,

In the lower societies … the group regularly produces an intellectual and moral uniformity of which we find only rare examples in the more advanced societies … Since all consciousnesses are pulled along in the same current, the individual type virtually confounds the generic type. At the same time all is uniform, all is simple … everything is boiled down to what is absolutely indispensable [and] because the facts are simpler, the relations between them are more apparent.[16]

Aboriginal life promised the two key ingredients that Durkheim required. It was both *simple enough* to give up its truths to a scientific investigator and *universal enough* to 'explain a portion of reality that is near to us and thus capable of affecting our modern ideas and actions.'[17] Durkheim had travelled a distance from *The Division of Labour in Society* and now thought that collective belief systems held the keys to social integration. In his earlier system, Durkheim counterposed the mechanical solidarity of shared value systems with an organic solidarity rooted in modern economic interdependency. The idea of integrating communities around shared beliefs was originally deemed to be on the wane, as fellow feeling was supposed to emerge from an enlightened sense of our debts to each other in the capitalist economy. Given the conflict and competition that actually characterise capitalism, this was never likely to occur and Durkheim gradually concluded that new forms of mechanical solidarity would be needed if his beloved Republic was to hold together. It is in this context that *The Elementary Forms of Religious Life* takes on its modern significance as the religious integration of 'primitive' societies became the template for integration in early twentieth-century France.

Having selected Aboriginal beliefs and rituals as his object of investigation, Durkheim's next task was to define religion in a way that suited his project. Aware that most of his readers were likely to have been influenced by Christianity, Durkheim once again wants to challenge their preconceived ideas. This meant shifting the focus away from the idea of the Supernatural and/or God to the *social activities of believers themselves*. He therefore makes four key arguments against the idea that religion can be defined by the 'mysterious' or the 'supernatural'. The first of these is based on the historical evidence. According to Durkheim, the idea of tying religion to mysterious things only appears 'very late in the history of religions.'[18] In Christianity, for example, it took the development of modern science in the seventeenth century to force their doctrines beyond the realm of nature into the speculative realm of Gods and spirits. Far from being foundational or elementary, the very idea of a 'supernatural realm' is therefore modern in its development. Following on from this, Durkheim's second point is that to be 'able to call certain facts supernatural, one must already have an awareness that there is a *natural order of things*. In other words, that the phenomena of the universe are internally linked according to necessary relationships called laws.'[19] To have the idea of a supernatural realm is to have the idea of natural laws which really only come into society through positive science. Once again the major chasm that separates the natural from the supernatural is really a function of the modern mind rather than the primitive one.

Durkheim's third point is related to this. He argues that when a modern observer witnesses 'primitive people' attempting to 'stop the rain' or 'move the stars' it can seem as if they are spellbound by forces that escape their reason. Yet for the 'primitives' themselves, these activities are perfectly rational as it is their most direct way of conceiving and influencing the world around them.[20] Durkheim's final argument is that primitive religions are not concerned with the exceptional or abnormal but with the normal and mundane. As a general rule, the primitive mind equates sacred or religious forces with the constancy and 'regularity of the universe, the movement of the stars, the annual growth of vegetation ... and so forth.'[21] Consequently, any notion that equates the earliest forms of religion with the 'mysterious' or the 'unexpected' is wide of the mark.

Having disposed of the supernatural, Durkheim turns his attention to the idea of Gods. Here the dominant contention was that the earliest religions were forged through a union of conscious minds in the earthly realm with a superior consciousness in the realm beyond. One important implication of this conception is that human beings must engage with their Gods through exclusively psychological means. If the Gods are conceived as conscious beings, the faithful must relate to them through conscious activities such as prayer, offerings and sacrifices. This suggests that there can be no religion except where the latter are at work, but, once again, this flies in the face of crucial evidence. Far from all religions being defined by conscious prayer, there are major popular religions such as Buddhism and Brahminism in which the latter are virtually absent. Instead of praying in the usual sense, Buddhists invariably withdraw into themselves in order to meditate. More to the point, the very idea of Gods and spirits are more or less absent from these Great World religions, showing that: 'religion cannot be defined exclusively in these terms.'[22]

With these rival definitions thus eliminated, Durkheim moved to his own definition of the elementary characteristics of religion. His first key claim is that no matter where they have occurred in the world, religions have always been complex systems made up of two interconnected parts: beliefs and rituals.[23] Beliefs are defined as collective representations that contain and transmit the central ideas of particular religious world-views. Rituals are the modes of action that flow from these ideas, helping to reproduce them in various ways. He also insists on a second key distinction, this time between the *sacred* and the *profane*. For Durkheim, this second distinction is absolutely fundamental in characterising *every form of religious thought*. He makes his case for the centrality of this distinction in the following remarks.

All known religious beliefs display a common feature: they presuppose a classification of the real or ideal things that men conceive into two classes – two opposite genera – that are widely designated by two distinct terms, which the words profane and sacred translate fairly well. The division of the world into two domains, one containing all that is sacred and the other all that is profane – such is the distinctive trait of all religious thought.[24]

Religious beliefs and rituals are those that express and are articulated towards the sacred. They are separated absolutely from the profane or mundane and protected by prohibitions, sanctions and interdictions. It follows that for Durkheim, religions are 'unified systems of beliefs and practices … relative to sacred things … which unite into one single moral community called a Church, all those who adhere to them.'[25]

Table 6.1 A Summary of Competing Claims about the Elementary Aspects of Religion

Competing Claims about the Elementary Aspects of Religion	Durkheim's Assessment
Religion is defined by the Supernatural	Presupposes science and so comes with modernity
Religion is defined by Gods	Presupposes conscious prayer when many of the major religions don't exhibit this
Religion is defined by beliefs and rituals which are sacred rather than profane.	Every religion has collective beliefs and rituals that separate the world into non-religious profane objects and religious or sacred objects.

NEITHER ANIMISM NOR NATURISM

With this definition of religion firmly in hand, Durkheim felt that he had successfully achieved his opening objective. By focusing his investigation around real world activities, *The Elementary Forms of Religious Life* was challenging those preconceptions that sought to tie religion primarily to the worship of 'other worldly beings'. This helped to undercut the potential prejudices of his Christian readers, but he still had to contend with the dominant views of 'primitive religions' propagated by ethnographers, anthropologists and philologists. These fell into two key categories: animism and naturism.

For the animists, the whole of primitive religion could be explained on the basis of the Soul. The theory was made popular by Edward Burnett Tylor and Herbert Spencer, who, each in their own way, argued that primitive religion hinged on the idea of an anthropomorphised nature, animated with spirits and souls with human-like qualities. To account for the origin of animism, Tylor argues that 'primitive' people attach great significance to their experiences whilst dreaming.[26] In the 'primitive worldview', the experiences one had whilst asleep are no less real than those had whilst awake. If the mind travels to far off places during dreams, for example, there must literally be a 'second self' that is really experiencing them. At death, this second self (Soul) detaches itself from the body before taking up residence in a spirit realm just outside the realm of experience. Because these souls were once part of human beings, they continue to involve themselves in the lives of the living. In this way, they gradually became sanctified as forces capable of offering great help or causing great harm depending on their predilections. To curry favour with these spirits, 'primitive' people began to worship them in various ways, thus creating the earliest forms of offerings, sacrifices and prayers.

Reflecting on all of this, Durkheim notes a supposed historical progression from souls 'being merely a life principle animating the human body, to being a [good or evil] spirit [or] even a deity.'[27] In time, the whole of nature was assumed to be populated with these spiritual 'second selves'. Primitive thinking had moved from the animated lives of human beings to natural phenomena – wind, rivers and seas – that were assumed to be similarly animated. This idea of 'primitive people' assuming that nature had human-like emotions proved immensely popular with investigators, but Durkheim found at least four major problems with it. In the first place, he points out that for animism to hold, dream-like states must be liable to but one interpretation, when in fact they are open to almost endless possibilities. Second, Durkheim asks why it is that primitive people, who had proven themselves so unreflective in their general lives, would be so driven to 'explain' their dreams. Third, Durkheim doubted that tribal people could be so primitive as to equate in significance their dream-like experiences with the reality they experienced when conscious and awake. Finally, and most importantly, Durkheim rejected the idea that something as powerful, as fundamental and as permanent as religion could have rested on the flimsy basis of individual hallucinations. For animism to hold, religion would have to rest on dreams, but as Durkheim quite rightly protests, it is literally 'unthinkable that systems of ideas which have had such a large place in history … could be mere fabrics of illusion.'[28]

In contrast to animism, one of the strengths of naturism is its insistence that religion must rest on something real. Its key advocate was a German philologist named Max Müller, who argued that: 'religion must begin, as does all of our knowledge with sense experience.'[29] The experience in question is the utter awe and amazement felt by primitive minds when confronted with the forces of nature. According to Müller, and his contemporary Adalbert Kuhn, men cannot enter into relations with nature without gaining a sense of its infinity and immensity. Human life must have seemed positively insignificant in comparison, leading to feelings of wonder, surprise, marvel and fear. To make sense of these experiences, human beings relied on their language. The earliest tribal languages were inevitably preoccupied with practical activities such as pushing, lighting, climbing and walking.[30] Such action verbs were essential for rudimentary communication, but they could also be illegitimately transferred onto the forces of nature. Over time, natural forces did indeed become anthropomorphised though the use of language – with the 'pulling of the wind' or the 'lighting of the sun' becoming seen as the outcomes of conscious intentions.

Once natural forces had been successfully transformed into personal agents, moreover, their very scale and immensity made them prime candidates for sanctification. Thus it was that:

> upon the physical world, as it is revealed to our senses, language superimposed a new world … comprising only spiritual beings that it had created out of nothing and that were from then on regarded as the determining causes of physical phenomena.[31]

Eventually these Gods of nature could be detached from their physical manifestations to become objects of worship in their own right. It was from these processes that myths and legends purportedly grew up around the forces of nature.

As before, there is a certain plausibility in the ideas of naturism that had to be confronted if Durkheim was to justify his own perspective. Alongside his contention that many of the philological arguments made by Müller were incorrect, he therefore advanced three more substantive critiques. The first of these challenged the empirical claims underpinning naturism. Although Müller claimed to found his system based on real experiences, Durkheim argues that it actually relies on an 'immense system of hallucinatory images'.[32] Naturism may begin with the raw material of the senses, but it immediately distorts them through 'the magical workings of primitive language … into bizarre ideas'.[33] This leaves the theory open to the same charge of unreality previously levelled at the animists. Durkheim's second argument calls into question the idea that primitive people were necessarily in awe of the forces of nature. Far from being awesome or mysterious, Durkheim argues that the rhythm of nature is generally so uniform that: 'it shaded off into monotony'. More importantly, primitive people generally assumed control over nature, making it unlikely that they would deify its forces in the way that Müller had insisted.[34] Durkheim's final argument rested on the fact that it was not the major forces of nature that had initially become the objects of worship, but the simplest plants and the humblest animals. This being the case, their 'objective properties surely could not have been the origin of the religious feelings they inspired.'[35] Arguing through his usual 'method of elimination', Durkheim therefore insisted that naturism was no more able to explain the elementary forms of religion than animism had been. This left only one candidate for the job – his own theory of totemism.

Starting as far back as 1791, adventurers on the Western Frontier of the United States noted a peculiar set of beliefs that came to be defined as totemism.[36] Over the course of the nineteenth century, American totemism became widely investigated, with a host of studies emerging in the 1870s. J.F. McLennan's *The Worship of Plants and Animals* (1869–70) was particularly influential in arguing that totemism was a primitive religion from which other, more advanced forms may have originated. Given the 'simplicity' of the clan groups with which it was associated, McLennan's assertion chimed perfectly with the prejudices of the imperialist era. Meanwhile, L.H. Morgan's *Ancient Society* (1877) also tied totemic religion to the 'simple' societies that Durkheim had investigated in *The Division of Labour in Society*.[37] By the late 1880s, however, an even simpler version of totemism had been discovered amongst the Aborigines of Central Australia. James Frazer summarised much of the relevant material in his *Totemism* of 1887, but it was Robertson Smith's interpretation of totemism as the *origin of sacrifice* that really grabbed Durkheim's attention.[38] In 1899, Baldwin Spencer and F.J. Gillen published what became the definitive empirical investigation of Aboriginal practices and together with Robertson Smith's more theoretical analysis, their *Native Tribes of Central Australia* convinced Durkheim that he now had the raw material and the theoretical categories to construct a radically new interpretation of religion. Thanks largely to the work of Spencer and Gillen, the records of Australian totemic institutions were easily the most complete on record. No less importantly, Australian Aborigines lived in the simplest – single segment – societies that currently existed, making them the perfect starting place to look for the elementary forms of religion life.

TOTEMIC BELIEFS – THE POWER OF THE SYMBOL

At first glance, totemic beliefs must have seemed strange to their Western observers. In modern societies, people generally have special bonds with family members or those in their immediate social networks. People with the same nationality, the same creed or the same interests may also elicit special bonds on the basis of a shared identity. Aboriginal clan groups also shared identities but these are created and sustained in a way that seems outwardly peculiar. Instead of forming their closest bonds on the basis of blood ties or close proximity, tribal members feel themselves part of wider communities based on *their links to a given plant or animal species*. In other words, they become related to each other because they each share the same totem.[39] Durkheim explains his initial observations of totemism in the following way,

> What distinguishes the Australian clan is that the name it bears is also that of a definite species of material things with which it thinks it has special relations … in particular, relations of kinship. The species of things that serves to designate the clan collectively is called its totem. The clan's totem is also that of each of its members.[40]

The idea that humans could believe in a shared kinship with plants or animals rather than their blood relatives seems hard to understand. Perhaps the most obvious way to explain these beliefs would be to write them off as rudimentary or irrational. Such an interpretation would have chimed with the prejudices of the colonial era, but to his credit, Durkheim saw more in totemic beliefs than that which meets the eye. Instead of ridiculing a belief system that seems outlandish in empirical terms, Durkheim sought to explain it with a provocative question – how could something that seems so irrational, be rational to those who live and believe it? This, in turn, led to a multi-layered and complex investigation of the social forces underpinning Aboriginal society.

Durkheim's first key insight centred on the *symbolic nature of totemic beliefs*. On first appearance, it may seem like the plant or animal is the primary focus but on closer inspection this is not actually the case. It is more accurate to see clan members, their ancestors, given plants or animals and their totemic symbols as inextricably bound together in a form of *imagined community*.[41] To put this slightly differently, it is the symbol of the plant or animal that demands the greatest respect. Understood in this way, the totem moves from the physical attributes of particular species to becoming a 'coat of arms' under which all of the tribal members feel similarly united. This makes totemism about identity, community and belonging. For this reason, Durkheim insists that: 'the totem is not simply a name; it is an emblem, a true coat of arms … [With] each person authorized to wear it as proof of the identity of the family to which he belongs.'[42]

Similar forms of representation and identity remain commonplace in modern societies. Consider the difference between standing at a table to arrange the dishes and standing at the same table when it serves as an altar. In both cases the physical attributes remain identical, but the social beliefs surrounding the object are fundamentally different. In the first case, the object is used in a utilitarian way to meet a basic physical need – this explains why it remains profane. In the second case, the object is sacred, representing in physical form the moral beliefs of the religious community. The same could be said for the national flag or a whole host of other – otherwise innocuous – material objects. Moreover, just as Aborigines give themselves the outward appearance of their totems through body art or imprints on their prized possessions, so modern people often wear national jerseys, crucifixes or headscarfs as a sign of their identity. For Durkheim, this suggests that it is the forms of representation that really count, rather than the physical objects which are being represented. Aboriginals may have considered totemic animals or plants to be sacred, but this is no more than modern minds believe in relation to pieces of coloured cloth. Appreciating this symbolism advances Durkheim's investigation in two important directions.

In the first place, he now has the means to establish the presence of abstract reasoning amongst supposedly primitive people. In the strictly visible sense, there is nothing that could link 'white cockatoos' or 'bush snakes' to their human relations, suggesting that it is the power of symbolism that overrides these visible differences, making them seem inconsequential.[43] As Karen Fields describes it, 'to be alike is not spontaneously given in reality, but stems from an intellectual process of abstraction.'[44] This aids Durkheim's overarching claim that religious ideas were the most important forerunner to modern science. In the second place, it allows him to ask questions about religious symbolism without thereby dismissing it completely. To Durkheim's mind, the idea that Aborigines have a natural kinship with cockatoos is clearly ridiculous, *but the social forces that create forms of identity are fundamental to life.*

This argument leads to the centrepiece of Durkheim's entire investigation and must be approached with considerable care. If the object of the religious worship is not an illusion and if people genuinely feel they are under its influence, it must be because there is a power hanging over each individual. This sacred power could only be society itself. What is being adored in religious ceremonies is not the totem itself but the social forces that turn these profane objects into sacred symbols of identity. When people feel close to their given totem, they are actually experiencing the closeness of each other. When they bow down before the sacred power of their totems they are really worshiping society itself. Durkheim explains his thesis in the following remarks,

> The totem is above all a symbol … but of what? It follows from the analysis that the totem expresses and symbolises two different kinds of things. From one point of view, it is the outward and visible form of what I have called the totemic principle or god; and from another, it is also a symbol of a particular society that is called a clan … Thus, if the totem is the symbol of both the god and society is this not because the god and the society are one and the same … The god of the clan can be none other than the clan itself, but the clan transfigured and imagined in the physical form of the plant or animal that serves as totem.[45]

Although Durkheim uses the term 'god' here for shorthand, he is actually referring to 'an anonymous and impersonal social force that is identifiable in each of the [sacred objects] but identical to none of them.'[46] This force, variously described as *mana* or *waken* is neither personal nor individualised, but a kind of collective energy that touches everything defined as being sacred. Thus it is, that participation in clan life creates and diffuses a form of social energy manifest as collective representations and beliefs. Such beliefs hinge on the fact that humans, plants, animals and symbolic objects are equally united into one sacred totemic system.

To build his case, Durkheim stresses that society is so superior to individuals, both physically and morally, that it is exactly the kind of external phenomenon that is capable of being worshipped. Yet for this to happen, tribal members need a complex set of shared beliefs alongside tangible expression of this in their social environment. Because it is easier to place respect onto physical objects than nebulous energies, tribal members inevitably reify their totemic symbols. In consequence, respect for society is expressed in a religious form that aboriginal people can more readily understand – that of their symbolic connection through totemic objects. Alun Jones gives a useful explanation of this process:

> The individual who is transported from his profane to a sacred existence in a social gathering ... seeks some explanation for his altered elevated state. The gathering of the clan is the real cause, though one too complex for the primitive mind to comprehend; but all around him the clan member sees symbols of precisely that cause – the carved engraved images of the totem – and fixes his confused sentiments on these clear concrete objects from which the physical power and moral authority of society seem to originate.[47]

All of this proves just how complex Durkheim's interpretation of totemic beliefs really is. As a scientist, he insists that religious beliefs must be rooted in something real and permanent, given their prominence throughout the entirety of human history. He further suggests that this reality is society itself, although this is neither consciously understood nor directly expressed. Table 6.2 summarises the key claims that Durkheim is making.

Far from imagining their kinship, moreover, Aboriginal people really do encounter fellow feeling in their direct experience, particularly during collective rituals. Participating in the latter fills tribal members with a joyousness that is enough to confirm the fact that they have been in the presence of significant forces, which they naturally assume come from the plants and animals being worshipped. This makes the reproduction of religious rituals extremely important for life in Aboriginal society.

Table 6.2   The Complex Layers of Totemic Religion

Physical Objects that Become Directly Sacred	Plants, animals, initiated tribal members and ancestors
Symbolic Representation of these Plants and Animals	Engravings of totemic plants and animals on bodies and other sacred objects
Ultimate Objects of Religious Worship	The social relationships between tribal members symbolised by the totemic plants, animals and their coats of arms

TOTEMIC RITUALS – THE REPRODUCTION OF LIFE IN SOCIETY

One implication of Durkheim's theory of religion is the precariousness of such beliefs in the absence of rituals. Any tribe that repeatedly failed to *represent its kinship to itself* would risk loosening the social bonds that make it whole, but the tribe also needs to find ways to reproduce itself physically. On the one hand, people are material beings with physical requirements for food, shelter and clothing. On the other hand, they are moral beings with requirements for social interaction, moral rules and collective ideals.[48] Life in Aboriginal societies is consequently structured so as to reproduce these different needs at pre-arranged intervals of time. These needs are also the basis for the most important division of human thought categories – the sacred and the profane – with the profane standing for the individual, the material and the economic; the sacred standing for the social, the ideal and the religious. In Durkheim's estimation, tribal life *must alternate* between meeting physical needs for economic resources and spiritual needs for social solidarity. Another way of expressing this, is the absolute necessity to keep sacred objects temporally and spatially apart from the profane. Moreover, the sacredness inhering in particular objects, Durkheim argues, is extremely contagious. The mere touch of a sacred object can be enough to contract its sacred power. This consideration is key to understanding what Durkheim terms as 'negative cults'.[49]

In order to separate the sacred and the profane, a whole series of interdictions, rules and taboos emerge. According to Durkheim, negative cults 'do not mandate obligations to be carried out by the faithful, but instead prohibit certain ways of acting.'[50] Prohibitions centred on physical contact are particularly important, with profane individuals not permitted to touch anything sacred. These prohibitions apply to sacred objects such as 'churingas', an oblong piece of wood that made a whirring sound that was used in some Aboriginal ceremonies. He also refers to the consumption of food as an act that is full of religious taboos. It is nearly always sacrilegious to eat animals or plants serving as totems for example. Because speech is another form of human contact, those defined as profane are often barred from speaking directly to the sacred or even speaking in their presence. By far the most important separation is that between profane acts in the service of material needs and sacred acts designed to reinforce the collective consciousness. For this reason, religious sites must be physically separated from the economic life of the tribe and only visited at pre-ordained times of the year. This interdiction has its modern significance when one thinks of churches and mosques and of the various periods set aside for worship – Sunday in the Catholic Church, the Holy Month of Ramadan, etc. Negative cults are also often a means of transforming someone (thing) profane into someone (thing) sacred as Durkheim explains in the following way:

> The negative cult is a means to an end; it is the precondition of access to the positive cult. Not confined to protecting the sacred beings from ordinary contact, it acts upon the worshipper himself and modifies his state positively. Through multiple prohibitions ... he gains a quality of sacredness. From now on he is admitted into the society of men; he takes part in the rites and has gained the quality of sacredness. So complete is the metamorphosis that it is often defined as a second birth.[51]

This period of initiation must be filled with hardship and deprivations, if it is to transform the uninitiated into someone sacred. Becoming a full member of society elevates human beings above their natural appetites, but it also does violence to that side of their personality that rests on egoistic desires.[52] The initiation ceremony must prepare tribal members for the cultivation of the higher, social side of their personality. Society therefore demands a form of asceticism which is mirrored in the asceticism of the initiation ceremony.

Shifting his attention to *positive cults*, Durkheim focuses on the *Intichuma ceremonies* of the Arunta tribe of Central Australia.

Rather than preparing members through initiation or hardship, these ceremonies rely on the joyous celebrations of the renewed vitality of the clan. In Central Australia, there are two sharply divided seasons – a dry season that lasts a long time and a rainy season that is short and irregular. As soon as the rain comes, life is revitalised with animals multiplying and plants and grasses springing up all around. The Intichuma ceremony celebrates this return of life in two successive phases. In the first phase, stones and rocks are struck by tribal members in order to release the souls of their tribal ancestors. As the dust settles in the surrounding area, it is assumed to impregnate plants and animals with life-giving energy. The second phase begins with an increase in interdictions and this is then followed by a feast involving tribal members sharing their totemic species with their gods. The aim of the ritual is to ensure the continued well-being of these plants and animals, but it is important not to view this through utilitarian lenses.[53]

This view of Intichuma ceremonies had been put forward by Edward Burnett Tylor and James Frazer of the Anthropological School. According to their interpretation, the ceremony was overwhelmingly economic as sacrifices were made to the gods to ensure the physical reproduction of sacred plants and animals. Durkheim felt that such interpretations were mistaken in two key areas. In the first place, there was often a general taboo against eating totemic species outside the ceremony. The celebration of their continued vitality was, thus, rooted in shared kinship rather than physical needs. Second, the fact that the tribal members partook in the ceremonial feast meant that it was much less a sacrifice rooted in fear and much more a celebration rooted in shared community. Once again this showed totemic gods as reified expressions of an 'imagined community'[54] made up of shared beliefs, actions and symbols. Durkheim captures this in the following remarks: 'it is man who makes his gods, one can say, or at least, it is man who makes them endure; but at the same time, it is through them that he himself endures.'[55] Alongside the Intichuma ceremony, Durkheim lists three more positive cults: imitative, representative and piacular or brutalisation.

Imitative ceremonies work on the basis that 'like produces like'. They involve tribal members mimicking the actions of their totem in order to reproduce them. By mimicking totemic behaviours, tribal members think they are physically increasing their sacred species, but once again Durkheim wants his readers to avoid economic interpretations of this ritual. The reality of these rituals is based in kinship and fellow feeling rather than utilitarian needs for extra resources. During these imitative ceremonies, moreover, tribal members really do create these bonds of kinship – although these are social and religious bonds rather than physical ones. Durkheim summarises his view by stating,

> We know that apart from the presumed effect on the totemic species, it has a profound influence on the souls of the faithful ... who come away from it with an impression whose causes they do not see but that is well founded.[56]

It follows that the 'true justification of religious practices is not in the apparent ends they pursue, but in the visible influence over consciousness and in their manner of affecting our states of mind.'[57]

Representative rituals mean that social symbols are projected onto the past. Everything takes place 'in dramatic performances that have no purpose other than to make the clans mythical past present in people's minds.'[58] Durkheim took special pleasure in elaborating the nature of these rituals as they were clearly not economic, individualistic or utilitarian. Rather they were designed to arouse feelings that are held in unison by all those within the group.

Finally, Durkheim investigated piacular rites, or those involving the brutalisation of clan members in the face of tragedy. In many ways, these were the mirror image of the joyousness, but they in no way invalidated Durkheim's basic theses. When tribal members felt compelled to burn, beat or lacerate themselves, these were not acts of individual mourning, but the social group reaffirming itself through pain and torture. For the clan to witness death without mourning, for example, would be to decisively undermine the collective consciousness. Society cannot allow such a course of action to occur and so it enforces piacular rituals to show society the importance of its fallen members. Durkheim writes that: 'when a society is going through events that sadden, distress or anger it, it pushes its members to give witness to their sadness, distress or anger though expressive actions.'[59] Like the other rituals, this has a positive influence on the collective consciousness as clan members feel renewed confidence to face their hardship after the ceremony.

Durkheim's theory of totemic rituals is now complete. Whether it is joyous celebrations, imitation, representation or mourning, totemic rituals work to affirm the group's common belief systems, their shared identity and their mutual kinship in an imagined community. It is for these reasons that they have persisted through time, occupying a central role in Aboriginal life right into the twentieth century.

PROBLEMS IN DURKHEIM'S METHODS AND ETHNOGRAPHY

As so often in his major works, Durkheim's methodology in *The Elementary Forms of Religious Life* hinges on procedures that pull him in different directions – a positivism that is duty bound to search out universal laws and an empiricism that claims to take Aboriginal beliefs completely on their own terms. From the outset, Durkheim tells his readers that his investigation is dedicated to explaining a fundamental aspect of our current reality through a detailed reconstruction of something archaic. He claims that all religions have common features that allow them to be classified together. External resemblances between them presuppose deeper ones that necessarily constitute something more fundamental. Because of this universal aspect, he draws a link between Aboriginal religions and those of his own society. He understands his task to be one of 'explaining a present reality that is near to us and capable of affecting our ideas and actions – that reality is ... present day man.'[60] This search for universal laws helped to inoculate Durkheim against the worst prejudices of the colonial era.[61] When ethnographers and anthropologists were deriding so-called 'primitive people' for their seemingly irrational behaviours, Durkheim was looking for universal traits common amongst his Parisian readers and his Aboriginal subjects. This was a progressive move rooted in the strictures of positive science, but it impaled Durkheim on the horns of a methodological dilemma.

To make any sense of Aboriginal beliefs, Durkheim had to move significantly beyond that which was empirically observable. When tribal members mimic cockatoos, for example, there is clearly more going on than meets the eye, *but how are we to be sure that what is going on for tribal members is captured authentically through Durkheim's categories?* Throughout *The Elementary Forms of Religious Life*, Durkheim insists that Aboriginal belief systems are socially grounded and socially mediated.[62] Totemism is accordingly revealed to be a complex system of symbolic representations generated *within the particular social conditions of the Aboriginal clan environment*. To make sense of their outward behaviours, Durkheim insists that totemic symbols are clearly rational for those who believe them, yet how is he able to properly interrogate them? His own socialisation occurred in the nineteenth-century French Academy, making it hard to see how he can move beyond surface descriptions without imposing his own prejudices upon that which he is observing. If all meaning is socially constructed, then Durkheim's ability to apply objective categories to a completely different social reality becomes considerably compromised. Rather than successfully excavating some eternal essence in every religion, Durkheim imposes categories onto people who would scarcely recognise them in their own activities. Indeed, the entire search for some universal 'religious holy grail' is, in the words of Clifford Geertz, 'palpable nonsense'.[63] Against the strictures of Durkheim's sociological positivism, there is no Archimedean point from which to view the rest of reality.[64]

Meanwhile, his ability to apply his theory of religion outside the experimental conditions of Aboriginal societies proved no more successful. At the outset of *The Elementary Forms of Religious Life*, Durkheim insists that his experiment works because all religions are species of the same class, responding to the same needs, playing the same roles and depending upon the same social causes wherever they are present.[65] This claim is essential for Durkheim, if he is to generalise the results of his experiment, yet as Fernando Uricoechea quite rightly points out, such transhistorical continuity is merely imposed as 'an a priori postulate' rather than emerging from detailed historical investigation.[66] There is no evidence presented to suggest that Aboriginal religion can be generalised to other social types and insofar as Durkheim implies this, he breaks two of the seminal rules established in his earlier methodological treatise. In *The Rules of Sociological Method*, Durkheim repeatedly stresses the need to take observations of *every social type*, if one is to come to a settled view of any important sociological variable. He stressed that: 'one cannot explain a social fact of any complexity except by following its *complete development through all social species*', yet here he was claiming to extend his analysis without any further empirical justification.[67] Had he sought this justification, moreover, he never would have found it. This fact is born out in the secondary literature.[68]

According to Steven Lukes, for example, Durkheim's assumption that he was involved in a crucial experiment that would validate all religious belief involved him in marshalling the specific evidence to suit his own purposes. Drawing on the empirical work of Evans-Pritchard, Stanner and van Gennep, Lukes makes at least eight empirical claims against Durkheim's account of Aboriginal religion. First, among the Aboriginal Australians, it is the tribe which constitutes the most important social organisation, rather than the clans emphasised by Durkheim. Second, the totemism of Central Australia that takes centre stage in Durkheim's investigation is highly atypical even within Australia itself. To take one important example, Durkheim delighted in the fact that the Intichuma ceremony was non-utilitarian, being focused on celebrations of kinship and familial representations. Yet the Intichuma had very different significance in the rest of Australia and often didn't even exist elsewhere on the continent. Third, there is no good evidence that Australian totemism was the earliest form of religion – let alone of religion itself.

Fourth, there is evidence that totemism is not associated with the simplest forms of social organisation and technology. Fifth, there is evidence against Durkheim's central equation of totemism and the clan – there are clans without totems and totems without clans. Sixth, there is significant evidence that counts against Durkheim's overarching emphasis on the symbolic nature of totemic beliefs. Indeed, most totemic systems are not represented by the symbolic carvings upon which Durkheim laid so much weight. Seventh, there is no evidence that the impersonal force of *mana* or *waken* is derived from the notion of the totemic principle.

Eight, and most importantly, there is no evidence that the distinction between the sacred and the profane was one that made any sense to those who actually practised totemism.[69] On the basis of these various discrepancies, van Gennep argued that Durkheim's system could not stand up to empirical scrutiny. He summarised his views in this statement:

> I will not deny the ingenuity of this whole construction, which in its breadth and simplicity, is the equal of the best constructions of the Hindu metaphysicians, the Muslim commentators and the Scholastic Catholics taken together. But as for recognising in it any scientific reality and truth, that appears to me to be difficult, given above all, that it is entirely based on analyses and interpretations whose accuracy ethnographers could not accept.[70]

The lack of evidence for any distinction between the sacred and the profane is particularly damaging given the weight attached to it throughout *The Elementary Forms of Religious Life*. Indeed, so essential was this aspect of Durkheim's theory of religion, that Stanner spent many months during the 1960s looking for evidence of it among Aboriginal people. He eventually began to question his own competence before concluding that the facts on the ground simply refuted it.[71] Aboriginal people did not divide their world into two mutually exclusive categories, setting 'sacred objects' aside in the name of their own society. This was rather something that Durkheim himself had repeatedly carried out in his sociological investigations.

To take some of the most important examples, Durkheim's sociology divides human beings into two mutually exclusive elements (*homo duplex*) with an individualistic, egoistic side counterposed to a moral altruism, embodying a person's social inheritance.[72] His categories in *The Division of Labour in Society* similarly exhibit binary oppositions, with a 'primitive society' underpinned by 'mechanical forms of solidarity', counterposed to an 'advanced society' characterised by 'organic solidarity'. The causes of self-destruction in *Suicide* are also marshalled into opposing categories: that between egoistic and altruistic suicide and that between anomic and fatalistic suicide. Perhaps more importantly, Durkheim had come to his own distinction between sacred and profane objects as far back as 1898 – a full 13 years before he *applied* it to his Aboriginal subject matter. Thus, in his 'Individualism and Intellectuals', he writes,

This human person, the definition of which is like the touchstone which distinguishes good from evil is considered sacred in the ritual sense of the word. It partakes of the transcendent mystery that churches of all times have attributed to their gods; it is conceived of as being invested with that mysterious power which creates a void about sacred things, which removes them from vulgar contacts and withdraws them from common circulation.[73]

Rather than discovering the sacred–profane distinction in the daily lives of Aboriginal people this shows that Durkheim imposed a set of sociological categories that had previously been employed in his work. Indeed, the hallmark of Durkheim's writings, taken as a whole, is his radical distinction of the collective and moral side of reality from the economic, the individualistic and the profane. This distinction was crucial in both his critique of utilitarianism and his critique of historical materialism. It was also central to his insistence that collective representations were so superior to individuals that they commanded authority and respect. To challenge the views of his theoretical opponents, Durkheim consistently played down the importance of the economic factor in social life in favour of morality. This explains why he divides the world into separate categories whilst simultaneously elevating one above the other. It is consequently Durkheim that separates the world into sacred rules and profane materiality – not the Aboriginal people of Central Australia. This completely invalidated his ethnographical assertions and much of his argument.

PROBLEMS IN DURKHEIM'S THEORY OF RELIGION

The substantive theory of religion developed in *The Elementary Forms of Religious Life* is no less problematic. With the tensions in his own society working as the backdrop, Durkheim was anxious to emphasise the potentially integrative functions of collective beliefs and practices. Yet in order to achieve this aim, his book takes a highly atypical society as its object of investigation, namely, one depicted as classless, geographically isolated and internally cohesive. This allowed a distorted picture of religion to emerge as totemism becomes a byword for the harmonious interaction of successfully socialised individuals. This obviously reflected the wider aspirations of Durkheimian sociology, but it is dangerously one sided when benchmarked against the historical reality of religious institutions. If Durkheim is right to insist on the fact that religion has historically had the ability to bind individuals into well-integrated communities, he simultaneously ignores two crucial factors: the class-based differences between how rulers and ruled relate to religion; and the undeniable fact that throughout much of human history, religion has been the spur to mass violence and social conflict. To put this latter point slightly differently, Durkheim pays no attention to the clashes that have historically occurred between people holding different and often competing belief systems. Taking up this point, Andrew Lisa argues that:

> If there is a single concurrent theme that unites the entire Medieval era – the approximate millennium between the fall of the Roman Empire and the beginning of the 16th century in the Western World – it is religious conflict. The era was marred by pagan barbarian incursions and ongoing violence between Christians and Muslims, as well as infighting among sects within the two dominant faiths. Jews, for the entirety of the Medieval period, were targeted and scapegoated by factions within both warring religions.[74]

From the fifth century BC until 1453, Muslim armies repeatedly invaded the Christian parts of the Byzantine Empire, initially capturing Egypt and Syria before eventually taking Constantinople. In response, Christian Europe launched six separate incursions – known as the Crusades – between 1096 and 1229, as a series of Popes called on Western Christians to reclaim their territory. Enormous atrocities were committed by both sides until Muslim armies finally drove the crusaders out and regained control of the modern-day Middle East.[75] From 1524 until 1648, Europe itself was convulsed by religious wars as Protestantism became the spiritual banner of the rising commercial and industrial classes. More than 8 million people died in the Thirty Years' War alone (1618–1648) as the Holy Roman Empire sought to maintain its control over the European continent. Peter Wilson has described this war, with some justification, as one of the longest and most destructive conflicts in European history.[76] The rise of Western Imperialism in the late nineteenth century also used religion as its spiritual banner, with Christian Europe often justifying its enslavement of foreign people on the basis of the need to 'save their souls'. When George Bush invaded Iraq in 2003, he famously argued that his Christian God had told him to do it. Similar claims were made by Al-Qaeda when it retaliated, attacking Western civilians in the name of Allah. Indeed, whether we assess the terror unleashed by the Spanish Inquisition, the brutality of the Ku Klux Klan or the atrocities of Islamic State today, religion has repeatedly proven itself compatible with barbaric conflict, violence and disorder. This is particularly true when material (class) interests are brought into the theoretical picture – yet, none of this is visible in Durkheim's study of religion in the atypical social conditions of Central Australia.

In class societies such as Durkheim's own, religion has typically worked to bind rulers and ruled collectively to their conditions of existence. For the elites, this meant reinforcing their power and privilege as Durkheim himself regularly bemoaned in relation to the Monarchy in the *ancient régime*. For the working classes, it meant constructing a false unity in which exploitation and oppression are necessarily covered over by other worldly harmony. Reflecting on the late medieval period, Richard H. Tawney notes the deeply ideological role played by the Catholic Church in attempting to uphold the power of the feudal aristocracy.[77] As the owners of vast amounts of land, the Catholic hierarchy traditionally preached the complementary doctrines of *Organicism* and the *Divine Rule of Kings*.[78] The latter argued that God had made the world in his own image, placing the King at the head of his flock on earth. Organicism was a more general variant of this narrative, which argued that the various classes in society operated as an organic whole: with the aristocracy – including the church – making up the head; the army and knights making up the hands; and the peasants and wage labourers making up the feet. From the other side, Protestantism, and particularly Calvinism, preached the ideals which suited the newly emerging industrialists. It championed the importance of self-directed initiative, thriftiness and the accumulation of material wealth to be used in the celebration of God. Protestantism also challenged the Catholic ban on the lending of money – an activity that was to prove essential to the rise of merchants and industrialists.

The clashes that emerged in this period were fought under religious banners that sucked millions of people into conflicts over who would have the right to rule them. Regardless of the outcome, the working classes were to remain oppressed and exploited either by feudal landlords or the newly emerging industrial bosses. In this context, it is useful to counterpose Durkheim's overwhelmingly positive account of religion with Karl Marx's socialist critique. Because he refuses to see any class dimension in religious integration, Durkheim argues that: 'faith above all is warmth, life, enthusiasm, enhancement of all mental activity, uplift of the individual above himself'.[79] On the one hand, religion helps to raise the individual above their egoistic desires. On the other hand, it offers fortitude to believers in the face of life's unrelenting hardships.

Challenging similar beliefs more than fifty years earlier, Marx argued that it is the economic structures of class societies that create the need for spiritual refuge in a world characterised by exploitation and oppression. For Marx, religion is the 'heart in a heartless world and the soul in soulless conditions', making it imperative to overthrow these material conditions rather than finding a new set of spiritual beliefs – such as modern-day nationalism – to soften the pain.[80] If religion fulfils our genuine need for community and solidarity, it does so in a distorted way that sustains the pain and suffering it is meant to alleviate. To bind people together on the basis of imagined beliefs is to trap them in mystification and inauthenticity.[81]

This shows the problems in trying to separate the cognitive from the practical aspects of religious beliefs in the way that Durkheim ultimately wants to. Durkheim's atheism meant that he challenged the truth claims of religious institutions at the same time as his republicanism looked to collective beliefs as the template for resolving – class-based – conflicts within his own society. Instead of critiquing religion, Durkheim therefore glorified it as the social institution most capable of fulfilling fundamental conditions of human existence.[82]

Yet there is something objectionable in refuting the truth of a set of ideas, whilst nevertheless looking to uphold them. Genuine emancipation surely relies on becoming increasingly aware of our actual reality, not bowing down to collective myths that rob humanity of its power and its dignity. By glorifying the integrating power of an imagined solidarity amongst rulers and ruled, Durkheim failed to look at the alternative possibility of genuine understanding and genuine solidarity amongst working people. For all of its penetrating insights, *The Elementary Forms of Religious Life* ultimately failed in its two most basic aims – it failed to explain the essence of religious belief and it failed to act as a template for social harmony in the French Third Republic.

7

Educating Republican Citizens

The practical implications of Durkheim's sociology are evident in his writings on education. He wrote three key texts which are not usually examined in many sociology courses. These are *Education and Sociology*, *Moral Education* and *The Evolution of French Educational Thought*. They deal with the purpose of education and the pedagogical methods to be deployed. The main reason for their neglect is that they do not fit neatly into courses on classical sociological theory because they deal with practical measures. This is unfortunate because, as Bourdieu and Passeron put it, Durkheim 'most clearly reveals his social philosophy when dealing with the sociology of education, the privileged locus of the illusion of consensus.'[1]

Durkheim believed that education was the key to forming good republican and obedient citizens. He worried about the natural instinct of people to rebel against political authority, noting that: 'spontaneously, man was not inclined to submit to a political authority, to respect a moral discipline, to dedicate himself, to be self-sacrificing.'[2] The purpose of education, therefore, was to transform 'the egoistic and asocial being that has just been born' and render him or her 'capable of leading a moral and social life.'[3] The equation of rebellion against political authority with an 'egoistic and asocial outlook' was fundamental to his outlook. It allowed for an ambiguity between the integration of individuals into society and an acceptance of the established order. Durkheim's project was the creation of solidarity between the social classes and he saw this as the key to social stability. His definition of education reflects this aspiration:

> Education is the influence exercised by adult generations on those that are not yet ready for social life. Its object is to arouse and to develop in the child a certain number of physical, intellectual and moral states which are demanded of him *by both the political society as a whole and the special milieu for which he is specifically destined.*[4] [emphasis added]

Durkheim wanted to use education to produce citizens who responded to the needs of their state and who also accepted their position in the social hierarchy.

Durkheim was closely connected to key officials who were in charge of education in France's Third Republic. He was a protégé of the director of higher education, Louis Liard, who was pushing through a major reform programme in French education because he thought that it was too focused on classical learning. He argued that: 'a national teaching which refused to be thoroughly modern in substance and spirit would not simply be an inoffensive anachronism: it would be a national danger.'[5] Durkheim was subsequently appointed as a junior lecturer in Bordeaux in 1887 to a post that was specially created for him by Eugène Spuller, the minister for education. Spuller had taken advice from Liard, who had suggested Durkheim because of his republican idealism.[6] The purpose of his position in Bordeaux was to give future primary school teachers a sense of their republican mission by generating a more scientific rather than religious outlook. In 1902, Durkheim moved to the New Sorbonne in Paris to replace Ferdinand Buisson, who was professor of educational science when the latter was elected to the national assembly. His appointment was part of a wider strategy to establish republican hegemony at the centre of French higher education. Liard had become the Vice-Rector of the Academy of Paris and he insisted that Durkheim's lectures be obligatory for all teaching candidates at the university. As a result, Durkheim's sociology became an established feature of teacher training. To understand its full import, it is necessary to discuss the politics of education that operated at the time.

SECULARISM AND FRENCH EDUCATION

The French education system was shaped in the shadow of defeat in the Franco-Prussian War of 1870–71. Despite earlier revanchist rhetoric, the republican elite moved away from any thought of immediate revenge against Prussia. Instead, they adopted a longer term strategy of improving the education system as a means of restoring French greatness. They thought that the war's outcome was really 'a victory for the Prussian schoolmaster', who had produced a higher level of technique and morale in the Prussian army. They, therefore, hoped to build a more efficient school system in France to 'nurture national pride, literacy and numeracy' in order to 'generate efficient soldiers and productive workers'.[7] One of the key republican organisations in the forefront of educational reform was the Ligue de l'enseignement, which had been founded by Jean Macé in 1866. The Ligue wanted to expel the church from education, blaming them for a system where 'patriotism is frequently ignored, or worse, spat upon ... [books] appear to have been written less to mould enlightened citizens respectful of laws and institutions of their country than to raise a generation of servile clods.'[8] In a new era of universal male suffrage, the republicans were determined to create a citizenry in their own image – all the better to prepare for French expansion and defence. In Gambetta's words, 'our obsession with the extension of education is a commitment to social defence.'[9]

The republican transformation of French education began in earnest with the Ferry laws. The first of these, in 1880, introduced free attendance at all public primary schools and a year later attendance became compulsory. This greatly expanded access to education but very few students went beyond primary level. Even as late as 1910, only 3.8 per cent of boys and girls attended secondary education.[10] In 1882, all explicitly religious teaching was removed from the curriculum and in 1886, a further law was passed phasing out Catholic teaching personnel from the schools. The curriculum of the primary schools placed particular emphasis on history and geography as well as moral education. The purpose was to instil a sense of civic values in pupils so that they would appreciate the greatness of France. The republican schoolteacher was to dethrone the priest and preparation for a heavenly paradise was to be replaced with ardour for the earthly fatherland.

The social philosophy which guided the new generation of teachers was best expressed by Ferdinand Buisson, who was the director of primary education and who co-ordinated the writing of *Dictionnaire de pédagogie et d'instruction primaire*, the 'bible' of French pedagogy. He suggested that the republicans were trying to create 'a new social order founded on reason and justice' and that the schoolteacher was 'a sort of vanguard' in bringing this about.[11] These lofty ideals provided the ideological framework for the more specific goals of the French state. Pupils were to learn 'respect for the law and the cult of the flag'.[12] The teacher should teach the horror of war, but he nevertheless prepares his pupils to be 'good soldiers, capable of someday being heroes'.[13] This nationalist ethos was, however, wrapped in a noble rhetoric. Pupils were to be encouraged to believe that French civilisation was a gift to the wider world. They should understand that: 'serving France [was] a way of serving humanity'.[14]

In order to achieve these goals the new school system set out to overcome three main sources of division.

The first was the cleavage between the clergy and free thinkers. The republicans had viewed the Catholic Church as a bastion of royalty, aristocracy and conservatism. They wanted to displace the priests from the schools in order to build a new political culture based on science and reason. However, they were deeply sceptical of the British utilitarian view that if everyone pursued their own self-interest, the 'invisible hand' of the market would ensure that society benefited. The republicans insisted instead that moral education be taught in schools so that pupils learn a loyalty to society and the French nation. Despite their opposition to the Catholic clergy, they thought that religion had been useful for instilling morality in the population. They, therefore, wanted to create a scientific basis for this morality in order to replace a religious foundation. In doing so, they had no intention of changing a moral order that stressed duty and obligation. Their aim was only to give it a non-religious basis and to shift the target of obedience from the church to the state. As Ferry explained in his circular to teachers, 'properly speaking you will not be teaching anything new … [You will] transmit, along with what is called school learning, that good old morality which we received from our fathers.'[15]

The second aim was to overcome linguistic and cultural differences. Before the 1870s, there was a large linguistic diversity in France and in several departments, local languages were spoken, which were alien to French. The census of 1863 showed that one-quarter of the population spoke no French and the historian, Eugen Weber, concluded that up to half of all children regarded French as a foreign language.[16] This linguistic diversity had mattered little to the monarchy in pre-revolutionary France as they sought loyalty to the personhood of the king. Republican France, however, aimed to turn subjects into citizens and forge a loyalty to the nation state. Compulsory attendance of children at primary school was viewed as the means to impose both linguistic uniformity and a respect for French civilisation. This homogenisation of the population around language and culture was viewed as essential not only for national unity but for the pursuit of France's imperialist project. From the 1890s onwards, France embarked on colonial conquests in West Africa and Asia but did so under a very particular ideology. It saw itself as having a unique mission to bring French civilisation to backward people. As Ferry put it, 'if Providence deigned to confer on us a mission by making us masters of the earth, this mission consists ... of simply spreading or awakening among other races the superior notions of which we are guardians.'[17]

The third aim was to overcome class division. The republicans were terrified by any repeat of the insurrectionary instincts displayed by the working class during the Paris Commune. They viewed with horror the growing popularity of syndicalist and Marxist ideas and attacked the very notion of class war. One of the key goals of the education system was to instil in the children of workers a republican ethos rather than a class consciousness. Buisson spelled this out when he suggested that teachers were to show 'sympathy for the people but not class hatred'.

> The teacher should inspire in the pupil the spirit of association and co-operation. Thus he will arm them against so called revolutionary methods which can only retard the real economic revolution; against the general strike; against sabotage; against illegal and violent action ... in short against all forms of anarchy which do more harm to the democratic and social republic than to any other society.[18]

Durkheim gave these goals a more theoretical perspective. His purpose was to inspire student teachers with a deeper understanding in order to carry them out. Few of his ideas on education were original. They reflected more general republican thinking but he gave them a timeless, ahistorical gloss. While sociologists have been reluctant to explore the political roots of his thought, at least one historian has done so. In her survey of France's educational reformers, Katherine Auspitz, pointed to Durkheim's role. 'His work as a whole,' she claimed, 'vindicated Radical politics – and was so intended. Insofar as a triumphant radicalism was able to give a theoretical account of itself, that account was provided by Durkheim.'[19]

OUT WITH THE OLD

Moral Education is based on lectures which Durkheim gave at the Sorbonne in 1902–03 while *The Evolution of French Educational Thought* arose from lectures first given in 1904–05. In other words, these books were based on the experience of 20 years of the secular education system, inaugurated by the Ferry laws. Durkheim was fully supportive of these laws but he thought there was a crisis of 'serious proportions' in the system.[20] The main reason was the republican administration had been over-confident in thinking that it was enough to 'teach the old morality of our fathers' by simply taking out its supernatural element.[21] The task was far more complex, according to Durkheim, because morality must have a quasi-sacred character – even if that did not derive from religion. Morality could not arise simply from the exercise of reason. It must have an aura that arose from a superior reality that went beyond the individual. Teachers of morality also needed a certain authority in order 'to stir the heart and stimulate the mind' of their pupils.[22] They could only gain these qualities if they had a deeper understanding of the social roots of secular morality and the context in which the French educational system developed.

Durkheim's focus in *The Evolution of French Educational Thought* is the different educational theories that had underpinned secondary education. He notes that from the fourteenth century onwards, the 'most important intellectual forces of the nation were formed in the secondary schools' and, as a consequence, he was also writing a history of the French intellectual.[23] His narrative describes how educational theory evolved by incorporating the best of earlier traditions and evolving over time to a new understanding. To do so, he had to find contradictory elements in earlier traditions, some of which were preserved into the future.

The earliest intellectual culture in France, according to Durkheim, came from the Roman Empire. However, it came via the path of the Christian Church which won the allegiance of the uncivilised Franks. Christianity differed from other religions in that its adherents did not simply carry out duties according to traditional rituals. It was fundamentally about shared beliefs and accepting ideas about the nature of man and his relationship to God. Christianity set out to create a certain type of man with 'a general disposition of mind and will which will make him see things in general in a particular light.'[24] The Christian tradition, therefore, placed a particular emphasis on education in order to cultivate 'a certain attitude of the soul, a certain *habitus* of our moral being.'[25] Durkheim's own secular society had abandoned the confessional aims of the Christian Church but he still agreed that schooling should not simply be a matter of 'decorating the mind' but rather of 'getting down to the deepest recesses of the soul.'[26] The technique used by the early Christian Church was to take over the child and immerse him or her in its religious culture. In the more modern scientific age, this could be achieved by a form of sociology that saw the school as a community.

A number of developments within the Christian tradition led, according to Durkheim, to a greater use of reason. The first was Scholastic philosophy, which was an early attempt to confront faith with reason. It did not deny the truth of religious dogmas but sought to present them in a more rational and understandable form. The second was the great academic movement that gave rise to the University of Paris. Durkheim argues that the Papacy played a progressive role by forging an alliance with its teaching body and giving them immunity from local secular justice. As teachers gained greater autonomy, the university became neither an exclusively ecclesiastical or secular institution. There was an 'interpenetration of faith and reason' which, according to Durkheim, made this an interesting age because there was no attempt made to create a barrier between the 'two inseparable aspects of human life'.[27] As a result of these developments, Paris became 'the intellectual capital, not only of the kingdom but of the whole of Christendom'.[28] Even if there was no understanding of science, Durkheim believed that a tradition of argument through dialectic and debate was fundamentally progressive.

However, from the sixteenth century to the end of the eighteenth century, there was a partial regression. Durkheim is deeply sceptical of the Renaissance which, he claimed, helped to form the mentality of pre-revolutionary France. Although formally the Renaissance sought a return to the culture of ancient Rome and Greece, Durkheim argues that it rapidly degenerated either into an 'inordinate taste for erudition' or a belief that 'the whole principle of human culture' could be reduced to a literary culture.[29] This led to an over-reverence of the Latin and Greek languages and to an emphasis on literary style and modes of speech which were simply 'glittering decorations'.[30] This was not just a matter of poor educational practice. It also helped to erode the moral order because, as Durkheim put it, any culture that is 'exclusively aesthetic contains within itself the germ of immorality, or at least of inferior morality'.[31] The Renaissance weakened the link between morality and duty, which had been a key element of Christianity. The 'ideal of the Christian way of life is to do one's duty because it is one's duty, to obey rules because they are the rules'.[32] In place of this form of morality, there was a partial return to the eudemonic ethics of the ancient Greek philosophers, which promoted the happiness of humanity as its main rationale.

Durkheim's attack on Renaissance culture was, in reality, a thinly disguised attack on aristocratic France. The emphasis on style, literary expression and the downgrading of the French language as a medium of instruction was distasteful to this ardent French republican. His particular venom was reserved for the Jesuit order which, he claimed, had opportunistically adopted some of the forms of Renaissance culture rather than its content. The primary purpose of the Jesuits was a reactionary defence of Roman Catholicism but they adopted the 'elegant frivolousness of the leisured class' as a means of winning support.[33] This led to a form of schooling which promoted classical literature to 'the virtually complete exclusion of national literature'.[34] This had little to do with getting pupils to understand classical civilisation but rather its aim was to teach them to speak Latin and Greek. The Jesuits prized oratory, written expression and stylistic formalism as a means to turn their pupils into faithful Catholics who respected tradition.

Against this form of education, Durkheim wants to retain the earlier Christian emphasis on morality as duty – even if this morality is shorn of its religious foundation – and to combine it with a new emphasis on the French language, science and practical reasoning. Instead of producing good Christians, the school system would try to 'create good citizens who would be capable of usefully fulfilling the function which society would one day assign them'.[35] The Lutheran tradition in Germany had gone further than France in breaking from classical formalism and building an intellectual culture of studying 'the world of things, the world of reality'.[36] France needed to follow this path and to develop an education system which would study man and his external environment.

This required a break from the concept of a timeless human nature, which was universally and eternally the same. The Christian tradition was based on this concept and so too, ironically, were the *philosophes* who inspired the French Revolution. The latter sought an original human nature which would be liberated from the constraint of a corrupt society. Against this outmoded idea, Durkheim asserted that history teaches us that humanity was in an interminable process of evolution and that therefore, 'there are as many moral systems as there are types of society'.[37] The morality required by twentieth-century France with its cult of the individual person is fundamentally different from those of ancient Rome or Greece. Students should therefore be taught about the diversity of human types but they should also know that there is:

one type of humanity which is of crucial importance that we understand, namely our own; the one towards which we aspire, the one which we as Frenchmen and, more generally, as members of civilised society in the twentieth century take as our model.[38]

The second objective of modern education should be to give students a grounding in scientific reasoning. It should teach the relationship between man and nature, so that students understand the role they have to play in the natural order. This approach meant that science would cease to be a lifeless subject divorced from human concerns. Durkheim also taught that students needed an immersion in the methodology of science. They needed to find in science 'a kind of exemplary rationality which is the ideal model on which our individual rationalities should seek to model themselves.'[39] This would involve a shift away from a thinking based formal rationality to a greater reliance on observation, experimental reasoning and an appreciation of complexity. This, Durkheim suggests, would be wholly beneficial for the French national character.

Durkheim's political objectives should be clear from this brief summary of the book. He was situating the republican project within a wider historical context. His narrative combined an emphasis on the positive elements of the French intellectual character with an identification of weaknesses that needed to be addressed. The main cause of that weakness was the classical system of education which was devised for an aristocratic culture which promoted intellectual erudition as a stylistic decoration. The chief culprit was the Jesuits, to whom Durkheim devotes three chapters. It is hardly coincidental that one of the first measures that Ferry took in 1880 was the dissolution of the Jesuit order and their expulsion from France. However, while Durkheim's narrative sees a logical progression to a more scientific form of education, he also wants to retain a central element of the Christian tradition – a concept of morality that is rooted in duty.

HOW PRIMARY SCHOOLS TEACH MORALITY

Moral Education is more a practical manual for how teachers should instil this morality in their pupils. Durkheim starts by seeking to 'ferret out those basic sentiments that are the foundation of our moral dispositions.'[40] He suggests that moral behaviour is primarily about conformity to pre-established rules. This emphasis on pre-established norms is designed to encourage conformity to existing social arrangements. The rules he refers to are by no means abstract or universal. They do not arise from a general rational understanding, for example, that morality is based on treating others like one would desire for oneself. The basis of morality is: 'specific rules applying uniquely to the special situation that they govern.'[41] Durkheim is not concerned about morality in general but a morality that is appropriate for French culture and society.

He identifies three main elements of a moral disposition. The first element is *regularity* because, he claims, morality must imply a certain ability to develop habits. 'Transients' who do not have such habits have a 'defective' moral temperament. So too have those who disdain customary behaviour or who feel some compulsion to remain 'free'.[42] The second element of morality is *authority*. Rules become a moral power that we acknowledge as superior to us. They must be obeyed for their own sake. The third element is *discipline*. For Durkheim, discipline is good for people, regardless of its actual content.

These three elements of morality flow from Durkheim's particular view of the human psyche. He thought that the human appetites need to be constrained and that: 'the inability to restrict one's self within certain limits is a sign of disease.'[43] This stricture applies not just to desires but to intellectual activity itself. People needed to accept a limit to their rational capacity and should not continually ask 'why?'. If they do so, they will become 'abnormal subjects which doctors call *douteurs*'.[44] In his own contemporary historical period, he thought, there was also a 'malady of infinite aspiration'.[45] One example of this malady is the 'unleashing' of passions which had arisen because of the weakening of the rules on 'conjugal morality'. Such passions, Durkheim baldly asserts, 'entail a disillusionment which translates itself graphically into statistics on suicide.'[46] More generally, Durkheim loathed the 'anarchist' tendencies of modern society. He acknowledged that some 'moral innovators' had a legitimate need for change but this had 'degenerated into something like anarchy'.[47]

The primary schools were the key arena in which these problems could be overcome. The school is of greater importance than the family in inculcating morality because it can train children in the demands of society. The school system can convince the child of the need for boundaries and limits to their individual aspirations. It can also impose impersonal objectives on the child which reflect the needs of the wider society. By society, Durkheim means three concentric spheres: the family, the nation and wider humanity. However, the nation enjoys a primacy over the others.[48] Each particular country, according to Durkheim, represents 'a special point of view' towards mankind.[49] Provided that the nation is not 'solely pre-occupied with expansion and self-aggrandizement',[50] it has a right to demand the allegiance of its citizens. In the case of France, there is a fortunate harmony between the national interest and that of humanity as whole because the French national character is 'universalist'. When the French work out a constitution, they do not see it for their exclusive use but for mankind as a whole.[51] The school, therefore, is 'the only moral agent through which the child is able systematically to learn to know the love of his country'.[52]

Durkheim's method of inculcating French patriotism shows a degree of sophistication that most other nationalists did not possess. He assumed that France had a gift of civilisation to bestow on the world and, therefore, did not need to engage in any aggressive expansion. This allows him to equate love of country with love of humanity. The same sophistication is evident in his argument on the dutiful nature of morality. Initially, the moral order is imposed from the outside, but one of the purposes of schools is to give children an understanding of morality's rational basis. A secular education system shows pupils that the moral voice within them does not arise from a superhuman being – but from society itself. They need to know that: 'when conscience speaks, it is society speaking within us'.[53] Once pupils arrive at this understanding, their conformity to moral rules 'will not amount to passive resignation but to enlightened allegiance'.[54] As society has now become part of them, they develop an autonomy with respect to moral acts.

But how to bring this about? Durkheim suggests that the impersonal order of school with its timetable and its rules about classroom behaviour imposes a regularity and consistency on the pupils which they did not originally have. Moreover, 'by respecting school rules ... the child learns to respect rules in general'.[55] Interestingly, Durkheim associates the untrained mind of the child with 'primitives', who are also volatile and unpredictable. The second source of morality for the child is the authority of the teacher but this will require lay teachers to have a sense of their mission. In the past, he suggests, the priest thought that he spoke in the name of God and this gave him an aura of authority. The lay teacher must also develop his authority by seeing himself as 'the instrument of a great moral reality which surpasses him. Just as the priest is the interpreter of God, he is the great moral interpreter of his time and his country'.[56] He must project his authority as coming not from his own personality but as deriving from a society of which he is an instrument. If he does so, he will inculcate in his pupils a respect for impersonal law.

Durkheim thinks this task is vital because the 'only thing that survives in a society where the prestige of class and dynasties is no longer recognised is the impersonal authority of the law.'[57]

Just as the school becomes the arena for asserting two of the key elements of morality – regularity and authority – so too it must impose discipline by a systematic approach to punishment. Like most republicans, Durkheim was opposed to the use of corporal punishment – except in societies that are still 'uncivilised'.[58] His approach to punishment arises directly from his sociological understanding of the dichotomy between the sacred and the profane. Children need to see the school rules,

> as a sacred and inviolable thing quite beyond their control ... Where a rule is breached, it ceases to appear as inviolable; a sacred thing profaned no longer seems sacred if nothing new develops to restore its nature.[59]

The function of punishment is to restore the sacred character of the school rules and from this follows the specific methods of punishment. He recommends it consist of 'putting the guilty on the *index*, holding him at a distance, ostracizing him, making a void around him, and separating him from decent people.'[60] These psychological techniques are designed to convey to the child a language through which the general social conscience expresses its feeling about the infraction of a rule.

Schools must also encourage in children an attachment to wider social groups. They can do this by projecting themselves as a collective community. Durkheim calls this a development of 'altruistic instincts', which he believes can be as deeply rooted as egoistic instincts. The school has a special role to play in forging an awareness of political society – or the nation. This is because the nation does not derive from either blood relations or free choice and the school resembles this nature of association. Hence, the stronger the common life of the school is, the better it prepares the child to become citizens. Durkheim worries, however, that there is an inclination towards a 'fierce individualism' in the French national temperament.[61] The reason is that intermediate organisations between the individual and the state were never cultivated.

Both the absolutist monarchy and the French Revolution forged a strong, centralised state and placed obstacles in the way of intermediate groups. Durkheim believes that this tendency was broadly progressive, but that the disappearance of these groups 'impaired public morality'.[62]

The main forms of human activity developed outside social groups and so the spirit of association – the main medium through which morality was conveyed – was weakened. He contrasts Germany where 'everything is done in a group' with France where 'the principle, was that of isolation'.[63] The only way to overcome this weakness in the French national character was to 'get hold of the child when he leaves his family and enters school and instil in him the inclination for collective life.'[64]

Durkheim's primary concern was not collective life in general but patriotism for France. When discussing history teaching in school, he rejects interpretations which see key influences emanating from individuals such as Napoleon or Louis XIV. This, he suggests, stops children from 'recognizing in society a definite nature of its own'.[65] The pupil should understand instead that:

Rights accorded him today, the liberties he enjoys, the moral dignity he feels – all this is the work not of such and such an individual or such and such a generation but of that being, personal and impersonal at the same time, we call France.[66]

History teaching is the means of putting children in touch with this 'collective spirit'.[67] It is a way of bringing them into a 'close intimacy with the collective conscience'.[68] It provides a way of highlighting the French national character because 'what is the history of a people if not the genius of that people developing over time?'[69] This type of teaching, however, assumes that the teacher is imbued with a clear idea of what the French character is. And one of the reasons *Moral Education* was written was to ensure that teachers took on this mission with a deeper understanding.

CRITICISM

Durkheim's writings on education almost speak for themselves. There is little pretence of academic objectivity and they are partisan publications to promote the republican agenda. Nevertheless, they draw on his wider theories about the collective conscience and the sacred and the profane. These concepts are not treated as elements in an abstract theory and so the writings on education reveal the precise use they serve for his political agenda.

Durkheim's concept of morality arises from his class position in early twentieth-century France. He was a defender of a bourgeois order that had long passed its revolutionary stage. He wants to defend freedom for the individual but combine it with the repression of desire. So on the one hand, there is a rejection of the liberal view, which sees moral principles as being entirely independent of historical conditions. The liberal sees morality as a result of autonomous choices that cannot be justified with any appeal to facts. From this arises the standard injunction that one can never move from 'is' to 'ought'. Against this, individual-based moral choice, Durkheim substitutes an overarching concern for duty and respect – for rules for their own sake.

On the other hand, Durkheim can find no basis for these rules, except that they arise from the collective conscience or, more specifically, they grow out of the French national character. As MacIntyre pointed out, this is akin to a situation where primitive taboos survive, but people have forgotten what the point is.[70] Durkheim, however, does not want to ask 'what is the point?' because he wants to retain an element of the secularised Protestant tradition that he derives from Kant; namely, that morality is about repression of desire – it is about duty and hence rules must be respected for their own sake. In place of Kant's rational individual, however, Durkheim substitutes Society and asserts that people need to have their desire curbed.

One can, however, envisage a different morality that is not based on repression of the desires of the majority. This could have as its goal the promotion of the general well-being of both the individual and humanity. Such a morality would link human desire to the historic possibilities for their society. It would be based on a discovery that what we as individuals want most is what we have in common with others. From this perspective, rules might be a mechanism to curb our short-term selfishness to help serve the general desires of all. They would not simply be a mechanism for repression but a mechanism to help guide us to the possibility of realising our humanity.[71]

Durkheim's morality is precisely the opposite of this – and for good reason. He wanted to close down any possibility of a moral critique of his society. He wanted a morality that could be used to urge conformity to the unequal social relations. Far from presenting a scientific analysis, he develops an elaborate argument for why repression of the desires of the majority is necessary. And just as the priests used to claim it was 'for their own good', Durkheim also wants to give similar reassurance. He is correct to assert that, historically, there are different moral systems. But these do not reflect society in general rather than the needs of particular classes within them. Durkheim's own morality is that of a nineteenth-century French bourgeois republican.

His approach to pedagogy also reflects this outlook. The Swiss psychologist, Jean Piaget, has characterised Durkheim's approach as 'extremely conservative'.[72] This is because Durkheim conceives of the learning process as a one-way street between the teacher as authority figure and the child. He assumes that school is an institution whereby adult society transmits its values to children. This means, as Piaget points out, that Durkheim 'entirely ignored the existence of sponta-neously formed children's societies'.[73] There is no understanding that children also learn from their peers or that there can be a clash between the official culture of the school and the values children develop from their own social groups. Children do not simply imbibe the rules laid down by the school – they also develop their own rules through play. Piaget has called these respectively 'rules due to unilateral respect' and 'rules due to mutual respect'.[74] In activity based learning, children are encouraged to play because there is a belief that self-government and autonomous learning help to develop social relations based on mutual respect. Durkheim, however, wants a more authoritarian system because he is frightened that any other avenue will undermine his concept of duty. This is why Piaget accuses him of seeing the school 'as a monarchy founded on divine right'.[75]

Finally, there is a certain falsity to Durkheim's benign patriotism. At the time he was delivering his lectures, Durkheim could present an apparent harmony of interests between France's *mission civilisatrice* and humanity at large. As Conklin pointed out, the notion of a civilising mission was a way in which the republican regime 'struggled to reconcile its aggressive imperialism with its republican ideals'.[76] However, behind this ideological cover was a naked scramble to subjugate non-European countries to colonial rule. France was by no means alone in this and eventually the European desire for conquest led to a war between the imperialist powers themselves. The result was the horrific slaughter of the First World War when 17 million people were killed.

Once the war broke out, the mask hiding Durkheim's support for France's imperialism dropped and he deployed his academic skills to promote the war effort. This resulted in two publications which can only be characterised as war propaganda, *Who Wanted War?*[77] and *Germany*

Above All. In the latter publication, the same themes evident in *Moral Education* are revisited – only this time with a negative sign added when there is contrast with Germany. France is still presented as a moral nation, which respects international law and the rights of small nations. This is because it understands that morality is superior to the state and that although morality consists of ideas, 'these ideas are forces which move and dominate man.'[78]

The German mentality, however, is entirely different. It has a 'morbid character' because it is based on the idea that the State should not be subject to moral rules. 'The State is above Morality; it knows no higher end than itself; it is in itself its own end.'[79] This, Durkheim claims, leads to:

> the passion of Germany for conquest and annexation. She cares so little for what men may feel or desire. All she asks is that they should submit to the law of the conqueror, and she herself will see to it that it is obeyed.[80]

These claims are deployed to advance the interests of French imperialism above German imperialism. Durkheim took the religious motto – 'God is on our side' – and simply gave it a secular twist. Germany's 'social pathology' meant that France and her allies could have a 'legitimate confidence of victory', for 'there can be no greater source of strength than to have the nature of things on one's side.'[81]

Today, when hindsight has discredited the war propaganda of all sides in the First World War, this statement appears as highly facetious. However, it is important to recognise a certain unity in Durkheim's thought rather than dismissing his war propaganda as an aberration. The reality is that he was deploying a particular morality to advance the cause of republican France and to enforce a conformity among workers so that they turned their backs on class war. In peaceful times, this project could be presented in a somewhat benign and academic fashion. In war time, the same methodology is deployed in a more overt and propagandistic fashion. But behind both is a use of morality to promote the same class view of the world.

8

Socialism and Saint-Simon

In 1895–96, Durkheim gave a series of lectures on socialism. He had long maintained an interest in the subject as is evident from the original title of this PhD thesis, which was 'The Relations between Individualism and Socialism'.[1] He was a personal friend of Jean Jaurès, the former radical republican who had embraced the socialist cause just three years earlier. Durkheim had planned a three-year course on socialism, starting with the early ideas of Saint-Simon, devoting the second year to Fourier and Proudhon and culminating in a discussion on Marx, Lassalle and German socialism. However, he changed his mind after the first year and returned to 'pure science' to write on suicide. Nevertheless, the lecture series gave rise to a book which was subsequently published under the title *Socialism and Saint-Simon* – and issued simply as *Socialism* in the USA. It gives an insight into both the political agenda and the sociology of its author.

The context in which the lectures were given is all important. By the mid-1890s, there was a qualitative growth of Marxist ideas and a break between the workers movement and French Republicanism. The growth of the left had been hampered by the relatively low level of French industrialisation and the calamitous defeat of the Paris Commune. During the Third Republic, land-based activities accounted for between 40 and 45 per cent of the working population and a third of workers were employed in enterprises of less than five people.[2] Thousands of left-wing activists had been exiled after the Paris Commune and only gained an amnesty in 1880. All of this meant that the socialist movement developed at a much slower pace than in Germany.

Yet develop it did. The Parti Ouvrier was founded in 1880 and adopted a programme written in collaboration with Marx. Led by Jules Guesde, it propagated a dogmatic and somewhat sectarian version of Marxism, but nevertheless defined itself as a revolutionary party founded on class politics. For most of the 1880s, it remained a relatively small party, with probably no more than 2,000 members. But after a major upsurge of

working-class militancy, it began to grow significantly and while comparatively weak in Paris won a significant base in other towns. In 1892, the
Guesdist party won majorities in 23 municipal councils and when other
socialist groups were counted, there were 60 councils under left-wing
control.[3] Some of Durkheim's closest collaborators, including his nephew
Marcel Mauss, were attracted to this new hard left. In Bordeaux, where
Durkheim was based, the Guesdists had a strong foothold and there
were many debates between them and the followers of Jean Jaurès, who
maintained a closer connection to the French Republican tradition.[4]

By the mid-1890s, when Durkheim undertook his lecture series,
'everyone from activists to professors, in salons and in the streets was
talking about socialism.'[5] The Parti Ouvrier were building a mass,
working-class party that resembled the SPD in Germany and increasingly
adopting an electoral approach. They were being challenged by both a
vibrant anarcho-syndicalist movement and a more reformist 'possibilist'
movement. One of the key issues which divided this rising left was their
attitude towards republicans. Originally, the republicans had helped
to reawaken the French labour movement because it saw workers
as an ally against any possible monarchist reaction. However, when
working-class militancy grew, the republicans became more wary. They
adopted a rhetoric that was 'politically radical but not socially radical, a
socio-political orientation ideally calculated to confuse and seduce the
Guesdist working class electorate.'[6] They used a language of 'the people'
versus the 'elite' and abhorred any form of class politics. Many of the
Guesdists had originally come from the republican camp but this only
made their rivalry even more visceral. 'Class war is the *raison d'être* of
the Parti Ouvrier, without it (the party) would just become a fraction of
republicanism,' one of its correspondents noted.[7]

Durkheim's lecture course was a political intervention in these
debates. He aimed to halt the drift towards class politics and restore
unity around la République. To do so, he conveyed an impression of
sympathy with elements of socialism, all the better to target those who
promoted class struggle. But in order to gain a certain authority and to
be effective, he donned the air of an objective scientist examining the
malaise in society. The result is a book that comes in two halves. The
first half involves a torturous, obtuse argumentation designed to separate
socialism from class struggle. The second part is more interesting, as it
involves a genuinely learned and engaged debate with the ideas of Henri
de Saint-Simon.

SOCIALISM

Durkheim mocks the idea that there could be a scientific socialism. Socialism, he suggests, seeks an ideal, a future society and therefore could not be based on a scientific examination of current societies. It may make certain claims about social conditions but it does not reflect them accurately. It is like a sick person, who 'faultily interprets the feelings that he experiences and most often attributes them to a cause which is not even a true one.'[8] It is impossible to refute the overall philosophy because as soon as the doctrines of a Fourier, Saint-Simon or Marx are disproved, others spring up to take their place. Durkheim reserves his special contempt for Marx. He, apparently, established 'the entire theory of value in a few lines'.[9] He did not provide proper statistical data to solve many of the issues he discusses. His research studies are only undertaken 'to establish a doctrine that had previously (been) conceived'.[10]

Having dismissed the scientific claims of Marxists, Durkheim dons the familiar mantle of a scientist and a doctor. As usual, he apparently engages in a rigorous exercise to arrive at a definition of his object of scientific inquiry. He informs his readers that he has grouped together phenomena under their distinctive characteristics. This then allows him to 'study socialism as we did suicide, the family, marriage, crime, punishment, responsibility and religion.'[11] His methodology, however, barely conceals a deeply patronising strategy. Socialist ideas will not be contested, debated or challenged in Durkheim's book. They will be treated simply as a 'cry of grief' from those who suffer from our 'collective malaise'.[12] In other words, the ideas are so confused that – at least according to Durkheim's scientific standards – they will be treated only as symptoms of wider problems.

> Socialism is to the facts which produce it, what the groans of a sick man are to the illness with which he is afflicted, to the needs that torment him. But what would one say of a doctor who accepted the replies or desires of his patient as scientific truth?[13]

After this somewhat torturous exercise, Durkheim produces a definition of socialism, which is fairly close to his own concerns. Socialism, he asserts, is not about alleviating the plight of workers. It cannot be reduced to a workers' question, he repeats several times. Neither is socialism about 'collectivised' state ownership. It is not even about denying the principle of private ownership. Socialism, according to Durkheim, is founded on 'those theories which demand a more or less complete connection of all economic functions or of certain of them, though diffused, with the directing and knowing organs of society.'[14] Moreover, Durkheim stresses that the key word is 'connecting' economic activities to the state rather than 'subordinating' them to it.[15] The definition contains so many qualifications as to be almost open ended.

Durkheim's next move is to distinguish socialism from communism. This raises some difficulties for the modern reader because the word 'communism' is normally connected to the regime that emerged in the USSR after the 1917 revolution. As Durkheim died in the same year as that revolution, he was not applying the term 'communist' to anything resembling these regimes. Instead, he asserts that all communist theories are derived – with some minor variations – from Plato.[16] Communism, he states, is a doctrine that calls for the abolition of all private property because it sees it as the source of all immorality. It is a timeless doctrine that calls for a return to primitive society. It is promoted by 'secluded men whose words seem only to awaken feeble echoes among the masses surrounding them.'[17] Socialism, by contrast, is practical and of the present age. It is focused on industry and commerce and seeks to 'regulate the productive organs (so) that they co-operate harmoniously.'[18]

However, since the French Revolution, there has been a certain reinvigoration of communist ideals and these have tended to contaminate socialism. The growth of this abstract, philosophical and utopian doctrine has led to an over-focus on equality. It takes the concept of fraternity too far and turns it into a 'compulsory charity', a 'current of pity and sympathy'[19] for the poor and this has become an obstacle to socialism. Communism fails to recognise the essential problem with the human condition – that our appetites are unlimited. They do not see that,

It is in vain that one will create privileges for workers which neutralise in part those enjoyed by employers; in vain will the working day be decreased or even wages legally increased. We will not succeed in pacifying roused appetites, because they will acquire new force in the measure they are appeased.[20]

The implication could hardly be clearer. Socialism needs to break from these abstract philosophers and focus on the practical steps of bringing the productive system into harmony with the rest of society. It should even stop promoting wage increases or a shorter working week.

Durkheim's argument is so contrived that it barely requires a critique. But there are four obvious problems with it.

First, his definition of socialism is entirely arbitrary and there is nothing scientific about it. No detailed evidence is provided to show that it derives from the main currents of the socialist movement. Defining socialism as simply seeking to 'connect' some, or all, economic activities to the state would render nearly all politicians as socialists. It is a definition designed to incorporate the term socialism into the lexicon of French republicanism.

Second, Durkheim may *wish* to cut the connection between socialism and the workers' movement, but empirically there were no grounds for this. The main socialist party in France was called 'The Workers' Party' and promoted 'revolutionary action of the class of producers – the proletariat – organised in an independent party.'[21] Anarcho-syndicalists endlessly proclaimed their desire to build class struggle unions of workers. Even Jean Jaurès, who had more sympathy with the French republican tradition, saw an intrinsic link. He stated that:

> The Socialistic idea, the Communist idea, is strong enough to guide and co-ordinate successive efforts on the part of the proletariat. It is towards the accomplishment of that end, towards its gradual realization, that the proletariat is directing its organized effort.[22]

If all the main currents in France, saw socialism as arising out of the struggles of workers, then Durkheim was not engaged in objective analysis but wishful republican thinking.

Third, Durkheim's distinction between 'communism' and 'socialism' is based on a dishonest construction. His definition of 'communism' as originating from a form of utopian thinking is correct. But asserting that all varieties of communism derived from Plato – who coincidently, championed slave ownership – is absurd. Far from the term communism emerging from the minds of 'secluded theoreticians', it developed within the secret societies of the radical French working-class movement. Étienne Cabet is sometimes credited with inventing the term in 1839 and it was Marx's engagement with workers' clubs in Paris that convinced him to use the term. Engels explained the distinction between the two terms in an entirely different way to Durkheim:

By socialists, in 1847, were understood ... the adherents of various socialist systems ... [promoted] by men outside the working class movement, and looking to 'educate' these classes for support. Whatever portion of the working class had become convinced of the insufficiency of mere political movements, and had proclaimed the necessity of a total social change, that portion called itself Communist.[23]

However, the issue is not the peculiar lexicons of either Engels or Durkheim but rather Durkheim's implicit identification of Marxists with the term 'communist' and their consequent relegation to the status of impractical utopians. In his one direct attack on Guesde, Durkheim suggested that 'Marxist collectivism' was 'a simple extension of ancient communism'.[24] The reality, however, was very different. Marxism involved a break with both the utopian 'socialism' of Robert Owen and the utopian 'communism' of Étienne Cabet. It focused instead on the real movement of workers, advancing both an immediate practical programme for change and a wider goal of overthrowing capitalism. Durkheim ignores this reality, however, as he wanted to urge French socialists to break from the 'secluded philosophers' who promoted equality and to turn to practical matters of regulation. In brief, he wished to see a mild, reformist version of socialism that could be allied to the Republican cause. But to do so, he had to weave a web of obtuse, roundabout arguments.

Finally, Durkheim is using an aura of science and academic credentials to dismiss a powerful political philosophy rather than critically debate it. He is defining it, in advance, as irrational while establishing himself as a doctor with a cure for the malaise from which it grows. However, one could also simply reduce Durkheim's own sociology to a malaise that arises from the fears of the republican elite. Moreover, even if socialism or sociology might have arisen because of certain conditions, one still needs to critically discuss its ideas.

SAINT-SIMON

If Durkheim's argumentation on socialism is slipshod and instrumental, his discussion on Saint-Simon is enlightening and subtle. Saint-Simon was an extremely complex, progressive and sophisticated thinker whose theories contained the 'germs' of many later systems. Durkheim credits him – rather than Comte – with being the real founder of positivism and sociology. But equally, he recognises that Saint-Simon also inspired other diverse currents such as a new science of history, early forms of socialism and even an aspiration for a new religious revival. Engels concurs with Durkheim on one of these points, claiming that: 'almost all the ideas of later socialists that are not strictly economic are found in him in embryo.'[25] Disentangling the various strands of Saint-Simon's thinking and plotting their development from embryo to maturity was an arduous task. In doing so, Durkheim displays a considerable talent in exposition – even while stressing those aspects of Saint-Simon that lead to his own sociology rather than socialism. The following summary of Saint-Simon's life and ideas is drawn from Durkheim.

Claude Henri de Saint-Simon led an extraordinary life. Born into the aristocracy in 1750, he encountered the ideas of the Enlightenment at an early age and became an officer in the American revolutionary forces, who fought for separation from Britain. He welcomed the French Revolution enthusiastically but, after being involved in financial speculation, he was arrested and nearly lost his life on the guillotine. This experience led to support for radical Enlightenment ideas, even while abhorring the disorder that followed in their wake. After the revolution, he used his large fortune to embark on an education course and to create an open house for fellow intellectuals. By 1805, however, he had lost all his money and was reduced to abject poverty. Ironically, it was during this period that he produced most of his works. He also created around him a small group of followers, including Auguste Comte, who, Durkheim notes, 'owed him much more than he acknowledged.'[26] After his death in 1825, the Saint-Simon School eventually morphed into a group of engineers and bankers, who played an important role in the industrialisation of France.

The French Revolution was inspired by Enlightenment ideas which proclaimed a new age of reason. It promised to abolish feudal privilege and to establish the rational organisation of society. By the time that Saint-Simon was writing, however, bourgeois class privileges were in evidence and the 'sans culottes', who had driven through the revolution were suffering new oppressions. Far from Reason leading to social harmony, society was rent asunder with conflict. Saint-Simon's writings grapple with the failure of Reason to deliver a better society – and to propose some solutions. His starting point was the need for a positive philosophy that would be 'inventive and organizational' to replace the 'critical and revolutionary' outlook of the preceding century.[27] The new type of knowledge that was required was a science of man and societies – a 'social physiology'.[28]

Saint-Simon thought that society had a reality of its own, independent of the feelings, thoughts and action of individuals. It was 'a veritable organised machine'[29] and its development was not dependent on the arbitrary whims of a conglomerate of individuals. In brief, there was a social system whose parts interlocked to enable the functioning of the whole. There was a set of dominant beliefs, political structures and modes of wealth creation which constituted a central dynamic. Social systems were subject to 'the law of progress' and thus there were significant shifts. The central dynamic of feudal society was military conquest. Society was built on war and the enforced serfdom of a peasant class. The military class dominated its political structures and the clergy dominated the belief systems and both interlocked to create social stability.

However, the law of progress meant that these structures were eroded in time. The discoveries of Copernicus and Galileo undermined the theology that the earth had been created by God for man. Science and rational thought weakened the clergy's appeal to blind faith. Meanwhile in the urban communes, new forms of industry and commerce emerged. These eventually lead to a new society based on *industrialism*. Saint-Simon's central argument was that there were two key periods in human society. One was an 'organic' period where the varying parts of society worked in harmony – another was the 'critical period' where this has broken down. Thus for a long period during the Middle Ages, feudal society worked harmoniously but the critical period – that coincided with the Enlightenment and French Revolution – laid the foundations for a new society.

Saint-Simon's own society – and Durkheim's – had also entered one of those critical periods. Industrialism had broken through the barriers of feudalism to lay the basis for a modern society based on peaceful and productive activity. Instead of permanently seeking enemies, it needed a culture of collaboration and trust. Instead of superstition and blind faith, it required rational discussion. Yet these were not occurring in post-revolutionary France. Royal authority had been re-established after the defeat of Napoleon 'but these revivals did not constitute a solution.'[30] The revolution had destroyed the old beliefs but 'it did not attempt to elaborate a new body of rational beliefs that all minds could accept.'[31] Lawyers and 'metaphysicians', who spoke the language of 'the rights of man', had wedged themselves into the places once occupied by the aristocracy and clergy, but they were unable to provide harmony for society.[32]

There is much in the above account of Saint-Simon's ideas that Durkheim took over and developed. But there was one element of Saint-Simon's thinking that Durkheim was less happy about – his model of a producer-led society. Living in an age, when the privileged grand bourgeoisie of the Restoration were dominating society, Saint-Simon suggested that there remained a fundamental class division in modern society, namely, between 'idlers' and 'producers'. For Saint-Simon, 'the owner who is merely an owner and who does not himself exploit his capital' is simply a 'drone'.[33] He joins the ranks of the aristocratic idlers, who serve no useful social purpose. However, as Durkheim correctly points out, Saint-Simon is not suggesting that: 'all capitalists are placed beyond the pale of regular society, but only those who live on unearned income'.[34] The 'immense majority of the nation' – all the workers, but also the managers who are engaged in the production process as well as technicians – constitute the large class of 'producers'. Saint-Simon suggests that from their ranks is drawn the political representatives of the new society. The 'idlers' should not participate in political deliberation.

The governance structure of industrial society should be built on a supreme council of industry who would be assisted by a supreme council of the learned – a Council of Newton composed principally of social scientists. On one level – and Durkheim brings out this contradiction well – Saint-Simon is proposing a technocratic elite, who will manage the social tensions in society and create a new harmony. However, there is also an aspiration to reduce the role of the state. Like Durkheim subsequently, Saint-Simon thought that industrialism led to a greater division of social labour and hence greater dependence of each on the other. He thought there would still be a need for a 'directing agency' or a state but this would be engulfed by an economy, primarily based on producers. As long as the economy was organised through cooperation amongst these producers, government should be reduced to administration. Moreover, as the scientific ethos spread in society, political decision-making would flow naturally from this. 'Politics,' Saint-Simon suggested, 'will become the science of observation and political questions handled by those who would have studied the positive science of man.'[35] More specifically, 'scholars show what the laws of social hygiene are, then from among the measures they propose … the industrialists choose those which experience has proven most practical.'[36]

For a long period, Saint-Simon thought that the goal of the new society was simply to increase production. But gradually he came to realise that this was not sufficient and that a moral end was required because even in a well-organised society, selfishness and egoism would grow. Towards the end of his life, he proclaimed the need for a new religion – a new Christianity. Christianity has been historically progressive in promoting a wider love of humanity. There was a need to free 'the Christian idea that is the moral idea, of all alloys which debase it, to re-establish it in its original purity and make it the single basis of the religious system.'[37] According to Durkheim, Saint-Simon's new emphasis did not mean that he embraced the idea of a personal living God. The proposal was more akin to a pantheistic religion which placed morality at its core. In this new religion, 'The best theologian will simply be the best moralist,' Durkheim claims.[38]

This brief summary gives some indication of the debt that Durkheim owed to Saint-Simon. Essentially, he removed many of the latter's ideas from their original encasing, reconfigured some of them and surrounded them with the aura of academic science. Durkheim's claim that organic solidarity arose with a modern division of labour came straight from Saint-Simon's notion of industrial society as peaceful and collaborative. Both thinkers were optimists, who thought that greater interdependence could lead to a higher form of solidarity. Using social science to lead society also came from Saint-Simon. But Durkheim expressed the matter in more modest and cautious terms. Instead of creating a council of scholars to advise industrialists, he called for a science of morality that could be taught in schools. Nevertheless, both Durkheim and Saint-Simon went to some lengths to justify a science of society which could reduce social conflict and restore harmony. The notion of a time lag between the shift to industry and the lack of social integration also came from Saint-Simon. Both thinkers make use of the model of a social fit between belief systems and an underlying central dynamic. They both draw on the concept of a 'critical period' – or, in Durkheim's words, a period of social malaise – to suggest a role for social science. Durkheim developed this by looking for specific indicators – such as incidences of suicide – to provide more empirical evidence that society was indeed in a critical period.

However, just as Durkheim borrowed from Saint-Simon, he also criticised him and added his own conservative twist.

First, he challenged Saint-Simon's materialism with a metaphysical view of human nature. Saint-Simon had suggested that a new society was developing from an objective historical process. Instead of seeing reason as the driving force which might create historical change, Saint-Simon looked to economic development as the motor. He described how industry and science had grown, but maintained that they were still trapped in a power structure that was regressive – in other words, the type of revivals brought on by the restoration of the monarchy in France. Saint-Simon pressed for the downfall of these power structures in order to assure industry of its supremacy. But according to Durkheim he was 'mistaken' and his remedy led only to an 'aggravation of the evil'.[39] The cause of this mistake was his failure to recognise that human appetites are insatiable. Even if all workers were equal, Durkheim asserts, social conflict would still emerge because some wanted more. In other words, Saint-Simon has leaned too heavily towards a materialist understanding. Durkheim's critique is metaphysical as there is no scientific evidence to prove his theory of insatiable need. It is rather a secular version of the doctrine of original sin, proposing a timeless design fault in the human make-up.

Naturally, this leads Durkheim to welcome Saint-Simon's later embrace of religion as the idealist glue that binds people together. However, he claims that Saint-Simon does not go far enough. Durkheim's reasoning here betrays his deep-seated fear of working-class militancy. Saint-Simon's new religion, he suggests, 'If it curbs the wealthy by assigning as their goal the well-being of the poor, it does not restrain the latter – and the desires of these should be no less regulated than the needs of others.'[40] In other words, the target of Saint-Simon's moral imperative was the wealthy, but for Durkheim the main problem – because they were in the majority – was the insatiable appetites of the poor. Durkheim finds Saint-Simon's embrace of religion to be hesitant and too directed towards the salvation of the poor. He himself went on to identify religion as the primary causal factor in giving shape to society and to root the human categories of knowledge in religion.

Due in some part to his materialism, Saint-Simon's theories involve a degree of class struggle, even if his categories were somewhat vague. Moreover, at the core of his argument is a suggestion that the revolution, which brought about modern capitalism, has not been completed. The historic process is pushing society towards a new stage whereby the 'producers' rule. This implies quite a damming critique of capitalism

– even if Saint-Simon did not discard the role of individual capitalists. Durkheim, however, is deeply uneasy with this view. He abhors any form of class conflict as a pathology that needs to be cured. He promotes the stability of the existing social system without analysing which class dominates it. In practice, this means encouraging the poor to know their place by getting them to embrace an official morality. Nowhere in Durkheim's sociology is found a critique of the 'idlers' that Saint-Simon pioneered. In an age where owners are even more distant from the production process and greater amounts of the world's resources are devoted to speculation, this critique might have even more validity today. It certainly explains why Engels regarded Saint-Simon as an early precursor of socialism, even if he was critical of his limitations.

Finally, Durkheim discards Saint-Simon's aspiration for a new society. Saint-Simon's somewhat mechanical notion of the 'law of progress' implied that there was further social development in the offing. History had not ended with the creation of capitalism but could move on towards a producer-driven society. Durkheim, by contrast, wanted to end talk of a new society or 'a feeling of subversive hatred'.[41] He states that in his own theories,

> It is not a matter of putting in a completely new society in the place of the existing one, but of adapting the latter to the new social conditions. At least it no longer stirs questions of classes; it no longer opposes rich to poor, employers to workers – as if the only possible solution consisted of diminishing the portion of one in order to augment that of the other ... Put differently, the social question ... is not a question of money; it is a question of moral agents.[42]

Durkheim's account of his difference with Saint-Simon yet again reveals the true motivation of his own sociology – how to maintain the Republican order in France.

9

The Limits to Durkheim's Republican Sociology

In his monumental study, Steven Lukes argues that the relationship between the individual and society is the centre point around which Durkheim's entire sociology revolves.[1] Lukes' point is that everything that Durkheim did sociologically was ultimately concerned with the cohesion of his own society. Like many intellectuals, Durkheim fretted about the rising levels of conflict in the Third Republic, yet he parted ways with much contemporary opinion with his view of social science as a diagnostic tool that could bring remedies. Unlike de Tocqueville's pessimistic approach, for example, Durkheim had absolute faith in the ability of sociology to foster new forms of solidarity. This faith drove his sociology forward, influencing the selection of his central problems, the construction of his categories and the nature of his sociological prescriptions.[2]

The best lens through which to view Durkheim's sociology is his republican politics. Durkheim was not only trained in the pre-eminent republican institution of his day – the École Normale Supérieure – he was also a direct beneficiary of state patronage at various stages of his academic career. He supported the legacy of the French Revolution against the Catholic Church and the aristocracy even if he recoiled from its radicalism. He was a French patriot who wanted to see the rebirth of his country after its defeat in the Franco-Prussian War. He thought that the concept of individual rights, which was proclaimed in the Declaration of the Rights of Man and of the Citizen, was a gift which French civilisation brought to the world. Coming from a Jewish family, Durkheim also traced religious freedom to the French Revolution, although his adherence to the values of French republicanism ran deeper than self-interest. It was, rather, heartfelt and enduring. Throughout his life, Durkheim believed passionately in the republican precepts of reason, liberty and bourgeois democracy.

Yet rather than engaging directly in politics, Durkheim donned the mantle of the neutral scientist, rooting pronouncements in the 'nature of the facts'. Against the clericalism of the monarchist right and what he perceived as the utopianism of the revolutionary left, Durkheim posited republican ideals as flowing from the nature of reality itself. His greatest theoretical achievement was thus to translate the class interests of the French elites into a scientific framework that claimed universal application. Indeed, in many ways, it was his ability to present republican values as neutral and objective that made his sociology so successful. It also made it deeply ideological.

Like much Enlightenment thinking, French Republicanism rested on a glaring contradiction between its promised ideals and the harshness of its outcomes. The French Revolution was fought under the banner of *liberty, equality* and *solidarity*, but the reality of nineteenth-century French society was oppression, inequality and class-based conflict. Three quick examples will remind us of this.

The first is the drowning of the Paris Commune in a river of blood. This was one of the great massacres of the nineteenth century, as the state unleashed untold terror against its fellow citizens. Similar levels of state violence were often mirrored in the French colonies, giving a lie to the value supposedly placed on human liberty.

The republican record on equality was scarcely any better. Prior to the revolution of 1789, France had been a notoriously unequal country, with the landed aristocracy and the Catholic hierarchy usually exempted from paying taxes. One of the rallying calls by the revolutionary bourgeoisie had been greater equality, but this never materialised. Indeed, the rising influence of republicanism throughout the nineteenth century did virtually nothing to redistribute wealth to the working classes.[3] Rather, as capitalism became more firmly embedded, it simply replaced the privileges of the landed aristocracy with the privileges of industrialists and financiers. If we look at the first and last columns in Table 9.1, the inequality of the *ancient régime* was more or less equalled by Durkheim's beloved republic.

In these conditions, genuine solidarity also became a pipe dream. Between 1789 and 1880, France enacted 14 different constitutions in an indication of just how fractious the country had become. Throughout the century, right-wing forces continually agitated for counter-revolution and by the mid-1880s, they were joined by a qualitative growth in revolutionary socialism. Republicans genuinely wanted to resolve these conflicts, but they were not prepared to challenge the social and economic structures that were responsible for creating them. Instead of addressing the clashing interests of property owners and the working classes, republican politicians believed in binding rulers and ruled together through equal citizenship and collective ideals. This resulted in a hollow form of social solidarity wrought through ideology and state oppression.

Table 9.1   Income Inequality in France was Relatively Stable Across the Nineteenth Century

Income Group	1780	1831	1866	1894
Top 10%	51–53	45	49	48
Bottom 40%	10–11	18	16	9.5

Source: Christian Morrisson and Wayne Snyder, 'The Income Inequality of France in Historical Perspective'. *European Review of Economic History* 4 (2000): 59–83.

With the realities of capitalism clashing so violently with the stated values of the French Revolution, scientists and intellectuals were also left with a dilemma. Should they accept the evidence from their own society or should they ignore this reality and seek to wash over these structural problems through moral education and strategies to develop a solidarity between all classes of French society? Durkheim unambiguously chose the second option, decisively weakening the objectivity of his sociology. Instead of exposing the causes of the conflicts that he witnessed in society, Durkheim used his considerable influence to buttress the institutions of the status quo. This can be seen in the nature of the problems Durkheim posed, the nature of the concepts he used and the way that he chose to marshal his evidence.

DURKHEIM'S RESEARCH AGENDA

Durkheim's blending of republicanism with his sociology is particularly evident in the way that he approached each of his major works.[4] At first glance, there doesn't seem to be anything linking studies into the division of labour, the methodology of sociology, suicide and aboriginal religion. However, Durkheim's search for a scientifically informed republican morality is the ever-present constant. The American sociologist, Robert Nisbet, partially grasped this when he suggested that Durkheim's greatest sociological achievement was to 'take the conservative view of society out of what was essentially a speculative framework ... before translating it into certain hypotheses which he sought to verify.'[5]

The Division of Labour in Society is a case in point. The rise of industrial society was so sudden that it immediately demanded scientific investigation. Liberals and Marxists differed profoundly in their assessment of the merits of capitalism, but they were united in offering an explicitly materialist analysis of their object of inquiry. In each case, the way the economy was organised had decisive effects on the rest of society. Thus Adam Smith's defence of capitalism rested on his iconic vision of self-interested competition. In a doctrine that was to prove immensely popular in liberal circles, Smith insisted that capitalist production relations were responsible for fostering individual freedom, rising productivity and increasing the levels of social harmony. The other pole in this debate was occupied by revolutionary socialists. Pointing to the sharp increase in exploitation associated with the new society, Karl Marx protested that the capitalist division of labour was making life unbearable for much of the working class. The limited paternalism of the feudal period was being replaced with ruthless self-interest and the result was far from the utopia envisaged by liberals. Instead, industrialists were using their growing power to force workers into poverty and exhaustion. This, in turn, led to social strife and ongoing conflict.

Like their liberal counterparts, French republicans were committed to capitalism, but they worried about the instability that it was creating. Between 1890 and 1900, labour unrest increased considerably in France, as more than 9 million strike days were lost in 1,309 separate actions.[6] There was also a qualitative growth in Marxist ideas following the founding of the Parti Ouvrier in 1880. The republican response to this growing militancy was to create a network of corporatist organisations that would seek to bind workers back into French society. The idea was to regulate the worst excesses of capitalist exploitation, whilst fostering new forms of social solidarity. Durkheim's original PhD thesis was tailor-made to give theoretical expression to this political project.

Wading into an existing debate about the merits of capitalism, Durkheim announced that his primary aim is to 'treat the facts of moral life according to the methods of the positive sciences.'[7] This seems a strange claim in a book titled *The Division of Labour in Society*, but it highlights perfectly the central objective of Durkheim's first major investigation. Whereas Marx and Smith were concerned with the nature of the economic relations, Durkheim's key task was to investigate the potential social solidarity in industrial society. His conclusion was highly optimistic, suggesting that growing economic interdependence would produce newer forms of solidarity. In this analysis, the division of labour becomes a causal variable for different forms of moral solidarity. This unusual approach allowed Durkheim to develop a republican slant on the division of labour. Essentially, his argument was that capitalism had created new, more positive conditions for wider social cohesion. Moreover, it did so while creating a cult of individuality that guaranteed personal freedom. In other words, it was possible to have both liberal values and social solidarity. All that was required was that capitalism needed to be regulated in the interests of every class.

However, Durkheim's argument was not without its complications. The most obvious was the persistence of economic conflict. Durkheim's solution was to relegate the observable evidence into a transitory pathology that was soon to be eradicated. The reality was character-ised by anomie, inequality and social conflict but all these features were deemed to be transitory and abnormal. They were not an essential or normal feature of modern society. This meant that, against his own argument on how to conduct a scientific inquiry, Durkheim arbitrarily re-categorised the existing evidence to suit his defence of the status quo.

Then, having insisted that economic interdependence would normally lead to organic solidarity, Durkheim dropped this argument in all of his subsequent published work. From *Suicide* onwards, Durkheim never again invoked the idea of organic solidarity emerging from within the relations of the capitalist economy. Instead, he increasingly pinned his hopes on new forms of solidarity coming from collective ideals and imposed in society through moral education. This, it should be remembered, was precisely what he termed 'mechanical solidarity' and this supposedly belonged to pre-modern traditional societies. This shift towards moral idealism became the central strand of Durkheimian sociology from the mid-1890s onwards. Before this, however, he set out to justify the standing of his sociology with a methodological treatise.

One of the great folklores in republican France was the need to replace patronage and personal prejudice with faith in reason and belief in science. This ensured that republican intellectuals genuinely believed in scientific objectivity even as they used their writings to defend the interests of a propertied elite. As usual, Durkheim's *The Rules of Sociological Method* reflected these twin ideals more or less perfectly. On the one hand, he insisted on a sociological discipline geared to investigating the 'objective facts' of French society. This meant laying down methodological rules for aspiring sociologists that were supposedly designed to 'allow the facts to speak for themselves'.[8] For sociology to be truly effective, moreover, it had to be completely independent from practical doctrines such as individualism, communism and socialism. Overtly political theories were deemed to be devoid of all scientific value, 'since they tend not to directly express social facts but to seek to reform them'.[9] Genuine sociology had to confront reality without preconceptions, making observations, classifications and explanations in much the same way as physicists and chemists.

On the other hand, however, Durkheim stakes a claim for a diagnostic social science, explicitly geared to the maintenance of moral order and social stability. The sociologist was to act as society's doctor, able to cure the temporary ills and conflicts that might arise. This meant differentiating the 'normal' from the 'pathological' in the way that had supposedly been done in *The Division of Labour in Society*. It also meant orientating sociological investigation towards practical concerns once objective social facts had been thoroughly understood. Rather than standing aloof from practical questions, the social facts unearthed by sociologists should inform policy making in the French republic. Durkheim explains this practical aspect of his work in the following remarks,

> Sociology must abandon generalities and enter into a detailed examination of the facts ... Nevertheless this is not to say that sociology should profess no interest in practical questions. On the contrary, it has been seen that our constant preoccupation has been to guide it towards some practical outcome. It encounters these problems at the end of its investigations. But from the very fact that the problems do not manifest themselves until that moment, and that, consequently they arise out of the facts and not the passions, it may be predicted that they will present themselves to the sociologist in completely different terms than to the masses.[10]

By situating sociology above the fray of political considerations, Durkheim was attempting to establish himself as a social arbitrator. The idea was to objectively investigate social phenomena, before passing on important findings to the relevant authorities.[11] Durkheim believed this procedure was rigorously independent, but everything about his scientific detachment was inherently political. The distinction between 'normal' and 'pathological' phenomena is a case in point. The fact that no other major social thinker made this distinction undermines Durkheim's claim that his categories emerged spontaneously from the facts. Rather, it was obvious that he constructed these concepts to suit the reformist agenda of the Third Republic. It was only by privileging order as 'normal' and 'healthy' that Durkheim was able to relegate central features of his own society – class struggle, exploitation, anomie, etc. – to the status of the inessential and the transitory.[12]

This was a strategy that allowed him to quarantine problems in a way that suited piecemeal social reforms. It also showed that Durkheim's diagnostic view of science was imposed by the republican requirements of his own sociology. Thus, he insisted in *The Rules of Sociological Method* that any social phenomena that was 'general' throughout society should be regarded as 'normal'. However, he was willing to drop this assertion when it came to the *generalised conflict of the capitalist economy*. Lewis Coser takes up this aspect of Durkheim's procedure below,

> It is remarkable that Durkheim, although his sociology arises out of an awareness of the crises of his age, never really attempts to analyse such crises in their own terms. They are always seen as departures from the expected order and equilibrium; they are pathological and thus devoid of any inherent worth … [Yet] Durkheim does not always follow his own prescription. For example, he states in the *Division of Labour* that *all generally existing forms of labour division are pathological* even though he considered the general to be normal. In The Division of Labour *the normal turns out to be a utopian fiction* and not general at all.[13] [emphasis added]

Far from letting the facts speak for themselves, this shows that Durkheim continually sought to interpret them through the lens of his political intentions. There was nothing objective in his investigative procedures, merely a set of theoretical devices designed to reinforce the norms of social integration. Durkheim's separation of science from politics was a blatant attempt to delegitimise all forms of political activity except that of acting as advisors to the current – republican – administration.[14] Republican values were also deeply embedded within the school and university systems, meaning that when Durkheim argues that sociologists should restrict themselves to being 'educators' and 'advisors', he was 'lending legitimacy to the ascendant republican and secular forces and seeking to delegitimise alternative ideological positions – clericalism and integral nationalism on the right, revolutionary socialism and syndicalism on the left.'[15]

Similar biases and sleights of hand are evident in Durkheim's next major work – *Suicide*. In Chapter 5, we noted that the study of suicide appealed to Durkheim for two interrelated reasons. First, the idea of self-destruction seemed so utterly subjective, that if Durkheim could unearth social causes underlying national statistics, it would aid the case for sociology. Second, the French elites abhorred suicide as a sign of social disease striking at the vitality of the republic. This was then the perfect opportunity for Durkheim to engage in his first diagnostic examination of social ailments, before helping society to heal itself. To his credit, Durkheim rejected common sense explanations in favour of a deeper scientific reality, but his republicanism was once again evident in the way that he interpreted the empirical material. Durkheim's first major category was egoistic suicide.

To develop this category, he investigated what he felt were previously the central sources of integration within society – religion, the family and political cohesion. In traditional societies, each of these institutions helped to bind individuals securely into their surroundings, minimising the social compulsion to engage in self-destruction. The rise of individualism in modern societies had weakened the power of these institutions, however, making it more likely for egoistic suicide to occur. Because of this, Durkheim drew a theoretical conclusion that was full of political implications – suicide rates vary inversely with the degree of social integration and positively with the detachment of individuals from their social networks.[16] This placed his opening category in perfect alignment with republican values. The negative freedom championed by economic liberals was unlikely to lead to general well-being as atomism and egoism were often a recipe for social isolation. Instead, what was needed was the right balance of social integration and economic freedom bound together through civil networks and corporate institutions.

Durkheim's other major category – anomic suicide – was, if anything, even more political. Here, the issue was not the level of integration in society, but the correct levels of regulation. Although Durkheim previously used the term anomie to refer to the lack of regulation, in *Suicide* it describes a more general pathological state, afflicting those who have not placed sufficient curbs on their limitless appetites.[17] Drawing on the conservative tradition of Thomas Hobbes and Sigmund Freud, Durkheim argues that human nature requires strong discipline and external limits. This is a deeply pessimistic outlook that takes little account of the human potential for development and expansion of sensibilities. Durkheim's primary aim is to speak of the weakness of individuals when outside the moral guidance of social constraints. Contentment comes from understanding our debt to society and being regulated by superior social – and by implication, republican – institutions. In fairly crude terms, Durkheim is asserting that individuals should know their place and feel the better for it.[18] Although he speaks in general terms, it is clear that Durkheim once again has the struggles within his own society firmly in mind.

By arguing that the individual 'gets from society the best part of himself, all that gives him a distinct character ... his intellectual and moral culture,' Durkheim deliberately neglects the starkly unequal *levels of economic and political resources* that societies generate for different social classes. In republican France, nearly half the income flowed to the top tenth of the population, but Durkheim did not see this as a reason for workers to strive to improve their situation against their employers. Instead, there should be 'an upper limit to which the workman may aspire' within a regime 'that fixes with relative precision the maximum degree of ease to which each class may legitimately aspire.'[19] One obvious question for an objective scientist might possibly be: why are so many workers unable to attain even the minimal standards of economic security? Another more radical question might be: how could one move towards a more equal society where workers got a greater share of what they produced? But Durkheim was far less interested in either the causes of social inequality or strategies to reduce it. His prime concern is simply the moral framework which could contain conflicts over inequality.[20] This is clear in his purported solutions, which amount to the usual republican prescriptions of corporate groups and legal regulations.

Durkheim's views on gender in *Suicide* also equally displayed a sexist outlook, which undermines his claim to scientific status. Although he noted that women gained less from marriage than men – evident by lower rates of suicide for single women – he used a crude biological cause to explain this. Women's capacity for intellectual thought and imagination, he asserted, was less than men's. This apparently meant that they required less integration into social groups. This retreat to a biological explanation contravened the strictures against biological reductionism that he issued in *The Rules of Sociological Method*. This breach did not seem to bother him too much because, unfortunately, it was repeated in other works. His classic book, *The Division of Labour in Society* contains the following extraordinary claim, drawn from a Dr Le Bon,

> The volume of the crania of men and women, even when we compare subjects of equal age, of equal height and equal weight, shows considerable differences in favour of men, and this inequality grows with civilization, so that from the point of view of the mass of the brain, and correspondingly of intelligence, women tend to be more and more differentiated from the male sex.[21]

The sexism behind this claim is so shocking that it deserves a double take. It suggests that human intelligence is related to 'the volume of the crania', making women less intelligent than men. Further, that the gap between the relative size of the skulls – and accordingly the level of intelligence – grows with the progress of civilisation. So the gap in the skull volume between the average Parisian man and woman of the late 1900s is greater than that of ancient Egyptians. Presumably then the respective levels of intelligence have also widened – and has increased further since!

Durkheim's views on gender simply did not reflect his own time. They are far more conservative than many progressive views expressed at this time. In an article written in 1904, for example, Durkheim reviewed a book by Le Thoreau wherein the latter suggested that the inequality between men and women needs to be explained by social rather than biological causes and had to be remedied by legal change. Durkheim, unfortunately, rejected both of these propositions.[22] His views on children born outside marriage were equally shocking and anachronistic, even for his own age. He claimed that 'free unions' – as non-married couples were called – amounted to an 'immoral society' with 'children raised in such a milieu presenting great quantities of moral defect.'[23] Despite this, thousands of French couples lived in such arrangements at the time with no noticeable issues for their children. Durkheim was opposed to divorce by mutual consent and this political position influenced how he dealt with gender in his academic writings.

Durkheim's last major text took up the importance of mechanical solidarity in the experimental conditions of an Aboriginal society. Having spent his entire career studying social forces in the French republic, Durkheim shifts tack in *The Elementary Forms of Religious Life* by starting with a cohesive society, without any major social tension. Durkheim had initially insisted that anomie and social strife were merely symptoms of temporary adjustment to the worst aspects of industrialisation. Yet the more time he spent analysing modern society, the less confident he must have become. Throughout the 1890s, the Marxist inspired, Parti Ouvrier, took control of 23 municipal councils and was gaining members across the country. Added to this, a tradition of revolutionary syndicalism began to gain ground, with militant trade unionism posing as an 'alternative to the liberal, republican social order'.[24] Although republicans had initially helped to reawaken the French labour movement – as a bulwark against reactionary forces – they now increasingly feared its effects on internal stability.

Durkheim registered his own fear of this working-class militancy by dropping the idea of organic solidarity in favour of collective myths and national symbols. After *The Division of Labour in Society*, he came to the conclusion that nationalist feelings and patriotic fervour were the most likely route to social solidarity.[25] This mechanical form of fellow feeling should therefore be studied in its ideal state – the primitive tribal communities of Central Australia.

In spite of their obvious failings as systems of truth, Durkheim argued that primitive religions offered tribal people social stability and collective identities. Aborigines feel warmth and affinity for rules that are commanded by the wider society, and feel themselves 'morally complete' when they act in line with the moral precepts of their particular clan groups. As a proxy for society itself, religion initially raised people above their egoistic desires, giving them culture, language and scientific reason. Society is therefore the source of everything worthwhile in aboriginal communities and Durkheim wanted his readers to draw the modern-day conclusions.

In order to overcome their current state of anomie and moral degeneration, Durkheim's compatriots needed to believe in something beyond themselves. More than this, collective belief systems have always been the bedrock of harmonious communities rather than economic or political equality. This explicitly anti-Marxist conclusion had first been expounded decades before in Durkheim's review of the work of the Italian socialist Antonio Labriola.[26] Here, it was meant to make the most important of political assertions – we can overcome the current economic malaise by reviving the strength of the collective conscience.

This, yet again, chimed perfectly with the outlook and concerns of contemporary republicans. Since the Paris Commune, the architects of the Third Republic had been acutely aware of the need for a form of secular religion that would replace Catholicism, socialism and economic individualism. In 1879, they proclaimed *La Marseillaise* the national anthem. A year later, Bastille Day became a national holiday and the republican motto of 'Liberty, Equality and Fraternity' was inscribed onto all public buildings. In 1885, the Pantheon was taken over by the state and turned into a lay temple. The first of the 'great men' to be buried there was the republican hero, Victor Hugo in a monumental ceremony.[27] By highlighting the capacity of former societies to create a sense of collective ideals, Durkheim felt that he was revealing a 'fundamental and permanent aspect of reality. Yet the truth was that in writing *The Elementary Forms of Religious Life*, Durkheim was finally admitting defeat.

Throughout his career, Durkheim had consistently denigrated traditional forms of solidarity as claustrophobic. In stark contrast, the solidarity associated with modern societies was meant to blend the right amount of individual freedom with social cohesion. Unlike the all-embracing solidarity of traditional societies, modern France supposedly offered equality of opportunity, individual liberty and stable loyalties to intermediary groups and ultimately the state.[28] This was Durkheim's most deeply held conviction, but after a lifetime searching for modern forms of social solidarity, he had to retreat into tribal society to study it successfully. As a stand-alone text, *The Elementary Forms of Religious Life* challenged contemporary prejudices concerning the 'inferiority' of the Aboriginal people and offered useful insights into the ways that close-knit social groups constructed their identities.

As part of his overall sociological project, however, *The Elementary Forms of Religious Life* was a sign of defeat. France in the early twentieth century was nothing like the close-knit groups of Central Australia. The class differentiation of society meant that an all-embracing solidarity born of a secular morality was neither feasible nor desirable. Seeking to bind people together in the context of oppression and exploitation was the ultimate act of political bad faith. It was never likely to work and nor should it have done. The way to sustain genuine individuality and social solidarity was to end the class divisions that were renting French society apart. But this would be to disavow the republican politics that inspired Durkheim at every stage of his academic development.

DURKHEIM'S CONTINUING RELEVANCE TODAY

Durkheim's work ends in a profound failing. Throughout his career, Durkheim celebrated the principles of scientific objectivity and impartiality, but his writings were frequently little more than a theoretical defence of contemporary social order. Instead of allowing the 'facts to speak for themselves', Durkheim repeatedly manipulated them, reclassified them and ultimately disregarded them, when they were not in line with his political ideals. For all of their problems, Durkheim credited the republican bourgeoisie with bringing scientific reason and liberal progress into modern France. Come what may, he therefore assumed the superiority of his own society, even as he registered its many pathologies. This coloured his judgement in crucial ways and forced him to reject the empirical evidence of class exploitation and oppression.

This was hardly in line with proper scientific procedures, but the contradictions in Durkheim's sociology actually mirrored those within his own society. It was for this reason that it proved so successful. The scientific revolution of the seventeenth century occurred within the economic structures of newly emerging capitalist societies.[29] The bourgeoisie celebrated scientific progress as universally beneficial, but in reality, the vast bulk of the advantages flowed to those with capital to deploy. Understanding nature was the route to competitive technologies that, in turn, were used to control the lives of working people. Reflecting on the ways that scientifically informed profiteering made life harder for working-class people, Bertrand Russell had this to say,

> the industrial revolution caused unspeakable misery both in England and in America … and this was due almost entirely to scientific technique. In Lancashire cotton mills … children had to be beaten to keep them from falling asleep while at work, in spite of this many failed to keep awake and rolled into the machinery, by which they were killed or mutilated. Parents had to submit to the infliction of these atrocities because they themselves were in a desperate plight. Handicraftsmen had been thrown out of work by the machines; rural labourers were compelled to migrate to the towns by the Enclosure acts, which used parliament to make landowners rich by making peasants destitute … such was the effect of machinery in England.[30]

Natural science and the development of machinery can benefit humanity but Russell's point is that it can be put to other uses in class-based societies. The more knowledge the bourgeoisie accumulated, the more effective they were in using it against the interests of the working classes. By virtue of their ability to turn science into oppressive technologies – machines, production lines, etc. – the bourgeoisie came to dominate the whole of society.

Similar considerations were at play in the social sciences. Although they genuinely wanted to understand the nature of their own society, the elites did not want that knowledge to threaten their economic position. Social knowledge had to be objective enough to reveal important features of modern society, but partial enough to defend the interests of the contemporary elites. As in the natural sciences, genuine understanding competed with a need for widespread manipulation and control. Durkheim's blend of republican sociology mirrored these needs more or less perfectly. Against what he saw as the ideological distortions of the left and right, Durkheim would take society as it was currently constituted before offering piecemeal solutions to its central problems. This was undoubtedly part of his wider appeal, as Durkheim offered detailed empirical research undertaken within the *strict parameters of the current system*. By taking an outwardly impartial perspective, moreover, Durkheim could mask the partisan nature of his politics behind the diagnostic aspects of his sociology. His greatest theoretical achievement was thus to translate the class interests of the French elites into a scientific framework that claimed universal application.

Durkheim's moderate critique of capitalist industrialisation has also proved useful and enduring. Like modern versions of social democracy, Durkheim wanted to blunt the worst excesses of the capitalist economy without challenging the class relations that caused these problems in the first place. This appealed to the most enlightened section of the republican elites, who had always accepted the need to tie workers into the system rather than launching an all-out attack on them directly. The modern industrial relations machinery in many states owes much to the spirit of Durkheimian sociology with its insistence that legal rules and regulations can harmonise the central conflict between capital and wage labour. Over the last one hundred years, Keynesian economic management, state regulations, trade unions laws and a host of charitable organisations have also been employed to ameliorate the worst aspects of the capitalist system.

Insofar as modern society still requires state regulation, Durkheim's work has something to offer. Insofar as the system still requires partisan social theory draped in impartiality, Durkheim's work remains indispensable. By carefully delimiting his analysis to what went on *within the structures of his own society*, Durkheim made sure that his sociology was as politically successful as it was scientifically compromised. This is the enduring legacy of Durkheim's work in social theory.

Notes

1. DURKHEIM DECLASSIFIED

1. E. Durkheim, *The Rules of Sociological Method* (New York: Free Press, 1982), 63.
2. Ibid., 39.
3. T.M. Kando, '*L'Année Sociologique*: From Durkheim to Today'. *The Pacific Sociological Review* 19 (2) (1975): 147–174.
4. C.J. Calhoun, *Classical Sociological Theory* (Oxford: Wiley Blackwell, 2002), 107.
5. Durkheim, *The Rules of Sociological Method*, 36.
6. T.N. Clark, *Prophets and Patrons: The French University and the Emergence of Social Sciences* (Cambridge, MA: Harvard University Press, 1973), 216.
7. T. Parsons, *The Structure of Social Action* (New York: Free Press, 1968), 5.
8. Ibid., 463.
9. Ibid., 467.
10. C. Calhoun and J. VanAntwerpen, 'Orthodoxy, Heterodoxy and Hierarchy: "Mainstream" Sociology and its Challengers' in C. Calhoun (ed.), *Sociology in America: A History* (Chicago, IL: University of Chicago Press, 2008), 390.
11. Ibid., 768.
12. R. Nisbet, 'Conservatism and Sociology'. *American Journal of Sociology* 58 (2) (1952): 167–175.
13. Ibid.
14. C.W. Mills, *The Sociological Imagination* (New York: Oxford University Press, 2000).
15. M. Nicolaus, 'Fat Cat Sociology', in Martin Oppenheimer, Martin J. Murray and Rhonda F. Levine (eds), *Radical Sociologists and the Movement* (Philadelphia, PA: Temple University Press, 1991), 251–254.
16. R. Collins, 'A Comparative Approach to Political Sociology', in R. Bendix (ed.), *State and Society: A Reader in Comparative Sociology* (Berkeley, CA: University of California Press, 1973), 42–69.
17. M. Nicolaus, 'The Professional Organisation of Sociology: A View from Below', in R. Blackburn (ed.), *Ideology and Social Science* (London: Fontana, 1978), 48.
18. H. Becker, 'Whose Side Are We On'. *Social Problems* 14 (3) (Winter 1967): 239–247.
19. Susan Stedman Jones, *Durkheim Reconsidered* (Cambridge: Polity Press, 2001), 18.

20. M. Gane, 'Institutional Socialism and the Sociological Critique of Communism', in M. Gane (ed.), *The Radical Sociology of Durkheim and Mauss* (London: Routledge, 1992), 158.

21. F. Pearce, *The Radical Durkheim* (Montreal: Canadian Scholars Press, 2001).

22. J. Alexander, 'The Inner Development of Durkheim's Sociological Theory: From Early Writings to Maturity', in J. Alexander and P. Smith, *The Cambridge Companion Guide to Durkheim* (Cambridge: Cambridge University Press, 2005), 153.

2. DURKHEIM'S FRENCH REPUBLICANISM

1. J. Merriman, *Massacre: The Life and Death of the Paris Commune* (New York: Basic Books, 2014).

2. S. Lukes, *Emile Durkheim: His Life and Work. A Historical and Critical Study* (London: Allen Lane, 1973), 47.

3. R.D. Anderson, *France 1870–1914: Politics and Society* (London: Routledge, 1977), Chapter 2.

4. T. Zeldin, *France 1848–1945: Politics and Anger* (Oxford: Oxford University Press, 1979), 251.

5. R. Magraw, *France 1800–1914: A Social History* (London: Pearson, 2002), 55.

6. G. Dupeux, *French Society 1789–1970* (London: Methuen, 1976), 158.

7. M. Fournier, *Émile Durkheim: A Biography*, translated by David Macey (Cambridge: Polity Press, 2013), 87.

8. M. Aguilhon, *The French Republic 1879–1992* (Oxford: Blackwell, 1993), 21.

9. E. Weber, *France: Fin de Siècle* (London: Belknap Press, 1986), 26.

10. Fournier, *Émile Durkheim*, 22–23.

11. E. Durkheim, 'The Principles of 1789 and Sociology', in R. Bellah (ed.). *Emile Durkheim on Morality and Society* (Chicago, IL: University of Chicago Press, 1973), 40.

12. Fournier, *Émile Durkheim*, 78.

13. C.D. Hazen, *Modern European History* (New York: Henry Holt, 1917), 400–401.

14. Fournier, *Émile Durkheim*, 107.

15. P. Stock-Morton, *Moral Education for a Secular Society* (New York: New York Press, 1988), 58.

16. Ibid., 59.

17. E. Durkheim, 'Replies to Objection', in *Sociology and Philosophy*, translated by D.F. Pocock (London: Cohen and West, 1965).

18. Ibid., 75.

19. Ibid., 71.

20. E. Durkheim, *Professional Ethics and Civic Morals* (London: Routledge, 2003), 23–24.

21. Durkheim, *Sociology and Philosophy*, 72.

22. Ibid.

23. E. Durkheim, 'The State and Patriotism', in A. Giddens (ed.), *Durkheim on Politics and the State* (Stanford, CA: Stanford University Press, 1986), 194.

24. Ibid.

25. Durkheim, *Professional Ethics and Civic Morals*, 68–69.

26. Ibid., 74.

27. S. Parker, 'Civic-Moral Teaching in French Secular Schools, Part 2', in *The Elementary School Journal* 20 (9) (1920): 662.

28. E. Durkheim, 'A Review of Ferdinand Tönnies's *Gemeinschaft und Gesellschaft: Abhandlung des Communismus und des Socialismus als empirischer Culturformen*'. *American Journal of Sociology* (1887 reprint) 77 (6) (May, 1972): 1197.

29. Ibid., 1198.

30. E. Durkheim, 'The Dualism of Human Nature and its Social Conditions', in *Durkheimian Studies* 2 (2005): 42.

31. Durkheim, *Sociology and Philosophy*, 92.

32. Ibid.

33. P. Nord, *The Republican Moment: Struggles for Democracy in Nineteenth-Century France* (Cambridge, MA: Harvard University Press, 1998), Chapter 8.

34. M. Pickering, *Auguste Comte: An Intellectual Biography*, Vol. 3 (Cambridge: Cambridge University Press, 2009), 50.

35. See A. Wernick, *Auguste Comte and the Religion of Humanity: The Post-Theistic Program of French Social Theory* (Cambridge: Cambridge University Press, 2001).

36. A. Elwit, *The Third Republic Defended: Bourgeois Reform in France, 1880–1914* (Baton Rouge, LA: Louisiana State University Press, 1986), 77.

37. Fournier, *Émile Durkheim*, 65.

38. Lukes, *Emile Durkheim*, 331.

39. Durkheim, *Professional Ethics and Civic Morals*, 42.

40. Ibid., 50.

41. Ibid., 53.

42. Ibid., 80.

43. Ibid., 64.

44. Ibid., 82.

45. Ibid., 89.

46. Ibid., 94.

47. Ibid., 99.

48. Ibid., 99.

49. Ibid., 100.

50. Ibid., 65.

51. Ibid., 63.

52. C. Brinton, *The Jacobins: An Essay in the New History* (Piscataway, NJ: Transaction Publishers, 2012), 145.

53. P. Mair, *Ruling the Void* (London: Verso, 2013).

54. R. Magraw, *France 1815–1914: The Bourgeois Century* (Oxford: Oxford University Press, 1983), 303.

55. R. Goldstein, *Political Repression in 19th Century Europe* (New York: Routledge, 1983), 275.

56. Fournier, *Émile Durkheim*, 161.

57. Magraw, *France 1815–1914*, 286.

58. E. Durkheim, The Definition of Socialism', in A. Giddens (ed.), *Durkheim on Politics and the State* (Stanford, CA: Stanford University Press 1986), 99.

59. Ibid.

60. Ibid., 102.

61. E. Durkheim, 'Review of Labriola Essay on a Materialist Conception of History', in A. Giddens (ed.), *Durkheim on Politics and the State* (Stanford, CA: Stanford University Press 1986), 132–133.

62. E. Durkheim, 'Review of Merlino, Forms and Essence of Socialism', in A. Giddens (ed.), *Durkheim on Politics and the State* (Stanford, CA: Stanford University Press 1986), 143.

63. Ibid., 148.

64. Durkheim, *Professional Ethics and Civic Morals*, 12.

65. See Elwitt, *The Third Republic Defended*, Chapter 5.

66. Fournier, *Émile Durkheim*, 709.

67. Ibid., 687.

3. THE DIVISION OF LABOUR

1. A. Smith, *The Wealth of Nations* (London: Penguin Classics, 1999).

2. Ibid., 110.

3. For the definitive statement of this socialist perspective, see K. Marx, *Capital Vol I–III* (London: Lawrence and Wishart, 2003).

4. E. Durkheim, *The Division of Labour in Society* (New York: Free Press, 1997), xxv.

5. Ibid., 122.

6. A. de Tocqueville, *The Old Regime and the Revolution*, trans. John Bonner (New York: Harper & Brothers, 1856).

7. Ibid., 122.

8. R. Aldrich, *Greater France: A History of French Overseas Expansion* (Santa Barbara, CA: Praeger Publishers, 1996), 304.

9. Melvin E. Page (ed.), *Colonialism: An International Social, Cultural, and Political Encyclopaedia* (Santa Barbara, CA: ABC-CLIO, 2003), 218.

10. Durkheim, *The Division of Labour in Society*, 89.

11. Ibid., 118.

12. Ibid., 24.

13. Ibid., 127.

14. Ibid., 105.

15. Ibid., 105.

16. Ibid., 127.

17. Ibid., 126.

18. Ibid., 116.

19. Ibid., 90.

20. Ibid., 61.
21. Ibid., 56.
22. Ibid., 142.
23. Ibid., 85.
24. Ibid., 61.
25. Ibid., 128.
26. Ibid., 63.
27. R.G. Perrin, 'Emile Durkheim's Division of Labour and the Shadow of Herbert Spencer', *The Sociological Quarterly* 36 (4) (1995): 798.
28. Ibid., 795.
29. T. Hobbes, *Leviathan* (London: Penguin Classics, 1985).
30. R. Nozick, *Anarchy, State and Utopia* (Oxford: Blackwell Publishers, 1974).
31. Durkheim, *The Division of Labour in Society*, 220.
32. Margaret Thatcher Interview by Douglas Keay. *Woman's Own*, 31 October 1987.
33. Ibid., 151.
34. Ibid., 463.
35. Ibid., 71.
36. Ibid., 203.
37. Ibid., 209.
38. Ibid., 105.
39. Ibid., 120.
40. Ibid., 122.
41. Ibid., xxx.
42. Ibid., 85.
43. Ibid., 221.
44. Ibid., 153.
45. Ibid., 102.
46. Ibid., 291.
47. H-P. Müller, 'Social Differentiation and Organic Solidarity: The "Division of Labour" Revisited'. *Sociological Forum* 9 (1) (1994): 80.
48. Durkheim, *The Division of Labour in Society*, 290.
49. Ibid., 292.
50. Ibid., 306.
51. Ibid., xxix.
52. Ibid., liii.
53. Ibid., 310.
54. Ibid., 312.
55. Ibid., 319.
56. Ibid., 320.
57. E. Faris, 'Emile Durkheim and the Division of Labor in Society'. Review in *American Journal of Sociology* 40 (3) (November, 1934): 376.
58. T.D. Kemper, 'Emile Durkheim and the Division of Labour'. *The Sociological Quarterly* 16 (2) (Spring 1975): 194.
59. Ibid.

60. L. Schnore, 'Social Anthropology and Human Ecology'. *American Journal of Sociology* 63 (6) (1958): 620–634.

61. R.D. Schwartz and J.C. Miller, 'Legal Evolution and Social Complexity'. *American Journal of Sociology* 7 (2) (1964): 159–169.

62. M. Fortes, *Kinship and the Social Order: The Legacy of Lewis Henry Morgan* (Chicago, IL: Aldeine, Galle, O. and K.E. Taeuber, 1969).

63. R. Bendix and G. Roth, *Scholarship and Partisanship: Essays on Max Weber* (Berkeley, CA: University of California Press, 1971).

64. B. Malinowski, *Magic, Science and Religion and Other Essays* (Glencoe, IL: Free Press, 1948).

65. R. Merton, 'Durkheim's Division of Labour in Society'. *Sociological Forum* 9 (1): 23.

66. S. Lukes, *Emile Durkheim: His Life and Work. A Historical and Critical Study* (London: Allen Lane, 1973), 298.

67. See J.A. Barnes, 'Durkheim's Division of Labour in Society'. *Man, New Series* 1 (2) (1966): 161; T. Bottomore, 'A Marxist Consideration of Durkheim'. *Social Forces* 59 (1981): 907.

68. Barnes, 'Durkheim's Division of Labour in Society', 161.

69. Ibid.

70. Merton, 'Durkheim's Division of Labour in Society', 21.

71. Whitney Pope and Barclay D. Johnson, 'Inside Organic Solidarity'. *American Sociological Review* 48 (5) (1983): 690.

72. Durkheim, *The Division of Labour in Society*, liii.

73. Ibid., xxxi.

74. E. Durkheim, *The Rules of Sociological Method* (New York: Free Press, 1982), 36.

75. Ibid.

76. H. Braverman, *Labor and Monopoly Capital: The Degradation of Work in the Twentieth* Century (New York: Monthly Review Press, 1999).

77. T. Piketty, *Capital in the 21ˢᵗ Century* (London: Belknap Press of Harvard University Press, 2014), 244.

78. Ibid., 438–439.

79. D. Hardoon, R. Fuentas-Nieva and S. Ayele, 'An Economy for the 1%: How Privilege and Power in the Economy Drive Extreme Inequality and How This can be Stopped'. *Oxfam International: Briefing Paper*, 18 January 2016, at: http://policy-practice.oxfam.org.uk/publications/an-economy-for-the-1-how-privilege-and-power-in-the-economy-drive-extreme-inequ-592643.

4. DURKHEIM'S METHOD OF SCIENTIFIC INQUIRY

1. E. Durkheim, *The Rules of Sociological Method* (New York: Free Press, 1982), 63.

2. S. Lukes, *Emile Durkheim: His Life and Work: His Life and Work. A Historical and Critical Study* (London: Allen Lane, 1973), 289 and 392.

3. Durkheim, *The Rules of Sociological Method*, 49.

4. W. Schmaus, 'Explanation and Essence in "The Rules of Sociological Method" and "The Division of Labour in Society"'. *Sociological Perspectives* 38 (1) (1995): 57.
5. Ibid., 57.
6. E. Durkheim, *The Elementary Forms of Religious Life* (New York: Free Press, 1995), 427.
7. C. Kelly, 'Methods of Reading and the Discipline of Sociology: The Case of Durkheim Studies'. *The Canadian Journal of Sociology* 15 (3) (1990): 304.
8. R.A. Jones, 'Ambivalent Cartesians: Durkheim, Montesquieu and Method'. *American Journal of Sociology* 100 (1) (1994): 4.
9. Ibid., 14.
10. E.A. Burtt, *The Metaphysical Foundations of Modern Science* (New York: Dover Publications, 2003).
11. Durkheim, *The Rules of Sociological Method*, 40.
12. Ibid., 51.
13. Ibid.
14. Ibid., 59.
15. Ibid., 37.
16. Ibid., 72.
17. Ibid., 63.
18. Ibid., 37.
19. Ibid., 75.
20. Ibid., 85.
21. Ibid., 96.
22. Ibid., 86.
23. Ibid., 91.
24. Ibid., 91 and 92.
25. Ibid., 94.
26. Ibid., 95.
27. Ibid., 115.
28. Aristotle, *Physics*, trans. Robin Waterfield (Oxford: Oxford University Press, 2008), 39.
29. Durkheim, *The Rules of Sociological Method*, 119.
30. Ibid., 125.
31. Ibid., 123.
32. Ibid., 129.
33. Ibid., 135.
34. Ibid., 138.
35. R.A. Jones, *Emile Durkheim: An Introduction to Four Major Works* (Beverly Hills, CA: Sage Publications, 1986), 68.
36. Durkheim, *The Rules of Sociological Method*, 149.
37. Ibid.
38. Ibid., 150.
39. Ibid., 151.
40. Ibid., 153.
41. Ibid., 153. Durkheim's analysis of suicide will be taken up in Chapter 5.

42. Ibid., 157.
43. Ibid., 159 and 160.
44. See W.V.O. Quine, *From a Logical Point of View* (Cambridge, MA: Harvard University Press, 1953); T. Kuhn, *The Structure of Scientific Revolutions* (Chicago, IL: University of Chicago Press, 1962); R. Bhaskar, *A Realist Theory of Science* (London: Verso, 1975).
45. Bhaskar, *A Realist Theory of Science*, 11.
46. B. Hessen, 'The Social and Economic Roots of Newton's Principia', in Boris Hessen, Henryk Grossmann, Gideon Freudenthal and Peter McLaughlin (eds), *The Social and Economic Roots of the Scientific Revolution: Texts by Boris Hessen and Henryk Grossmann* (London: Springer, 2009).
47. Jones, *Emile Durkheim*, 78.
48. S. Lukes, Introduction, *The Rules of Sociological Method* (New York: Free Press, 1982), 20.
49. Lukes, *Emile Durkheim*, 36.
50. E. Durkheim, *The Rules of Sociological Method* (New York: Free Press, 1982), 251.
51. P. Gisbert, 'Social Facts in Durkheim's System'. *Anthropose* 54 (3–4) (1959): 364.
52. T.N. Takla and W. Pope, 'The Force Imagery in Durkheim: The Integration of Theory, Metatheory and Method'. *Sociological Theory* 3 (1) (1985): 85.
53. T. De Laguna, 'The Sociological Method of Durkheim'. *The Philosophical Review* 29 (3) (1920): 220.
54. Durkheim, *The Rules of Sociological Method*, 95.
55. Schmaus, 'Explanation and Essence in "The Rules of Sociological Method" and "The Division of Labour in Society"', 60.
56. S.P. Turner, 'Durkheim's *The Rules of Sociological Method*: Is it a Classic?'. *Sociological Perspectives* 38 (1) (1995): 1.
57. C. Lemert, 'The Canonical Limits of Durkheim's First Classic'. *Sociological Forum* 9 (1) (1994): 87.
58. L.A. Coser, 'Durkheim's Conservatism and its Implications for his Social Theory', in Kurt H. Wolff (ed.), *Essays on Sociology and Philosophy by Emile Durkheim et al.* (New York: Harper Torchbooks, 1964), 211–232.
59. S.G. Stedman Jones, 'Charles Renouvier and Emile Durkheim: "Les Regles de la method Sociologique". *Sociological Perspectives* 38 (1) (1995): 28.
60. Lukes, *Emile Durkheim*, 177.

5. SUICIDE

1. C. Lemert, 'The Canonical Limits of Durkheim's First Classic'. *Sociological Forum* 9 (1) (1994): 87–92.
2. P. Besnard, 'The Fortunes of Durkheim's Suicide' in W.S.F. Pickering and G. Walford (eds), *Durkheim's Suicide: A Century of Research and Debate* (London: Routledge, 2000), 105 and 114.

3. E. Durkheim, 'Suicide and Fertility: A Study of Moral Statistics'. *European Journal of Population/Revue Europeene de Demographie* 8 (3) (1992): 175–197.

4. E. Camiscioli, *Reproducing the French Race: Immigration, Intimacy and Embodiment in the Early Twentieth Century* (Durham, NC: Duke University Press, 2009), 23.

5. P.V. Dutton, *Origins of the French Welfare State and the Struggle for Social Reform in France, 1914–1947* (Cambridge: Cambridge University Press, 2004), 17.

6. E. Durkheim, *Suicide: A Study in Sociology* (New York: Free Press, 1951), 333.

7. E. Garrison, 'Attitudes towards Suicide in Ancient Greece'. *Transactions of the American Philological Association* 121 (1991): 1–34.

8. G. Minois, *History of Suicide* (London and Baltimore, MD: Johns Hopkins University Press, 1999), 43.

9. M. Barbagli, *Farewell to the World* (Cambridge: Polity, 2015), 61.

10. Minois, *History of Suicide*, 29.

11. Barbagli, *Farewell to the World*, 45.

12. Ibid., 55.

13. A. Bahr, 'Between "Self-Murder" and "Suicide": The Modern Etymology of Self Killing'. *Journal of Social History* 46 (3) (2013): 620–632.

14. Barbagli, *Farewell to the World*, 98.

15. Ibid., 99.

16. I. Zeitlin, *Ideology and the Development of Sociological Theory* (Englewood Cliffs, NJ: Prentice-Hall, 1981), Chapters 6 and 7.

17. T. Porter, 'Statistical and Social Facts from Quetelet to Durkheim'. *Sociological Perspectives* 38 (1) (1995): 15–26.

18. J. Douglas, *The Social Meaning of Suicide* (Princeton, NJ: Princeton University Press, 1967), 15.

19. S. Turner, 'Durkheim among the Statisticians'. *Journal of the History of Behavioural Science* 32 (4) (1996): 354–378.

20. Quoted in M.J. Hawkins, 'Durkheim and Occupational Corporations: An Exegisis and Interpretation'. *Journal of the History of Ideas* 53 (3) (1994): 461–481.

21. Durkheim, *Suicide*, 37.

22. Ibid., 44.

23. Ibid., 51.

24. Ibid., 60.

25. Ibid., 169.

26. Ibid.

27. Ibid., 179.

28. Ibid., 189.

29. Ibid., 201.

30. Ibid., 208.

31. Ibid., 209.

32. Ibid., 214.

33. S. Stack, 'Emile Durkheim and Altruistic Suicide'. *Archives of Suicide Research* 8 (1) (2004): 9–22.
34. Durkheim, *Suicide*, 237.
35. Ibid., 254.
36. Ibid., 247.
37. Ibid., 249.
38. Ibid., 250.
39. Ibid.
40. Ibid., 253.
41. Ibid., 262.
42. Ibid., 272.
43. Ibid., 270.
44. Ibid., 309.
45. Ibid., 391.
46. Ibid., 366.
47. Ibid.
48. Ibid., 371.
49. Ibid., 383.
50. Ibid.
51. Quoted in Hawkins, 'Durkheim on Occupational Corporations'.
52. Durkheim, *Suicide*, 353.
53. Ibid., 386.
54. Douglas, *The Social Meaning of Suicide*, 209.
55. A. Cicourel, *The Social Organisation of Juvenile Justice* (New York: John Wiley, 1968).
56. S. Timmerans, 'Suicide Determination and the Professional Authority of Medical Examiners'. *American Sociological Review* 70 (2) (2005): 311–333.
57. B.A. Pescosolido and R. Mendelsohn, 'Social Causation or Social Construction of Suicide?: An Investigation into the Social Organization of Official Rates'. *American Sociological Review* 51 (1) (1986): 80–100.
58. C. Baudelot and R. Establet, *Suicide: The Hidden Side of Modernity* (Cambridge: Polity, 2008), 10–11.
59. A. Gestrich, E. Hurren and S. King, *Poverty and Sickness in Modern Europe: Narratives of Sick People, 1780–1938* (New York: Continuum Publishers, 2012), 149.
60. Baudelot and Establet, *Suicide*, Chapter 7.
61. Quoted in Baudelot and Establet, *Suicide*, 136.
62. J. Horton, 'The Dehumanization of Anomie and Alienation: A Problem in the Ideology of Sociology'. *British Journal of Sociology* 15 (1) (1964): 283–300.
63. K. Marx, *Economic and Philosophic Manuscripts* (Moscow: Progress Publishers, 1959).
64. Quoted in S. Lukes, 'Alienation and Anomie' in P. Laslett and W.G. Runciman (eds), *Philosophy, Politics and Society* Third Series (Oxford: Blackwell, 1967), 79.
65. Durkheim, *Suicide*, 369.

66. Ibid., 370.

67. Ibid., 276.

68. P. Besnard 'Anomie and Fatalism in Durkheim's Theory of Regulation', in Stephen P. Turner (ed.), *Emile Durkheim: Sociologist and Moralist* (London: Routledge, 1993), 51.

69. J.E. Pedersen, 'Sexual Politics in Comte and Durkheim: Feminism, History and the French Sociological Tradition'. *Signs: Journal of Women in Culture and Society* 27 (1) (Autumn 2001): 229–263.

70. E. Durkheim, 'Introduction to the Sociology of the Family', in M. Traugott (ed.), *Emile Durkheim on Institutional Analysis* (Chicago, IL: University of Chicago Press, 1994): 205–228.

71. Ibid.

72. M.A. Lamanna, *Emile Durkheim on the Family* (London: Sage, 2002), 177.

73. J.M. Lehmann, 'Durkheim's Theories of Deviance and Suicide: A Feminist Reconsideration'. *American Journal of Sociology* 100 (4) (1995): 904–930.

74. Durkheim, *Suicide*, 272.

75. E. Durkheim, 'Le divorce par consentement mutuel'. *Revue bleue* 44 (5) (1975): 549–554.

6. THE ELEMENTARY FORMS OF RELIGIOUS LIFE

1. S. Lukes, *Emile Durkheim: His Life and Work. A Historical and Critical Study* (London, Allen Lane, 1973), 36; R.A. Jones, *Emile Durkheim: An Introduction to Four Major Works* (Beverly Hills, CA: Sage Publications, 1986), 135; Erin Olson, 'Marx vs. Durkheim: Religion', with commentary by Antonino Palumbo, 5, www.erinolson.com/mar.pdf (accessed 12 May 2017).

2. R.H. Tawney, *Religion and the Rise of Capitalism: A Historical Study* (Harmondsworth: Penguin Press, 1961).

3. E. Durkheim, *The Elementary Forms of Religious Life* (New York: Free Press, 1995), 1.

4. N. Lobkowicz, 'Karl Marx's Attitude toward Religion'. *The Review of Politics* 26 (3) (1964): 320.

5. K. Fields, 'Introduction', in E. Durkheim, *The Elementary Forms of Religious Life* (New York: Free Press, 1995), xx.

6. R.A. Segal, 'Interpreting and Explaining Religion: Geertz and Durkheim'. *Soundings: An Interdisciplinary Journal* 71 (1) (1988): 35.

7. E. Durkheim, 'Marxism and Sociology: The Materialist Conception of History', in *The Rules of Sociological Method* (New York: Free Press, 1982), 167.

8. S. Taylor, 'Some Implications of the Contributions of Emile Durkheim to Religious Thought'. *Philosophy and Phenomenological Research* 24 (1) (1963): 125–134.

9. Durkheim, *The Elementary Forms of Religious Life*, 8–18.

10. R.A. Wallace, 'The Secular Ethic and the Spirit of Patriotism'. *Sociological Analysis* 34 (1) (1973): 3.

11. Ibid., 2.
12. Ibid., 21.
13. Ibid., 1.
14. Fields, 'Introduction', xxxviii.
15. Ibid., xxxviii.
16. Durkheim, *The Elementary Forms of Religious Life*, 5–6.
17. Ibid., 2.
18. Ibid., 23.
19. Ibid., 24.
20. Ibid.
21. Ibid., 26.
22. Ibid., 33.
23. Ibid., 34.
24. Ibid.
25. Ibid., 44.
26. Ibid., 47.
27. Ibid., 49.
28. Ibid., 66.
29. F.M. Müller, *Natural Religion* (London: Longmans, Green 1889), 114; Durkheim, *The Elementary Forms of Religious Life*, 70.
30. Ibid., 74.
31. Ibid., 75.
32. Ibid., 78.
33. Ibid.
34. Ibid., 83.
35. Ibid.
36. Jones, *Emile Durkheim*, 123.
37. Ibid.
38. R.A. Jones, 'Durkheim, Frazer, and Smith: The Role of Analogies and Exemplars in the Development of Durkheim's Sociology of Religion'. *American Journal of Sociology* 92 (3) (November 1986): 596–627.
39. Durkheim, *The Elementary Forms of Religious Life*, 100.
40. Ibid.
41. See B. Anderson, *Imagined Communities* (London: Verso, 1991).
42. Ibid., 108.
43. K. Fields, 'Durkheim and the Idea of Soul'. *Theory and Society* 25 (1996): 195.
44. Ibid.
45. Durkheim, *The Elementary Forms of Religious Life*, 208.
46. Ibid., 191; Fields, 'Durkheim and the Idea of Soul', 197.
47. Jones. *Emile Durkheim*, 126.
48. E. Durkheim, 'The Dualism of Human Nature and its Social Conditions', in *Essays on Sociology and Philosophy by Émile Durkheim, et al.* (New York: Harper Torchbooks, 1964).
49. Durkheim, *The Elementary Forms of Religious Life*, 303.
50. Ibid., 304.

51. Ibid., 315.
52. Ibid., 321.
53. Ibid., 333.
54. See Benedict Anderson, *Imagined Communities* (London: Verso, 1991).
55. Ibid., 345.
56. Ibid., 363.
57. Ibid., 364.
58. Ibid., 379.
59. Ibid., 415.
60. Ibid., 1.
61. Taylor, 'Some Implications of the Contributions of Emile Durkheim to Religious Thought', 127.
62. Fields, *Introduction*, l..
63. C. Geertz, *The Interpretation of Cultures: Selected Essays* (New York: Basic Books, 1973), 22.
64. W.S.F. Pickering, 'The Eternality of the Sacred: Durkheim's Error'. *Archives of the Social Sciences of Religion* 35 (69) (1990): 91–108.
65. Durkheim, *The Elementary Forms of Religious Life*, 2–3.
66. F. Uricoechea, 'Durkheim's Conception of the Religious Life: A Critique'. *Archives des sciences sociales des religions* 79 (July–September 1992): 158.
67. E. Durkheim, *The Rules of Sociological Method* (New York: Free Press, 1982), 157.
68. R. Stark, D.P. Doyle and J.L. Rushing, 'Beyond Durkheim: Suicide and Religion'. *Journal for the Scientific Study of Religion* 22 (2) (1983): 120.
69. Lukes, *Emile Durkheim*, 477 and 478.
70. W.E.H. Stanner, 'Reflections on Durkheim and Aboriginal Religion', in M. Freedman (ed.), *Social Organization: Essays Presented to Raymond Firth* (London: Frank and Cass Co., 1967), 240.
71. Jones, *Emile Durkheim*, 135.
72. Durkheim, 'The Dualism of Human Nature and its Social Conditions', 325.
73. E. Durkheim, 'Individualism and the Intellectuals'. *Revue Bleue* 4 (10) (1898): 8.
74. A. Lisa, 'Religious Conflicts During Medieval Times'. *People of our Everyday Life*, http://peopleof.oureverydaylife.com/religious-conflicts-during-medieval-times-7816.html (accessed 12 May 2017).
75. Ibid.
76. P.H. Wilson, *Europe's Tragedy: A New History of the Thirty Years War* (London: Penguin, 2010), 787.
77. Tawney, *Religion and the Rise of Capitalism*.
78. Ibid., 27.
79. Durkheim, *The Elementary Forms of Religious Life*, 427.
80. Lobkowicz, 'Karl Marx's Attitude toward Religion', 322.
81. Ibid.
82. E. Wallwork, 'Durkheim's Early Sociology of Religion'. *Sociological Analysis* 46 (3) (1974), 203.

7. EDUCATING REPUBLICAN CITIZENS

1. P. Bourdieu and J. Passeron, *Reproduction in Education, Society and Culture* (London: Sage Publications, 1990), 4.
2. E. Durkheim, *Education and Sociology* (New York: Free Press, 1956), 70.
3. Ibid.
4. Ibid., 70–71.
5. L. Greenberg, 'Architects of the New Sorbonne: Liard's Purpose and Durkheim's Role'. *History of Education Quarterly* 21 (1) (1981): 77–94.
6. S. Lukes, *Emile Durkheim: His Life and Work. A Historical and Critical Study* (London: Allen Lane 1973), 95.
7. R. Macgraw, *France 1800–1914: A Social History* (London: Pearson, 2002), 200.
8. Quoted in S. Elwitt, *The Making of the Third Republic: Class and Politics in France, 1868–1884*, (Baton Rouge, LA: Louisiana State University Press, 1986), 194.
9. Ibid., 178.
10. Macgraw, *France 1800–1914*, 225.
11. F. Buisson, 'The Schoolmaster as a Pioneer of Democracy', in F. Buisson and F.E. Farrington (eds), *French Educational Ideals of Today: An Anthology of the Molders of French Educational Thought of the Present* (Yonkers-on-Hudson, NY: World Book Company, 1919), 128 and 130.
12. Ibid., 131.
13. Ibid., 136.
14. Ibid., 135.
15. Quoted in B.H. Bergen, 'Secularizing the Schools in France, 1870–1900: Controversy, Continuity, and Consensus'. Working Paper 26 Baker Institute for Public Policy, Rice University, Houston, TX, no date.
16. E. Weber, *Peasants into Frenchmen: The Modernization of Rural France 1870–1914* (Stanford, CA: Stanford University Press, 1976), 67.
17. A. Conklin, *A Mission to Civilise: The Republican Idea of Empire in France and West Africa, 1895–1930* (Stanford, CA: Stanford University Press, 1997), 13.
18. Ibid., 134.
19. K. Auspitz, *The Radical Bourgeoisie: The Ligue de L'enseignement and the Origins of the Third Republic 1866–1885* (Cambridge: Cambridge University Press, 1982), 170.
20. E. Durkheim, *Moral Education* (New York: Dover Publications, 2002), 3.
21. Ibid., 8.
22. Ibid., 11.
23. E. Durkheim, *The Evolution of French Educational Thought* (London: Routledge Kegan Paul, 1977), 18.
24. Ibid., 29.
25. Ibid.
26. Ibid., 30.
27. Ibid., 97.

28. Ibid., 85.
29. Ibid., 202.
30. Ibid., 206.
31. Ibid., 207.
32. Ibid., 209.
33. Ibid., 233.
34. Ibid., 249.
35. Ibid., 285.
36. Ibid., 286.
37. Ibid., 324.
38. Ibid., 333.
39. Ibid., 340.
40. Durkheim, *Moral Education*, 21.
41. Ibid., 26.
42. Ibid., 27.
43. Ibid., 38.
44. Ibid., 39.
45. Ibid., 40.
46. Ibid., 42.
47. Ibid., 53.
48. Ibid., 79.
49. Ibid., 78.
50. Ibid., 79.
51. Ibid., 179.
52. Ibid., 79.
53. Ibid., 90.
54. Ibid., 115.
55. Ibid., 149.
56. Ibid., 155.
57. Ibid., 156.
58. Ibid., 182.
59. Ibid., 165.
60. Ibid., 175.
61. Ibid., 234.
62. Ibid., 238.
63. Ibid., 234.
64. Ibid., 239.
65. Ibid., 275.
66. Ibid., 277.
67. Ibid., 278.
68. Ibid.
69. Ibid.
70. A. MacIntyre, 'Notes from the Moral Wilderness', in K. Knight (eds), *The MacIntyre Reader* (Cambridge: Polity, 1998), 42.
71. Ibid., 47.

72. J. Piaget, *The Moral Judgement of the Child* (Glencoe, IL: Free Press, 1948), 350.
73. Ibid., 358.
74. Ibid., 365.
75. Ibid., 370.
76. Conklin, *A Mission to Civilise*, 1.
77. E. Durkheim and E. Denis, *Who Wanted the War?: The Origin of the War According to Diplomatic Documents* (Paris: Librairie Armand Colin, 1915).
78. E. Durkheim, *'Germany Above All': German Mentality and War* (Paris: Librairie Armand Colin, 1915), 18.
79. Ibid., 38.
80. Ibid., 40.
81. Ibid., 46.

8. SOCIALISM AND SAINT-SIMON

1. S. Lukes, *Emile Durkheim: His Life and Work. A Historical and Critical Study* (London: Allen Lane, 1973), 244.
2. A. Mayer, *Persistence of the Old Regime: Europe to the Great War* (New York: Pantheon, 1981), 30 and 49.
3. J.W. Scott, 'Social History and the History of Socialism: French Socialist Municipalities in the 1890's'. *Le Mouvement social* 111 (April–June 1980): 145–153.
4. M. Fournier, *Émile Durkheim: A Biography*, translated by David Macey (Cambridge: Polity, 2013), 211.
5. Ibid., 210.
6. R. Stuart, *Marxism at Work: Ideology and French Socialism during the Third Republic* (Cambridge: Cambridge University Press, 1992), 286.
7. Ibid., 286.
8. E. Durkheim, *Socialism and Saint-Simon* (London: Routledge and Kegan Paul, 1958), 42.
9. Ibid., 41.
10. Ibid.
11. Ibid., 44.
12. Ibid., 41.
13. Ibid.
14. Ibid., 56.
15. Ibid.
16. Ibid., 68.
17. Ibid., 73.
18. Ibid., 88.
19. Ibid., 92.
20. Ibid., 93.
21. K. Marx, 'Introduction to the Programme of the French Workers Party', in D. Fernbach (ed.), *The First International and After: Marx* (Harmondsworth: Penguin 1974), 376.

22. J. Jaurès, 'The General Strike and Revolution'. *Studies in Socialism* (London: G.P. Putnam, 1906), www.marxists.org/archive/jaures/1906/studies-socialism/ch12.htm (accessed 12 May 2017).

23. F. Engels, Preface to the first Russian edition of the *Communist Manifesto* (London: Verso, 2012), 85.

24. Durkheim, *Socialism and Saint-Simon*, 65.

25. F. Engels, *Socialism: Utopian and Scientific*, in *Karl Marx and Engels, Selected Works*, Vol. 3 (Moscow: Progress Publishers, 1970).

26. Durkheim, *Socialism and Saint-Simon*, 123.

27. Ibid., 130.

28. Ibid., 134.

29. Ibid., 136.

30. Ibid., 160.

31. Ibid., 159.

32. Ibid., 162.

33. Ibid., 174.

34. Ibid., 175.

35. Ibid., 137.

36. Ibid., 191.

37. Ibid., 230.

38. Ibid., 229.

39. Ibid., 145.

40. Ibid., 245.

41. Ibid., 246.

42. Ibid., 246–247.

9. THE LIMITS TO DURKHEIM'S REPUBLICAN SOCIOLOGY

1. S. Lukes, *Emile Durkheim: His Life and Work. A Historical and Critical Study* (London: Allen Lane, 1973), 22.

2. S. Lukes, 'Introduction', in E. Durkheim, *The Rules of Sociological Method* (New York: Free Press, 1982), 20–22.

3. C. Morrisson and W. Snyder, 'The Income Inequality of France in Historical Perspective'. *European Review of Economic History* 4 (2000): 59–83.

4. L.A. Coser, 'Durkheim's Conservatism and its Implications for his Sociological Theory', in Kurt H. Wolff (ed.), *Essays on Sociology and Philosophy by Émile Durkheim, et al.* (New York: Harper Torchbooks, 1964), 211–232.

5. R. Nisbet, 'Conservatism and Sociology'. *American Journal of Sociology* 58 (2) (1952): 165–175.

6. R. Magraw, *France 1815–1914: The Bourgeois Century* (Oxford: Oxford University Press, 1983), 303.

7. E. Durkheim, *The Division of Labour in Society* (New York: Free Press, 1997), xxv.

8. E. Durkheim, *The Rules of Sociological Method* (New York: Free Press, 1982), 69.

9. Ibid., 160.
10. Ibid.
11. M. Richter, 'Durkheim's Politics and Political Theory', in Kurt H. Wolff (ed.), *Essays on Sociology and Philosophy by Émile Durkheim, et al.* (New York: Harper Torchbooks, 1964), 186.
12. Lukes, 'Introduction', 20–22.
13. Coser, 'Durkheim's Conservatism and its Implications for his Sociological Theory', 214–215.
14. Lukes, 'Introduction'. *The Rules of Sociological Method*, 20–22.
15. Ibid.
16. E. Durkheim, *Suicide: A Study in Sociology* (New York: Free Press, 1951), 209.
17. Ibid., 247.
18. E. Durkheim, *Sociology and Philosophy* (London: Cohen and West, 1953), 72.
19. Durkheim, *Suicide*, 249–250.
20. A. Callinicos, *Social Theory: A Historical Introduction* (New York: New York University Press, 1999), 146.
21. Durkheim, *The Division of Labour in Society*, 57.
22. M.A. Lamanna, *Emile Durkheim on the Family* (London: Sage, 2002), 180.
23. Ibid., 143.
24. H.H. Chenut, *The Fabric of Gender: Working-Class Culture in Third Republic France* (University Park, PA: Pennsylvania State University Press, 2005), 2.
25. R.A. Wallace, 'The Secular Ethic and the Spirit of Patriotism'. *Sociological Analysis* 34 (1) (1973): 3.
26. E. Durkheim, 'Marxism and Sociology: The Materialist Conception of History', in *The Rules of Sociological Method* (New York: Free Press, 1982), 167–174.
27. P. Nord, *The Republican Moment: Struggles for Democracy in Nine-teenth-Century France* (Cambridge, MA: Harvard University Press, 1998), Chapter 8.
28. Lukes, *Emile Durkheim*, 83.
29. J. Henry, *The Scientific Revolution and the Origins of Modern Science* (Basingstoke: Palgrave Macmillan, 2008), 100.
30. B. Russell, *The Impact of Science on Society* (London: Unwin Paperbacks, 1976), 31.

Bibliography

Aguilhon, M. *The French Republic 1879–1992*. Oxford: Blackwell, 1993.

Aldrich, R. *Greater France: A History of French Overseas Expansion*. Santa Barbara, CA: Praeger Publishers, 1996.

Alexander, J. 'The Inner Development of Durkheim's Sociological Theory: From Early Writings to Maturity', in J. Alexander and P. Smith (eds), *The Cambridge Companion Guide to Durkheim*. Cambridge: Cambridge University Press, 2005.

Anderson, B. *Imagined Communities*. London: Verso, 1991.

Anderson, R.D. *France 1870–1914: Politics and Society*. London: Routledge, 1977.

Aristotle, *Physics*, trans. Robin Waterfield. Oxford: Oxford University Press, 2008.

Auspitz, K. *The Radical Bourgeoisie: The Ligue de L'enseignement and the Origins of the Third Republic 1866–1885*. Cambridge: Cambridge University Press, 1982.

Bahr, A. 'Between "Self-Murder" and "Suicide": The Modern Etymology of Self-Killing'. *Journal of Social History* 46 (3) (2013): 620–632.

Barbagli, M. *Farewell to the World*. Cambridge: Polity Press, 2015.

Barnes, J.A. 'Durkheim's Division of Labour in Society'. *Man, New Series* 1 (2) (1966): 158–175.

Baudelot, C. and Establet, R. *Suicide: The Hidden Side of Modernity*. Cambridge: Polity Press, 2008.

Becker, H. 'Whose Side Are We On'. *Social Problems* 14 (3) (Winter 1967): 239–247.

Bendix, R. and Roth, G. *Scholarship and Partisanship: Essays on Max Weber*. Berkeley, CA: University of California Press, 1971.

Bergen, B.H. 'Secularizing the Schools in France, 1870–1900: Controversy, Continuity, and Consensus'. Working Paper 26 Baker Institute for Public Policy, Rice University, Houston, TX, no date.

Besnard, P. 'Anomie and Fatalism in Durkheim's Theory of Regulation', in Stephen P. Turner (ed.), *Emile Durkheim: Sociologist and Moralist*. London: Routledge, 1993, 169–190.

Besnard, P. 'The Fortunes of Durkheim's Suicide' in W.S.F. Pickering and G. Walford (eds), *Durkheim's Suicide: A Century of Research and Debate*. London: Routledge, 2000.

Bhaskar, R. *A Realist Theory of Science*. London: Verso, 1975.

Bottomore, T. 'A Marxist Consideration of Durkheim'. *Social Forces* 59 (1981): 902–917.

Bourdieu, P. and Passeron, J. *Reproduction in Education, Society and Culture*. London: Sage Publications, 1990.

Braverman, H. *Labor and Monopoly Capital: The Degradation of Work in the Twentieth Century*. New York: Monthly Review Press, 1999.

Brinton, C. *The Jacobins: An Essay in the New History*. Piscataway, NJ: Transaction Publishers, 2012.

Buisson, F. and Farrington, F.E. (eds) *French Educational Ideals of Today: An Anthology of the Molders of French Educational Thought of the Present*. Yonkers-on-Hudson, NY: World Book Company, 1919.

Burtt, E.A. *The Metaphysical Foundations of Modern Science*. New York: Dover Publications, 2003.

Calhoun, C.J. *Classical Sociological Theory*. Oxford: Wiley Blackwell, 2002.

Calhoun, C.J. and VanAntwerpen, J. 'Orthodoxy, Heterodoxy and Hierarchy: "Mainstream" Sociology and its Challengers', in C. Calhoun (ed.), *Sociology in America: A History*. Chicago, IL: University of Chicago Press, 2008.

Callinicos, A. *Social Theory: A Historical Introduction*. New York: New York University Press, 1999.

Camiscioli, E. *Reproducing the French Race: Immigration, Intimacy and Embodiment in the Early Twentieth Century*. Durham, NC: Duke University Press, 2009.

Chenut, H.H. *The Fabric of Gender: Working-Class Culture in Third Republic France*. University Park, PA: Pennsylvania State University Press, 2005.

Cicourel, A. *The Social Organisation of Juvenile Justice*. New York: John Wiley, 1968.

Clark, T.N. *Prophets and Patrons: The French University and the Emergence of Social Sciences*. Cambridge, MA: Harvard University Press, 1973.

Collins, R. 'A Comparative Approach to Political Sociology', in R. Bendix (ed.), *State and Society: A Reader in Comparative Sociology*. Berkeley, CA: University of California Press, 1973, 42–69.

Conklin, A. *A Mission to Civilise: The Republican Idea of Empire in France and West Africa, 1895–1930*. Stanford, CA: Stanford University Press, 1997.

Coser, L.A. 'Durkheim's Conservatism and its Implications for his Sociological Theory', in Kurt H. Wolff (ed.), *Essays on Sociology and Philosophy by Émile Durkheim, et al.* New York: Harper Torchbooks, 1964, 211–232.

De Laguna, T. 'The Sociological Method of Durkheim'. *The Philosophical Review* 29 (3) (1920): 213–225.

Douglas, J. *The Social Meaning of Suicide*. Princeton, NJ: Princeton University Press, 1967.

Dupeux, G. *French Society 1789–1970*. London: Methuen, 1976.

Durkheim, E. 'Individualism and the Intellectuals'. *Revue Bleue* 4 (10) (1898): 14–30.

Durkheim, E. '*Germany Above All': German Mentality and War*. Paris: Librairie Armand Colin, 1915.

Durkheim, E. *Suicide: A Study in Sociology*. New York: Free Press, 1951.

Durkheim, E. *Sociology and Philosophy*. London: Cohen and West, 1953.

Durkheim, E. *Education and Sociology*. New York: Free Press, 1956.

Durkheim, E. *Socialism and Saint-Simon*. London: Routledge and Kegan Paul, 1958.

Durkheim, E. 'Replies to Objection', in *Sociology and Philosophy*, translated by D.F. Pocock. London: Cohen and West, 1965.

Durkheim, E. 'A Review of Ferdinand Tönnies's *Gemeinschaft und Gesellschaft: Abhandlung des Communismus und des Socialismus als empirischer Culturformen*'. *American Journal of Sociology* (1887 reprint) 77 (6) (May, 1972): 1190–1199.

Durkheim, E. 'The Principles of 1789 and Sociology', in R. Bellah (ed.), *Emile Durkheim on Morality and Society*. Chicago, IL: University of Chicago Press, 1973, 43–57.

Durkheim, E. 'Le divorce par consentement mutuel'. *Revue Bleue* 44 (5) (1975): 549–554.

Durkheim, E. *The Evolution of French Educational Thought*. London: Routledge Kegan Paul, 1977.

Durkheim, E. *The Rules of Sociological Method*. New York: Free Press, 1982.

Durkheim, E. 'The Concept and Nature of Socialism', in A. Giddens (ed.), *Durkheim on Politics and the State*. Stanford, CA: Stanford University Press, 1986, 97–120.

Durkheim, E. 'The Definition of Socialism', in A. Giddens (ed.), *Durkheim on Politics and the State,*. Stanford, CA: Stanford University Press 1986.

Durkheim, E. 'Review of Labriola Essay on a Materialist Conception of History', in Giddens (ed.), *Durkheim on Politics and the State*. Stanford, CA: Stanford University Press 1986.

Durkheim, E. 'Review of Merlino, Forms and Essence of Socialism', in A. Giddens (ed.), *Durkheim on Politics and the State*. Stanford, CA: Stanford University Press 1986.

Durkheim, E. 'The State and Patriotism', in A. Giddens (ed.), *Durkheim on Politics and the State*. Stanford, CA: Stanford University Press, 1986, 194–242.

Durkheim, E. 'Suicide and Fertility: A Study of Moral Statistics'. *European Journal of Population/Revue Europeene de Demographie* 8 (3) (1992): 175–197.

Durkheim, E. 'Introduction to the Sociology of the Family', in M. Traugott (ed.), *Emile Durkheim on Institutional Analysis*. Chicago, IL: University of Chicago Press, 1994, 205–228.

Durkheim, E. *The Elementary Forms of Religious Life*. New York: Free Press, 1995.

Durkheim, E. *The Division of Labour in Society*. New York: Free Press, 1997.

Durkheim, E. *Moral Education*. New York: Dover Publications, 2002.

Durkheim, E. *Professional Ethics and Civic Morals*. London: Routledge, 2003.

Durkheim, E. 'The Dualism of Human Nature and its Social Conditions' in *Durkheimian Studies* 2 (2005): 35–45.

Durkheim, E. and Denis, E. *Who Wanted the War?: The Origin of the War According to Diplomatic Documents*. Paris: Librairie Armand Colin, 1915.

Dutton, P.V. *Origins of the French Welfare State and the Struggle for Social Reform in France, 1914–1947*. Cambridge: Cambridge University Press, 2004.

Elwit, A. *The Third Republic Defended: Bourgeois Reform in France, 1880–1914*. Baton Rouge, LA: Louisiana State University Press, 1986.

Engels, F. *Socialism: Utopian and Scientific*, in *Karl Marx and Engels, Selected Works*, Vol. 3. Moscow: Progress Publishers, 1970.

Engels, F. 'Preface' 1st Russian edn, *Communist Manifesto*. London: Verso, 2012.

Faris, E. 'Emile Durkheim and the Division of Labor in Society'. Review in *American Journal of Sociology* 40 (3) (November, 1934): 319–328.

Fields, K. 'Introduction', in E. Durkheim, *The Elementary Forms of Religious Life*. New York: Free Press, 1995.

Fields, K. 'Durkheim and the Idea of Soul'. *Theory and Society* 25 (1996): 193–203.

Fortes, M. *Kinship and the Social Order: The Legacy of Lewis Henry Morgan*. Chicago, IL: Aldeine, Galle, O. and K.E. Taeuber, 1969.

Fournier, M. *Émile Durkheim: A Biography*, translated by David Macey. Cambridge: Polity Press, 2013.

Gane, M. 'Institutional Socialism and the Sociological Critique of Communism', in M. Gane (ed.), *The Radical Sociology of Durkheim and Mauss*. London: Routledge, 1992.

Garrison, E. 'Attitudes toward Suicide in Ancient Greece'. *Transactions of the American Philological Association* 121 (1991): 1–34.

Geertz, C. *The Interpretation of Cultures: Selected Essays*. New York: Basic Books, 1973.

Gestrich, A., Hurren, E. and King, S. *Poverty and Sickness in Modern Europe: Narratives of Sick People, 1780–1938*. New York: Continuum Publishers, 2012.

Giddens, A. *Durkheim on Politics and the State*. Stanford, CA: Stanford University Press, 1986.

Gisbert, P. 'Social Facts in Durkheim's System'. *Anthropose* 54 (3–4) (1959): 353–369.

Goldstein, R. *Political Repression in 19th Century Europe*. New York: Routledge, 1983.

Greenberg, L. 'Architects of the New Sorbonne: Liard's Purpose and Durkheim's Role'. *History of Education Quarterly* 21 (1) (Spring 1981): 77–94.

Hardoon, Deborah, Fuentas-Nieva, Ricardo and Ayele, Sophia. 'An Economy for the 1%: How Privilege and Power in the Economy Drive Extreme Inequality and How This can be Stopped'. *Oxfam International: Briefing Paper*, 18 January 2016, at: http://policy-practice.oxfam.org.uk/publications/an-economy-for-the-1-how-privilege-and-power-in-the-economy-drive-extreme-inequ-592643.

Hawkins, M.J. 'Durkheim and Occupational Corporations: An Exegesis and Interpretation'. *Journal of the History of Ideas* 53 (3) (1994): 461–481.

Hazen, C.D. *Modern European History*. New York: Henry Holt, 1917.

Henry, J. *The Scientific Revolution and the Origins of Modern Science*. Basingstoke: Palgrave Macmillan, 2008.

Hessen, B. 'The Social and Economic Roots of Newton's Principia', in Boris Hessen, Henryk Grossmann, Gideon Freudenthal and Peter McLaughlin (eds), *The Social and Economic Roots of the Scientific Revolution: Texts by Boris Hessen and Henryk Grossmann*. London: Springer, 2009.

Hobbes, T. *Leviathan*. London: Penguin Classics, 1985.

Horton, J. 'The Dehumanization of Anomie and Alienation: A Problem in the Ideology of Sociology'. *British Journal of Sociology* 15 (1) (1964): 283–300.

Jaurès, J. *Studies in Socialism*. London: G.P. Putnam, 1906.

Jones, R.A. 'Durkheim, Frazer, and Smith: The Role of Analogies and Exemplars in the Development of Durkheim's Sociology of Religion'. *American Journal of Sociology* 92 (3) (November 1986): 596–627.

Jones, R.A. *Emile Durkheim: An Introduction to Four Major Works*. Beverly Hills, CA: Sage Publications, 1986.

Jones. R.A. 'Ambivalent Cartesians: Durkheim, Montesquieu and Method'. *American Journal of Sociology* 100 (1) (1994): 1–39.

Kando, T.M. '*L'Année Sociologique*: From Durkheim to Today'. *The Pacific Sociological Review* 19 (2) (1975): 7–174.

Kelly, C. 'Methods of Reading and the Discipline of Sociology: The Case of Durkheim Studies'. *The Canadian Journal of Sociology* 15 (3) (1990): 301–324.

Kemper, T.D. 'Emile Durkheim and the Division of Labour'. *The Sociological Quarterly* 16 (2) (Spring 1975): 190–206.

Kuhn, T. *The Structure of Scientific Revolutions*. Chicago, IL: University of Chicago Press, 1962.

Lamanna, M.A. *Emile Durkheim on the Family*. London: Sage, 2002.

Lehmann, J.M. 'Durkheim's Theories of Deviance and Suicide: A Feminist Reconsideration'. *American Journal of Sociology* 100 (4) (1995): 904–930.

Lemert, C. 'The Canonical Limits of Durkheim's First Classic'. *Sociological Forum* 9 (1) (1994): 87–92.

Lisa, A. 'Religious Conflicts During Medieval Times'. *People of our Everyday Life*, http://peopleof.oureverydaylife.com/religious-conflicts-during-medieval-times-7816.html (accessed 12 May 2017).

Lobkowicz, N. 'Karl Marx's Attitude toward Religion'. *The Review of Politics* 26 (3) (1964): 319–352.

Lukes, S. 'Alienation and Anomie' in P. Laslett and W.G. Runciman (eds), *Philosophy, Politics and Society* Third Series. Oxford: Blackwell, 1967.

Lukes, S. *Emile Durkheim: His Life and Work. A Historical and Critical Study*. London: Allen Lane, 1973.

Lukes, S. 'Introduction', in *The Rules of Sociological Method*. New York: Free Press, 1982.

MacIntyre, A. 'Notes from the Moral Wilderness', in K. Knight (ed.), *The MacIntyre Reader*. Cambridge: Polity, 1998.

Magraw, R. *France 1815–1914: The Bourgeois Century*. Oxford: Oxford University Press, 1983.

Magraw, R. *France 1800–1914: A Social History*. London: Pearson, 2002.

Mair, P. *Ruling the Void*. London: Verso, 2013.

Malinowski, B. *Magic, Science and Religion and Other Essays*. Glencoe, IL: Free Press, 1948.

Marx, K. *Economic and Philosophic Manuscripts*. Moscow: Progress Publishers, 1959.

Marx, K. *Capital Vol I–III*. London: Lawrence and Wishart, 2003.

Mayer, A. *Persistence of the Old Regime: Europe to the Great War*. New York: Pantheon, 1981.

Merriman, J. *Massacre: The Life and Death of the Paris Commune*. New York: Basic Books, 2014.

Merton, R. 'Durkheim's Division of Labour in Society'. *Sociological Forum* 9 (1) (1994): 17–35.

Mills, C.W. *The Sociological Imagination*. New York: Oxford University Press, 2000.

Minois, G. *History of Suicide*. London and Baltimore, MD: Johns Hopkins University Press, 1999.

Morrisson, C. and Snyder, W. 'The Income Inequality of France in Historical Perspective'. *European Review of Economic History* 4 (2000): 59–83.

Müller, F.M. *Natural Religion*. London: Longmans, Green, 1889.

Müller, H.-P. 'Social Differentiation and Organic Solidarity: The "Division of Labour" Revisited', *Sociological Forum* 9 (1) (1994): 73–86.

Nicolaus, M. 'The Professional Organisation of Sociology: A View from Below', in R. Blackburn (ed.), *Ideology and Social Science*. London: Fontana, 1978.

Nicolaus, M. 'Fat Cat Sociology', in Martin Oppenheimer, Martin J. Murray and Rhonda F. Levine (eds), *Radical Sociologists and the Movement*. Philadelphia, PA: Temple University Press, 1991.

Nisbet, R. 'Conservatism and Sociology'. *American Journal of Sociology* 58 (2) (1952): 167–175.

Nord, P. *The Republican Moment: Struggles for Democracy in Nineteenth-Century France*. Cambridge, MA: Harvard University Press 1998.

Nozick, R. *Anarchy, State and Utopia*. Oxford: Blackwell Publishers, 1974.

Olson, E. 'Marx vs. Durkheim: Religion'. Commentary by Antonino Palumbo, www.erinolson.com/mar.pdf (accessed 12 May 2017).

Page, Melvin E. (ed.) *Colonialism: An International Social, Cultural, and Political Encyclopaedia*. Santa Barbara, CA: ABC-Clio, 2003.

Parker, S. 'Civic-Moral Teaching in French Secular Schools, Part 2'. *The Elementary School Journal* 20 (9) (1920): 660–669.

Parsons, T. *The Structure of Social Action*. New York: Free Press, 1968.

Pearce, F. *The Radical Durkheim*. Montreal: Canadian Scholars Press, 2001.

Pedersen, J.E. 'Sexual Politics in Comte and Durkheim: Feminism, History and the French Sociological Tradition'. *Signs: Journal of Women in Culture and Society* 27 (1) (Autumn 2001): 229–263.

Perrin, R.G. 'Emile Durkheim's Division of Labour and the Shadow of Herbert Spencer'. *The Sociological Quarterly* 36 (4) (1995): 791–808.

Pescosolido, B.A. and Mendelsohn, R. 'Social Causation or Social Construction of Suicide?: An Investigation into the Social Organization of Official Rates'. *American Sociological Review* 51 (1) (1986): 80–100.

Piaget, J. *The Moral Judgement of the Child*. Glencoe, IL: Free Press, 1948.

Pickering, M. *Auguste Comte: An Intellectual Biography*, Vol. 3. Cambridge: Cambridge University Press, 2009.

Pickering, W.S.F. 'The Eternality of the Sacred: Durkheim's Error'. *Archives of the Social Sciences of Religion* 35 (69) (1990): 91–108.

Piketty, T. *Capital in the 21st Century*. London: Belknap Press of Harvard University Press, 2014.

Pope, W. and Johnson, B.D. 'Inside Organic Solidarity'. *American Sociological Review* 48 (5) (1983): 681–692.

Porter, T. 'Statistical and Social Facts from Quetelet to Durkheim'. *Sociological Perspectives* 38 (1) (1995): 15–26.

Quine, W.V.O. *From a Logical Point of View*. Cambridge, MA: Harvard University Press, 1953.

Richter, M. 'Durkheim's Politics and Political Theory', in Kurt H. Wolff (ed.), *Essays on Sociology and Philosophy by Émile Durkheim, et al*. New York: Harper Torchbooks, 1964.

Russell, B. *The Impact of Science on Society*. London: Unwin Paperbacks, 1976.

Schmaus, W. 'Explanation and Essence in "The Rules of Sociological Method" and "The Division of Labour in Society"'. *Sociological Perspectives* 38 (1) (1995): 57–75.

Schnore, L. 'Social Anthropology and Human Ecology'. *American Journal of Sociology* 63 (6) (1958): 620–634.

Schwartz, R.D. and Miller, J.C. 'Legal Evolution and Social Complexity'. *American Journal of Sociology* 7 (2) (1964): 159–169.

Scott, J.W. 'Social History and the History of Socialism: French Socialist Municipalities in the 1890's'. *Le Mouvement social* 111 (April–June 1980): 145–153.

Segal, R.A. 'Interpreting and Explaining Religion: Geertz and Durkheim'. *Soundings: An Interdisciplinary Journal* 71 (1) (1988): 29–52.

Smith, A. *The Wealth of Nations*. London: Penguin Classics: 1999.

Stack, S. 'Emile Durkheim and Altruistic Suicide'. *Archives of Suicide Research* 8 (1) (2004): 9–22.

Stanner, W.E. 'Reflections on Durkheim and Aboriginal Religion', in M. Freedman (ed.), *Social Organization: Essays Presented to Raymond Firth*. London: Frank and Cass Co., 1967.

Stark, R., Doyle, D.P. and Rushing, J.L. 'Beyond Durkheim: Suicide and Religion'. *Journal for the Scientific Study of Religion* 22 (2) (1983): 120–131.

Stedman Jones, S.G. 'Charles Renouvier and Émile Durkheim: "Les Règles de la méthode sociologique"'. *Sociological Perspectives* 38 (1) (1995): 27–40.

Stedman Jones, S.G. *Durkheim Reconsidered*. Cambridge: Polity Press, 2001.

Stock-Morton, P. *Moral Education for a Secular Society*. New York: New York Press, 1988.

Stuart, R. *Marxism at Work: Ideology and French Socialism during the Third Republic*. Cambridge: Cambridge University Press, 1992.

Takla, T.A. and Pope, W. 'The Force Imagery in Durkheim: The Integration of Theory, Metatheory and Method'. *Sociological Theory* 3 (1) (1985): 74–88.

Tawney, R.H. *Religion and the Rise of Capitalism: A Historical Study*. Harmondsworth: Penguin Press, 1961.

Taylor, S. 'Some Implications of the Contributions of Emile Durkheim to Religious Thought'. *Philosophy and Phenomenological Research* 24 (1) (1963): 125–134.

Thatcher, M. Interview by Douglas Keay. *Woman's Own*, 31 October 1987.

Timmerans, A. 'Suicide Determination and the Professional Authority of Medical Examiners'. *American Sociological Review* 70 (2) (2005): 311–333.

de Tocqueville, A. *The Old Regime and the Revolution*, trans. John Bonner. New York: Harper & Brothers, 1856.

Turner, S. 'Durkheim among the Statisticians'. *Journal of the History of Behavioural Science* 32 (4) (1996): 354–378.

Turner, Stephen P. (ed.) *Emile Durkheim: Sociologist and Moralist*. London: Routledge, 1993.

Turner, S.P. 'Durkheim's *The Rules of Sociological Method*: Is it a Classic?'. *Sociological Perspectives* 38 (1) (1995): 1–13.

Uricoechea, F. 'Durkheim's Conception of the Religious Life: A Critique'. *Archives des sciences sociales des religions* 79 (July–September 1992): 155–166.

Wallace, R.A. 'The Secular Ethic and the Spirit of Patriotism'. *Sociological Analysis* 34 (1) (1973): 3–11.

Wallwork, E. 'Durkheim's Early Sociology of Religion'. *Sociological Analysis* 46 (3) (1974): 201–217.

Weber, E. *Peasants into Frenchmen: The Modernization of Rural France 1870–1914*. Stanford, CA: Stanford University Press, 1976.

Weber, E. *France: Fin de Siècle*. London: Belknap Press, 1986.

Wernick, A. *Auguste Comte and the Religion of Humanity: The Post-Theistic Program of French Social Theory*. Cambridge: Cambridge University Press, 2001.

Wilson, P.H. *Europe's Tragedy: A New History of the Thirty Years War*. London: Penguin, 2010.

Zeitlin, I. *Ideology and the Development of Sociological Theory*. Englewood Cliffs, NJ: Prentice-Hall, 1981.

Zeldin, T. *France 1848–1945: Politics and Anger*. Oxford: Oxford University Press, 1979.

Index

Printed and bound by CPI Group (UK) Ltd, Croydon, CR0 4YY

25/03/2025

14647331-0001